School Desegregation and Defended Neighborhoods

Lexington Books Politics of Education Series
Frederick M. Wirt, Editor

George R. LaNoue, Bruce L.R. Smith, *The Politics of School Decentralization*

John C. Hogan, *The Schools, the Courts, and the Public Interest*

Jerome T. Murphy, *State Education Agencies and Discretionary Funds: Grease The Squeaky Wheel*

James Hottois, Neal A. Milner, *The Sex Education Controversy: A Study of Politics, Education, and Morality*

Frederick M. Wirt, Ed., *The Polity of the School: New Research in Educational Politics*

Lawrence E. Gladieux, Thomas R. Wolanin, *Congress and the Colleges: The National Politics of Higher Education*

Dale Mann, *The Politics of Administrative Representation: School Administrators and Local Democracy*

Harrell R. Rodgers, Jr., Charles S. Bullock III, *Coercion to Compliance*

Richard A. Dershimer, *The Federal Government and Educational R&D*

Tyll van Geel, *Authority to Control the School Program*

Andrew Fishel, Janice Pottker, *National Politics and Sex Discrimination in Education*

Chester E. Finn, Jr., *Education and the Presidency*

Frank W. Lutz, Laurence Iannoccone, *Public Participation in Local School Districts*

Paul Goldstein, *Changing the American Schoolbook*

Everett F. Cataldo, Micheal W. Giles, Douglas S. Gatlin, *School Desegregation Policy: Compliance, Avoidance, and the Metropolitan Remedy*

William J. Grimshaw, *Union Rule in the Schools: Big-City Politics in Transformation*

David K. Wiles, *Energy, Winter, and Schools: Crisis and Decision Theory*

Robert H. Salisbury, *Citizen Participation in the Public Schools*

Douglas E. Mitchell, *Shaping Legislative Decisions: Education Policy and the Social Sciences*

Emmett H. Buell, Jr., *School Desegregation and Defended Neighborhoods: The Boston Controversy*

David L. Colton, Edith E. Graber, *Teacher Strikes and the Courts*

School Desegregation and Defended Neighborhoods

The Boston Controversy

Emmett H. Buell, Jr.
Denison University
with
Richard A. Brisbin, Jr.
Saint Mary's College

LexingtonBooks
D.C. Heath and Company
Lexington, Massachusetts
Toronto

To the memory of my mother and father

Library of Congress Cataloging in Publication Data

Buell, Emmett H.
    School desegregation and defended neighborhoods

    Includes index.
    1. Busing for school integration—Massachusetts—Boston. I. Brisbin,
Richard A II. Title.
LC214.523.B67B83   370.19'342   78-19589
ISBN 0-669-02646-8   AACR2

Copyright © 1982 by D.C. Heath and Company

Published simultaneously in Canada

Printed in the United States of America

International Standard Book Number: 0-669-02646-8

Library of Congress Catalog Card Number: 78-19589

Contents

List of Figures
and Tables

Acknowledgments

Many people helped in the course of this research. Foremost among them was Fred Wirt, the editor of this series, who first proposed a book and then gently guided it to conclusion. Several Denison University Research Foundation (DURF) grants made data collection, reproduction, and other project expenses easier to bear. Anthony J. Lisska, dean of the college at Denison University and Andrew Sterrett, formerly the dean, endorsed the book at several points through DURF grants. Jay Sloan of Western Kentucky University and Gordon Galloway, associate director of the Denison Computer Center, provided invaluable aid in obtaining and processing the busing opinion data analyzed in chapter 2. Gary Schlickeiser of the Reed College Computer Center wrote the Taeuber and Coleman programs used to produced the desegregation indexes discussed in chapter 9. Howard Griffith of the Denison Media Services Center never complained when asked to draw yet another map or chart; examples of his work appear in this book. John Cronin, chief librarian for the *Boston Herald-American,* was most helpful during the many weeks spent working through old newspaper clippings, and replied promptly to many permissions requests. Bert Useem generously supplied original data from his own study of Boston busing protest. Jeanne Hardy and Louis Perullo of the Boston School Department provided much essential data on the public schools, including enrollment statistics analyzed in chapter 9. Sister Mary Jude Waters, O.P., made available enrollments for Catholic schools in the Boston archdiocese. Charles Maurer and associates often expedited the Denison library acquisition process so that needed materials could be obtained swiftly, and helped in too many other ways to enumerate. The assistance of librarians in the Government Documents section of the Boston Public Library, the Special Collections division of the Boston College Library, the Boston University and Ohio State University libraries, and the Library of Congress, is also gratefully acknowledged.

Emmett Buell is particularly grateful to Sam Gove, director of the Institute of Government and Public Affairs at the University of Illinois for making available in January 1980 so stimulating and congenial a place to write; to South Boston landlady Isabel Newton for her wit, wisdom, and kindness never to be forgotten; to the staff of the Vanderbilt University Television News Archive for their help; to Peter and Maureen Steinberger and other Reed College colleagues who so encouraged him in the final stages of the project; and, hardly least, to the many Denison and Reed students who took an interest in the project and contributed to its growth with their ideas.

Richard Brisbin would like to thank David and Nancy Kramer for facilitating his Boston visits; Bridget Madigan for assistance in preparing the index; Craig Hartzer, Edward Heck, and former Denison colleagues for their advice and counsel.

Finally, both thank the fifty anti-busing activists, busing proponents, attorneys, public officials, journalists, clergymen, and others interviewed for this project. In order to safeguard some respondents, the names of none are given. No one acknowledged above is responsible for any errors of fact or omission.

Grateful acknowledgment is made to the following for permission to reprint from previously published material:

Basic Books, Inc.: Excerpt from Diane Ravitch, *The Great School Wars* (New York: Basic Books, 1974), p. 254. Copyright © 1974 by Basic Books, Inc.

Boston Globe: Neighborhood map from 1971 "Boston's Neighborhoods" series.

Boston Herald-American: Excerpts from the following newspapers:

"Mrs. Hicks Says Nix to Peabody Plea," *Boston Traveler,* 3 September 1963.

"Mrs. Hicks, Hub NAACP Clash on Vote's Meaning," *Boston Record,* 26 September 1963.

"Louise Days Hicks Offers 'Pat' to the NAACP," *Boston Record,* 25 October 1963.

"BC Panel Ignorant About Hub Schools—Mirs Hicks," *Boston Record,* 1 November 1963.

"Mrs. Hicks Sees Programs OKd," *Boston Record,* 7 November 1963.

" 'Repeal State's Imbalance Law' Urges Mrs. Hicks," *Boston Record,* 23 November 1963.

"Mrs. Hicks Sees Kids Pressured," *Boston Traveler,* 15 Februrary 1964.

"Boston School Heads Attack Racial Report," *Boston Traveler,* 15 April 1964.

"Flood of Mail Backs Stand of Mrs. Hicks," *Boston Record,* 19 April 1965.

"Mrs. Hicks Gets Murder Threat," *Boston Record,* 10 September 1965.

"Mrs. Hicks Challenges Bus Plan," *Boston Herald,* 19 February 1966.

"Just What's the Matter In Southie?" *Boston Advertiser,* 10 July 1966.

"Survey Predicts Mrs. Hicks Defeat," *Boston Herald,* 30 April 1967.

"Hicks to File Bill on Pupil Assignments," *Boston Record,* 17 July 1967.

"Hicks Files Imbalance Repeal Bid," *Boston Record,* 3 August 1967.

"Mrs. Hicks 'Woman of Year,' " *Boston Record* 18 October 1967.

"Hicks Would Hike Firemen's Pay," *Boston Record,* 20 October 1967.

"Mrs. Hicks Blasts Cohen," *Boston Herald,* 24 October 1967.

"Mrs. Hicks Calls Foe Outsider, 'Puppet,' " *Boston Record,* 6 November 1967.

"Imbalance Law Change Urged," *Boston Herald,* 20 February 1968.

"Mrs. Hicks Urges Spiritual Rebirth," *Boston Record,* 22 November 1968.

"Mrs. Hicks Raps Imbalance Law," *Boston Record-American* 4 December 1968.

"Mrs. Hicks Scores Sullivan on Busing," *Boston Record-American,* 27 March 1969.

"Pot, Booze Prevail in Southie," *Boston Record-American,* 20 April 1972.

"South Boston: The Voices of Reason," *Boston Herald-Advertiser,* 24 August 1975.

"Garrity Denies He is 'Running' City's Schools," *Boston Herald-American,* 26 March 1976.

"Anti-Bus Group Acts to Ruin Kennedy Politically," *Boston Herald American,* 8 April 1976.

"Cardinal Rejects City Leadership Role," *Boston Herald-Advertier,* 2 May 1976.

Editorial cartoon, *Boston Herald-American,* 8 June 1976.

Letter to editor, Boston Herald-American, 8 July 1976.

"South Boston High Crisis: Problems, No Visible Solutions," *Boston Herald-Advertiser,* 17 October 1976.

Boston Phoenix: Excerpts from "On Patrol: Night-Riding With the Marshals" by Dave O'Brian, 18 May 1976, pp. 6-7; and, page 8 of "Tug of ROAR" by Dianne Dumonski, 25 May 1976.

Dorsey Press: Excerpt from William A. Gamson, *Strategy of Social Protest.* Copyright © 1975 by the Dorsey Press.

E.P. Dutton & Co.: Excerpt from Andrew M. Greeley, *Why Can't They Be Like Us?* (New York: Dutton, 1975), pp. 96-98. Copyright © 1975 by E.P. Dutton & Company

Harvard University Press: Excerpt from Martin T. Katzman, *The Political Economy of Urban Schools (Cambridge, Mass.: MIT Press, 1971), p. 62. Copyright © 1971 by the Joint Center for Urban Studies of the Massachusetts Institute of Technology and Harvard University.*

MIT Press: Excerpt from Robert A. Woods and Albert J. Kennedy, Zone of Emergence (Cambridge, Mass.: MIT Press, 1962), pp. 168-169. Copyright © 1962 by the Joint Center for Urban Studies of the Massachusetts Institute of Technology and Harvard University.

Nashville Tennessean: Associated Press report "Anger Brews in LA Busing," 28 May 1978, p. 12-A.

The Oregonian: Excerpt from Associated Press report "Whites Stay Out of School," 7 October 1980, p. A-8.

Phi Delta Kappan: Excerpt from page 162 of "Magnet Education in Boston" by Charles B. McMillian, 59, November 1977.

The Real Paper: Excerpts from page 16 of "I Got My Job through ROAR and Louise Day Hicks" by Joe Conason, 16 June 1976; and page 3

of "South Group Threatens Left with Violence" by Joe Conason, 9 April 1977.

Transaction, Inc.: Excerpt from page 16 of "Negro Neighbors—Banned in Boston" by J.M. Ross, Thomas Crawford, and Thomas Pettigrew, published by permission of Transaction, Inc. from *Transaction* 3, no. 6. Copyright © 1966 by Transaction, Inc.

Berkeley: University of California Press, 1972, pp. 51-52.

University of Chicago Press: Excerpts from Gerald R. Suttles, *The Social Construction of Communities* Chicago: University of Chicago Press, 1972), pp. 36-37. Copyright © 1972 by the University of Chicago Press.

Grateful acknowledgment is also made to the Inter-University Consortium of Political and Social Research (ICPSR) for making available 1972, 1974, and 1976 U.S. national Election study data, and to the National Opinion Research Center (NORC) for General Social Survey Data, 1972-1978.

School Desegregation and Defended Neighborhoods

Days of Rage

The Wrong Time and Place

On 7 October 1974 André Jean-Louis, a Haitian immigrant, drove his car into South Boston en route to the laundry where his wife worked. A crowd of whites had assembled at the intersection of Old Colony and Dorchester streets to jeer and possibly stone passing schoolbuses returning black students to Roxbury and North Dorchester. Jean-Louis likely recognized the gravity of his situation instantly after stopping for a red light at this crossroads. For a few seconds the astonished whites eyed a visibly terrified Jean-Louis. Then someone yelled, "get the nigger," and the crowd was transformed into a mob, swarming over the car, pounding on the windows, dragging Jean-Louis out. A motorcycle policeman who intervened was knocked down. Temporarily breaking free from his assailants, an already bloodied Jean-Louis dashed toward the illusionary safety of a nearby porch. His pursuers caught him at the steps, grabbed his shirt, and jerked him back into their midst for more punishment. At this point, however, a police officer fired a warning shot and the mob retreated. Other police seized the moment to thrust Jean-Louis into a squad car and drive him safely out of South Boston.[1]

Signs of the Times

No one entering South Boston in January 1976 could fail to notice scores of messages expessing neighborhood opposition to the city's court-ordered school desegregation. Printed placards adorned perhaps one-third of the shop windows along Broadway, the chief commercial thoroughfare, exhorting inhabitants to "Resist," "Never" accept busing, and "Remember Black Tuesday," when South Boston High had been placed in federal receivership. Other merchants displayed less strident declarations of support for the South Boston Information Center, the local antibusing headquarters. Printed messages supplemented hundreds of inscriptions chalked or sprayed on walls, doors, lampposts, fences, sidewalks, and street intersections. One wall bore a promise in red letters three feet high: "We Shall Continue to Resist!"

Railing against the Wind

On a raw February afternoon in 1976 an elderly patron, stuffing clothes into a coin-operated washer at a South Boston laundromat, muttered to no one in particular, "Goddamned outsiders. This town was okay until the goddamned outsiders came in."

Frigid gusts lashed the shabby and exposed Broadway rapid transit station the following night, each new blast causing notable misery among shivering subway passengers waiting to transfer to City Point and Old Colony buses. A once-enclosed bench no longer defended against the wind because someone had kicked out its plexiglass panels. In this drab setting another elderly South Bostonian rasped: "One bus! One damned bus for South Boston! No Jews here. No niggers here. Jews get a bus every eight minutes, niggers every five. Southie gets one every three hours!"[2]

A Savage Spring

On 5 April 1976 about fifteen white South Boston and Charlestown teenagers assaulted a black labor representative outside City Hall in downtown Boston. The victim was on his way to the mayor's office when he encountered the teenagers, also entering the building for a meeting with Louise Day Hicks, a city councilwoman. During the unprovoked beating that followed, one strapping youngster clubbed the black man with a metal staff bearing the stars and stripes. This nationally publicized incident set off a spree of racial violence lasting into early summer.

Probably the most shocking episode of this violent period took place on 19 April, when rock-throwing black youths in Roxbury struck a white motorist, who lost control of his car and crashed into another vehicle. Some of his assailants then dragged him out and crushed his skull with paving stones. Police arrived to find the victim lying in the street surrounded by perhaps one hundred people, some of whom chanted "Let him die." Having sustained massive brain damage, the man lapsed into a coma and died several months later.[3] Across the city whites and blacks assailed one another with bats, tire irons, rocks, and fists.

A Fearsome Reputation

At the peak of this violence Humberto Cardinal Medeiros, Catholic archbishop of Boston, refused in a much-regretted newspaper interview to press personally for an end to racial violence in Boston. Cardinal Medeiros was especially unwilling to visit South Boston and implore its overwhelmingly Catholic population to abide by Christian principles. "Why should I go," he asked a reporter, "to get stoned?" Such a spectacle would hardly help matters, he insisted, and the visit would be pointless in any event: "I've been turned off in South Boston. . . . No one there is listening to me. Eighty percent of the Catholics in South Boston do not attend Mass . . . and it contributes to their attitude toward forced busing. People there are not learning the principles of true Christian living."[4]

The outcry following publication of his remarks soon induced Cardinal Medeiros to apologize publicly. He repented further by saying Christmas Mass at South Boston's Gate of Heaven Church. These gestures soothed some injured feelings in the neighborhood, but the initial comment had painfully reminded residents of their reputation in the outside world.[5]

"All We Want Is to Be Left Alone . . ."

Another response to this spring's violence was initiation of nightly vigilante car patrols in Charlestown and South Boston. Ostensibly the surveillance was undertaken to keep strangers out after dark. "There's no one gonna come in here and bother us," boasted a sentinel in South Boston, "we have the capacity to put thousands on the streets in a matter of minutes." "All we want is to be left alone," a comrade averred, "I wouldn't care if they put a fence around Southie so I'd never have to leave and no one could come in."[6]

School Days

Anyone hoping for lessened violence and tension when South Boston High began a third year of desegregation on 8 September 1976 was soon disappointed. Five people were sent to the hospital and several others arrested during the first month of classes, almost every day of which included interracial violence. School officials issued 196 suspensions of varying lengths in the first eighteen days of classes, 102 more than had been levied during the same period of the previous year.[7] Boston motorcycle police escorted buses transporting black students to and from the school, while state troopers patrolled hallways inside. Blacks and whites arrived in separate groups, filing past metal detectors as they entered different doorways. Teachers conducted "corridor sweeps" when classes were in session in an attempt to clear hallways of potential troublemakers; actual troublemakers were placed in separate "holding rooms" or suspended. Any point of white and black convergence was a potential flash point. Reporters often waited outside the school anticipating daily news of trouble. A journalist's notebook for 28 September described a fairly typical day:

8:12 a.m. White students slow on entering; black male student arrested for assaulting a teacher.

8:45 a.m. One-on-one fighting in lobby and on second floor during first period filing.

10:25 a.m. Black male students and white male students involved in confrontations on second floor; suspensions reported: four white males and two black males, five days for fighting; one white male, two black males and one black female, three days for fighting.

11:20 a.m. Suspensions reported: one white male, three days for fighting; one white male, five days for refusing to go to class; one black male, five days for possession of a weapon (nail).

1:05 p.m. Disruption in cafeteria during study period; books thrown but no injuries; some students sent to holding rooms.

3:00 p.m. Suspensions reported: three black males and one white male, three days for book throwing; one white male, three days for fighting.

3:10 p.m. Follow-up on fight this morning; teacher was taken to City Hospital for broken wrist.[8]

Sporadic fighting, frequent demonstrations, and oppressive tension characterized South Boston High's 1976-1977 academic year. In May black parents involved in the desegregation litigation asked the federal judge to close South Boston High and transfer its operations to a more neutral site outside the neighborhood. They complained the school was still identifiably white and representative of local resentment. The plaintiffs noted that South Boston High had been exempted from holding fire drills out of fear for the safety of black students who left the building.[9] Judge W. Arthur Garrity listened sympathetically but denied their request.

Recollections of a Hyde Park Parent

Hyde Park's leading antibusing spokesman recalled his compliance with Phase 1 of court-ordered busing in 1974 and the subsequent experiences of his son, who had been assigned to a local grade school:

I swore that if my children were assigned to the neighborhood schools . . . I didn't care who they went to school with. So I sent them. My boy caught it. . . . For the first time he gets shoved in the school yard, [and] his knees are all abrasions. So you say to yourself, "You're overreacting . . . calm down, it's not a racial incident, it's kids." So you call the school and try to straighten it out. . . . The second time he was shoved

down three stairs, not a whole flight, but three stairs, and whacks his head
and comes home with a big egg. So you say to yourself, "You're paranoid.
This is not racism, this is kids." The third time the [other] kid is
fourteen . . . and in the second grade, and he's strangling my kid. What do
you do? Do you keep your kid there? The next time it could be a knife, it
could be a pick, it could be anything. No way. . . . I took him out. . . . I
am not going to expose my children to that [anymore].[10]

Why Boston?

The anecdotes just recounted are only selective samplings of the furor
associated with Boston school desegregation during the 1970s. Tensions still
smouldered in a few places as the decade ended. In the fall of 1979, for example, a black high school football player was shot and crippled in
Charlestown. Racial violence flared in several schools for weeks after this
tragedy. South Boston High was forced to cancel classes on 2 October 1980
after a brawl between 100 white and black students. This outburst had been
preceded by two weeks of lesser violence and rising animosity. Whites
demanded reinstallation of recently removed metal detectors, but the
school's headmaster refused to take this symbolic step backward. "It would
be a big mistake to go back to metal detectors," he maintained, "we're not
running a concentration camp here."[11] White students boycotted in protest.

This book is a study of white opposition to busing and school
desegregation in Boston. Why did Boston experience so much turmoil over
busing? Why did resistance build to epic proportions in the city that gave
America its first public schools? What conditions impeded implementation
of federal court orders and rendered the local political system incapable of
resolving the conflict on its own? What lessons of national significance can
be learned from Boston's agony? These are our chief concerns in the present
study.

Understanding White Opposition to Busing

A simplistic analysis of opposition to busing begins and ends with white
racism. The Reverend Jesse Jackson and other black proponents of busing
take this view, invariably concluding "it's not the bus, it's us." Neo-
Marxists have argued similarly, often forsaking more traditional notions of
class struggle. One recent essay in this vein postulated fear of losing social
and economic advantages over blacks as the basis of white working-class
resistance to busing. "The issue is racism," the essay proclaimed, "and it
would be wrong to shift the debate away from it at this time."[12]

The U.S. Commission on Civil Rights also places much stock in the
white racism thesis, but emphasizes public ignorance of busing facts as well.

Numerous reports issued by this body condemn bigotry as a primary source of antibusing feeling, and strive to show that busing is the safest method of pupil transportation, that average distances bused for desegregation are shorter than previously, and that financial costs associated with busing for integration typically are not great.[13]

White reservations about busing for desegregation have been treated more sympathetically in accounts focusing on social class differences. Middle- and working-class parents are unlikely to approve of mixing their children with lower-class youth in any circumstances, it has been argued, and hence fears about busing are said to be grounded in class considerations. Recent media emphasis on violent crime in urban schools hardly reduces such concerns, as youth from the black underclass are unmistakably identified as a primary source of the problem. Diane Ravitch captured the mix of racial and class apprehensions in a description of how middle-class New Yorkers felt about cross-district busing:

> The more that middle-class parents read about the conditions in ghetto schools, the more frightened they were about any integration that might send their children into these schools. Some of the white fear was simply racist fantasy. But there was also a middle-class fear, common to both races, of sending their children to a school where there was a breakdown of discipline and adult authority, low academic standards, obscene language, and sporadic violence. Harrowing accounts of conditions in ghetto schools stirred the conscience of leading citizens who had no children in the public schools and heightened the anxiety of those who did.[14]

Such anxieties are not likely to disappear because of statistics about the safety of busing as a mode of student transportation or tepid academic findings that white achievement usually does not decline with school desegregation.[15] Even heroic attempts to upgrade staff, curricula, and physical plant in stigmatized schools may not be enough to overcome white (and black) middle-class fears.

Neoconservative intellectuals have depicted opposition to busing even more sympathetically as understandable resistance to governmental meddling and denial of personal freedom. For example, Robert Nisbet condemned "elaborate and labyrinthine programs of busing schoolchildren tens and tens of miles for no purpose other than that of meeting some bureaucratically arrived at quota."[16] Newspaper accounts often echo this perspective in reporting parental reactions to busing plans, as in the case of a Los Angeles mother who was notified her daughter would be bused for "about an hour" across the city rather than attend the school "across the street" from her home. "My feeling is that it's absolutely ridiculous," the mother said, "and it's just moving bodies."[17]

The present study explores yet another source of busing opposition as the most promising approach to analysis of events in Boston. Defense of neighborhood institutions against unwanted social change could be a fundamental reason for opposition to "forced busing," just as it is often said to underlie resistance to urban renewal, "gentrification," or some other plan to alter urban communities.

A "defended neighborhood" is not just any community where some or most inhabitants have been aroused. Rather it is a type of urban village no longer often found in metropolitan areas of the United States. Defended neighborhoods inside big cities enjoy reputations that cling to residents like shabby clothes, and exhibit patterns of relationships between inhabitants more typical of rural hamlets than of urban society. Such enclaves enjoy distinct identities reinforced by insider understandings of where neighborhood turf begins and ends. Within these unusual communities predominantly ethnic and blue-collar populations cling to certain advantages denied other urban districts, including notably more affluent ones. Inside defended neighborhoods most inhabitants feel personally safe and interact with neighbors on a relatively intimate basis. Hence their daily way of life enjoys aspects of community seldom found elsewhere in the city.

Understood in this way the defended neighborhood is to be viewed as a particularly recalcitrant environment for implementation of basic change. Those who formulate or applaud such changes may regard their plans and underlying biases as unassailable, but residents of a defended neighborhood seemingly threatened by their plans are unlikely to agree.[18] Appeals to the rule of law, social equality, or other norms probably will not offset what residents fear they will lose in exchange.

Although analytically distinct from other perspectives on busing opposition, the defended neighborhood view need not exclude elements of racism, class antagonism, ignorance, or suspicion of big government. As one urban scholar recently noted, "under cover of acting in the interests of the neighborhood, some people may give vent to the most unjustified and neurotic prejudices."[19] Indeed, it is difficult to imagine how those defending a neighborhood could remain free of prejudice or class hatred under some circumstances. Unless the dynamics of community conflict somehow have been repealed in school desegregation disputes, persistent strife over busing can only exacerbate racial bigotry and incorporate it into neighborhood defense. If the offending policy does not concern race, however, bigotry need not figure in neighborhood defense at all. In any case, although the specific threat shapes community response, the defended neighborhood is much more than situtionally-determined reaction. How much more is set out in greater detail subsequently.

Plan of the Book

The Boston school-desegregation controversy must be understood in context. National events and trends had an impact on what both sides thought and did. The federal district court decision that Boston schools were unlawfully segregated cannot be understood without first understanding the most important legal precedents handed down by the Supreme Court and lower federal courts elsewhere. Hence chapter 2 covers often familiar but still necessary material to construct a national-events context for understanding what happened in Boston. Chapter 3 sets out a general framework for analysis of judicial policy implementation and compliance, and then fits the defended-neighborhood concept within this framework. Chapter 4 is a history of South Boston, the archetypical defended neighborhood and district most mobilized against "forced busing." Chapter 5 chronicles the rise of Louise Day Hicks and the racial-imbalance dispute preceding the federal court's desegregation decision in 1974. Chapters 6 and 7 describe the way in which Boston's school desegregation lawsuit came about and detail the various judicial steps to implement desegregation in Boston schools. Chapter 8 analyzes defended-neighborhood protest against busing and draws upon several additional frameworks to enrich the explanation. Chapter 9 examines four antibusing claims that school desegregation caused unprecedented white flight, has already made racial imbalance worse than ever before, has destroyed educational quality in most Boston schools, and produced Boston's 1976 fiscal crisis and property tax increase. Chapter 10 summarizes leading findings by reviewing the questions raised in chapter 3, and offers policy recommendations for desegregating defended-neighborhood schools.

Notes

1. This account partly draws upon notes made during viewing videotaped television network news programs at the Vanderbilt University Television News Archive. Recorded in Central Standard Time (CST), the programs watched were the ABC Evening News, 7 October 1974, 5:22:50 p.m. to 5:23:59 p.m.; the CBS Evening News, 7 October 1974, 5:48:50 p.m. to 5:49:39 p.m.; and, the NBC Nightly News, 7 October 1974, 5:42:30 p.m. to 5:43:59 p.m. An account of the incident is also found in Jon Hillson, *The Battle of Boston* (New York: Pathfinder, 1977), pp. 15-18.

2. Notes by Buell in South Boston, 15 February 1976.

3. See "White Boston Man on Danger List After Beating by Blacks," *Boston Evening Globe,* 20 April 1976, p. 1; his death was noted in "Richard Poleet, in Coma Since '76 Beating, Dies," *Boston Herald-American,* 31 May 1978. The incident precipitating Boston's spring of racial violence is described in "Black Man Beaten by Young Busing Protesters," *Boston Globe* 6 April 1976, p. 1.

4. Quoted by Eleanor Roberts in "Cardinal Rejects City Leadership Role," *Boston Sunday Herald-Advertiser,* 2 May 1976, p. 1.

5. See "Cardinal Apologizes," *Boston Sunday Herald-Advertiser,* 9 May 1976, p. 1; and, "South Boston Welcomes Cardinal at Christmas," *Boston Globe,* 26 December 1976, p. 16.

6. Quoted by Dave O'Brian, "On Patrol: Night-Riding with the Marshals," *Boston Phoenix* 18 May 1976, pp. 6-7.

7. See Alan Eisner, "South Boston High Crisis: Problems, No Visible Solutions," *Boston Sunday Herald-Advertiser,* 17 October 1976, p. A-1.

8. Ibid., p. A-2. South Boston High violence has already inspired one novel; see Alan D. Burke, *Fire Watch* (Boston: Little, Brown, 1980). For an argument that press reports exaggerated busing-related violence in Boston, see Edwin Diamond, *Good News, Bad News* (Cambridge, Mass.: MIT Press, 1978), pp. 207-224.

9. "Blacks Give Up On Southie," *Boston Globe,* 4 May 1977, p. 12.

10. Interview by Buell, 11 July 1977.

11. Quoted in "Whites Stay Out of School," *The Oregonian,* 7 October 1980, p. A-8.

12. Jim Green and Allen Hunter, "Racism and Busing in Boston," in *Marxism and the Metropolis,* William K. Taub and Larry Sawyer, eds. (New York: Oxford University Press, 1978), p. 273.

13. See the following reports by the U.S. Commission on Civil Rights: *Public Knowledge and Busing Opposition* (Washington, D.C.: U.S. Government Printing Office, 1973); *Fulfilling the Letter and Spirit of the Law: Desegregating the Nation's Public Schools* (1976); and, *Statement on Metropolitan School Desegregation* (1977).

14. Diane Ravich, *The Great School Wars: New York City, 1805-1973* (New York: Basic Books, 1974), p. 254.

15. A good summary of research through the early 1970s is Nancy H. St. John, *School Desegregation: Outcomes for Children* (New York: Wiley, 1975). For more recent discussions, see *Law and Contemporary Problems* 42 (Summer 1978).

16. Robert Nisbet, *Twilight of Authority* (New York: Oxford University Press, 1976), p. 57. A more extensive case against busing is found in Nathan Glazer, *Affirmative Discrimination: Ethnic Inequality and Public Policy* (New York: Basic Books, 1975), pp. 77-129.

17. "Anger Brews in L.A. Busing, *Nashville Tennessean,* 28 May 1978, p. 12-A.

18. See Murray Edelman, *Political Language: Words That Succeed and Policies That Fail* (New York: Academic, 1977).

19. James Q. Wilson, *Thinking about Crime* (New York: Basic Books, 1975), p. 27.

2

The Boston Controversy in National Perspective

Transformation of a Symbol

Until the 1960s few symbols of American life were more innocuous than the yellow school bus. Long necessary to get children to rural schools, riding the bus also had become routine for suburban and inner-city pupils by the 1950s. In 1974-1975 just over half of all primary and secondary school students rode buses to class.[1]

Estimates vary, but all accounts agree that only a small fraction of all children bused since 1954 were bused for purposes of school desegregation. According to the Department of Transportation, less than one percent of the increased school busing from 1954 to 1975 was due to desegregation.[2]

When most Americans refer to busing today, however, they mean involuntary reassignment and transportation of students in order to lessen racial imbalance. "Busing" connotes much more than a mode of pupil transportation. For some it is the only practical way to desegregate urban schools; for others it represents an infringement upon personal choice and destruction of neighborhood schools. Hence the term has become shorthand for a fundamental debate over the meaning of American values. In the process this dispute has generated some of the most complicated litigation ever brought to the federal courts, pushed Congress into confrontations with the judiciary, enjoyed episodic importance in presidential and other campaigns, and commanded the attention of every significant opinion research institution in the nation.

Events in Boston cannot be understood in the absence of a national context. This is particularly the case with respect to federal judicial decisions, but is also true of presidential positions and public opinion data. An abundance of available and able descriptions of congressional actions on busing obviates an extensive discussion of legislation.[3]

The Federal Courts and Busing, 1954-1974

In order to assess the steps taken by Judge Arthur Garrity in Boston, we must first review the leading decisions by which lower federal courts were permitted to use equity powers in fashioning desegregation remedies.[4] Of course, the modern history of judicial desegregation policy begins with *Brown I,* in which a unanimous Supreme Court held *de jure* public school

11

segregation unconstitutional.[5] In *Brown II* the justices instructed lower federal courts to use their equity powers in bringing about desegregation. In so doing, courts could take account of physical conditions in the schools, the pupil transportation system, attendance and assignment zones, and local laws and regulations.[6]

Lower court judges in the South did not embrace this task with uniform enthusiasm. Some challenged *Brown I* outright, while others attempted to minimize it through narrow interpretations.[7] A few judges upheld *Brown* despite enormous pressures and thus effected a modicum of school desegregation.[8]

A new era began with passage of the 1964 Civil Rights Act. Title VI of the new law empowered the Department of Health, Education, and Welfare (HEW) to impose desegregation requirements on public school systems accepting federal funds. The law also provided a basis for initiation of school desegregation suits by federal attorneys.

The new period became evident in the judicial realm in 1968, when the Supreme Court indicated an end to patience with southern noncompliance and gradualism. Writing for a unanimous court in *Green* v. *County School Board of New Kent County,* Justice William Brennan rejected "freedom of choice" plans in favor of more immediate efforts to desegregate. "The burden of a school board today," Brennan declared, "is to come forward with a plan that promises realistically to work, and promises realistically to work now."[9]

Lower federal-court decisions affirmed this view. In Louisiana, for example, Judge Herbert Christenberry ordered officials in notoriously segregationist Plaquemines Parish to cease helping all-white private schools and start providing funds for public schools, while improving their curriculum and supplying other services stipulated by the court.[10] In Alabama Judge Frank Johnson ordered Montgomery County school administrators to alter bus routes, desegregate teaching and supportive staff, submit periodic reports on racial problems in the schools, and consult with him on all construction plans.[11]

It was clear by the end of the 1960s that southern dilatory tactics no longer had much chance in federal court. Moreover, the delay wrought by such recalcitrance had compelled federal judges to make extensive use of equitable remedies in overcoming segregation. Segregationists and integrationists alike recognized after *Green* that the school bus would likely become the vehicle of segregation's demise. When the Supreme Court agreed to hear a case involving the Charlotte-Mecklenburg school district of North Carolina, both sides realized a crucial juncture had been reached.

In 1969 the 550-square mile Charlotte-Mecklenburg district took in 107 schools and 84,000 students. Whites were about 71 percent of the combined city and county student population, while blacks made up the remaining 29 percent. Since the district's schools had been segregated by law, and more than two-thirds of the black pupils attended totally black schools, no one was surprised by a district court decision in favor of the black plaintiffs.[12]

The basic issue in this case was the extensive use of equitable powers by a district judge. Judge James McMillan ordered the Charlotte-Mecklenburg district to undertake substantial busing and group schools in clusters in order to balance most schools in the system. School officials appealed, partly on grounds that Judge McMillan's remedies exceeded his authority, and were upheld by the Fourth Circuit Court of Appeals, which judged McMillan's orders to be "overly harsh."[13]

Chief Justice Warren Burger wrote the Supreme Court's unanimous opinion in *Swann v. Charlotte—Mecklenburg Board of Education*.[14] When local officials defaulted in their obligation to end *de jure* segregation, he held, the fourteenth amendment's equal protection clause gave wide latitude to federal courts seeking to correct the situation. In this connection Burger upheld the racial balancing required of Charlotte-Mecklenburg schools, accepted busing said not to be dangerous to students or harmful to their education, and embraced school combinations even when "administratively awkward, inconvenient, and even bizarre in some situations."[15]

Yet Burger offered important qualifications as well. He declared that every school need not be racially balanced, allowing a "small number" of predominantly one-race schools if it could be proved their enrollments resulted from "genuinely non-discriminating" assignments. One indication of such procedures would be a transfer policy permitting blacks access to predominantly white schools.[16] He also raised the specter of "resegregation" because of what since has become known as "white flight." On this point Burger concluded, "neither school authorities nor federal district courts are constitutionally required to make year-by-year adjustments of student bodies once the affirmative duty to desegregate has been accomplished and racial discrimination through official action is eliminated from the system."[17]

This last point underscored the traditional distinction between *de jure* and *de facto* segregation. *De jure* segregation originated in official actions, most obviously manifested in state laws requiring racially separate schools. Though no less consequential, *de facto* segregation was said to arise out of unplanned conditions, such as residential patterns, where racial separation supposedly could not be attributed to official intent. At the time of the Charlotte-Mecklenburg decision, southern school segregation was said to be primarily *de jure* in origin, while most northern segregation was regarded as *de facto*.[18] Only a few northern school cases had been decided by lower federal courts, and the Supreme Court had refused to hear any challenge to *de facto* segregation.

The handful of lower federal court decisions involving northern schools did not form a coherent pattern. In a few cases judges deduced deliberate segregation from programmatic consequences. For example, Judge Irving Kaufman ruled that district boundary changes, pupil assignments, and student transfers in New Rochelle, New York had "intentionally created" a 90 percent black school.[19] Judge J. Skelly Wright did not deny valid educational purpose in neighborhood schools, tracking policies, new construction, and other Washington, D.C., programs, but held they discriminated against black students all the same. "If a valid purpose is in fact joined by a segregatory purpose," he declared, "the court has no doubt that a *de jure* case has been established."[20] But similar conditions were interpreted differently elsewhere, for example, rulings in favor of racially imbalanced schools in Gary, Cincinnati, and Kansas City because deliberate intent could not be found in existing laws.[21] Mixed results followed from cases arising in Chicago, Indianapolis, and, eventually, New York.[22]

This inconsistency underscored the need for a Supreme Court decision clarifying what constituted unlawful segregation. It was widely thought this point had been reached when the justices agreed to take a complicated Denver case from the Tenth Circuit Court of Appeals.

The major facts of the Denver case require brief discussion because of their direct relevance to later events in Boston. Black and Hispanic parents had protested racial isolation and other conditions in Park Hill district schools, and had been promised relief by the Denver school board. A newly elected board refused to implement these promises, however, and the parents brought suit in federal district court. After winning this case on *de jure* grounds,[23] the plaintiffs amended their suit to include all Denver schools. Their expanded case lost in both the district court and the Tenth Circuit Court, as deliberate official intent could not be proved for other schools in the system.[24]

In its decision the Supreme Court did not abolish the distinction between *de jure* and *de facto* segregation as some had anticipated, but the way in which the majority opinion reasoned that Denver officials had maintained unlawful segregation seemed to accomplish much the same result. Delivering this opinion, Justice Brennan noted the absence of statutory requirements, but found official intent nonetheless in various policies of the school board. Defining such intent by example, he pointed to manipulation of attendance zones, location of school construction sites in racially homogeneous areas, and neighborhood school designations conducive to residential segregation as deliberate and unlawful actions.

In terms momentous for Boston, Brennan now turned to remedies appropriate for an urban school system partly characterized by unlawful segregation. Appealing to "common sense," the justice argued that the consequences of unlawful segregation in a few schools were inevitably visited upon all other schools in the system. An overwhelmingly nonwhite school in one part of town meant fewer nonwhite students in other schools with similar grade structures. Hence deliberate segregation anywhere in the system "infected" all schools.[25]

Of course, such reasoning placed defendant school officials in desegregation suits at an enormous disadvantage. Not only could *de jure* segregation be inferred from nonstatutory circumstances, but, once intent was established for any school, the defendants somehow had to prove their actions (or those of predecessors) had not "contaminated" the rest of the system. In the likely event they were unsuccessful, district-wide remedies like those used in Charlotte-Mecklenburg were appropriate.

Since legal developments after the Denver decision had relatively little impact on the Boston litigation, our discussion of school-desegregation case law concludes at this point. Clearly, the Boston case came to Judge Garrity at the very time the federal courts had resolved to "grasp the nettle" of school segregation. Lower federal-court judges had developed and refined their equitable powers in desegregation cases largely because southern recalcitrance allowed them no other course. The Denver ruling demonstrated that northern school systems under less stringent interpretations of unlawful segregation were hardly immune from such remedies.

Presidential Policy on Busing, 1969–1974

In Boston, as elsewhere in the nation, citizens noted presidential pronouncements on important policy matters. The election of Richard Nixon placed an avowed opponent of busing and a gradualist on school desegregation in the White House at the very time lower federal-court judges were striking out against segregated schools. It was not long before the Nixon administration had taken issue with several judicial decisions, purged its own ranks of integrationists, and effectively ceased helping the courts to bring about school desegregation. Moreover, President Nixon was to voice virtually every antibusing argument later employed in Boston, Detroit, Pontiac, and other cities where school desegregation encountered resistance. The Nixon position on busing is best understood by analysis of two extensive presidential messages.

Perhaps the most comprehensive pronouncement on busing ever made by a president was released 24 March 1970 in the form of a written message.[26] According to Raymond Price, chief author of the final draft, Nixon's statement was intended to instruct the judiciary as well as sway public opinion.[27] The document expressed eight main points.

First, the president noted inconsistent federal and state court decisions on busing, some of which he characterized as "extreme," and pointed up the lack of a clear Supreme Court decision in the area. Given such ambiguity and the concomitant failure of Congress to resolve the problem, Nixon argued, it was his responsibility to determine national policy.[28]

Second, although affirming a commitment to *Brown*, Nixon interpreted the law in very conservative fashion. Only *de jure* segregation was a problem, and, even when discovered, local authorities were to be given every opportunity for voluntary compliance. Such compliance could take account of "cost, capacity, and convenience for pupils and parents," and desegregation was not to disrupt education, require precise racial balancing, or even compel reassignment of students beyond "normal geographical school zones."[29]

Having raised the topic of *de jure* segregation, the president now distinguished it from *de facto* segregation in a third section devoted to origins and remedies. Allowing that a single system could exhibit both types of segregation, Nixon concluded it was appropriate only to remedy the *de jure* situation "without insisting on a remedy for the lawful *de facto* portion."[30]

The influence of the famous Coleman report was much evident in a fourth section pertaining to educational disadvantages of minority pupils. In several paragraphs Nixon reiterated the view that home environment was far more important than race in determining individual success in school. He saw "inescapably racist overtones" in the assumption that an all-black school was necessarily substandard. "It is not really because they serve black children that most of these schools are inferior," he contended, "but rather because they serve poor children who often lack the home environment that encourages learning."[31]

A fifth part essayed the purpose of public schools; Nixon insisted this purpose was education rather than social reform. It was unfair to expect schools to build "a multi-racial society which the adult world has failed to achieve for itself," and further, it was shortsighted to promote integration at the expense of education.[32]

Antibusing activists across the nation would soon expand a sixth theme only briefly mentioned in Nixon's 1970 message. It was that involuntary school desegregation might create enough tension to cause "psychic injury" to sensitive children.[33]

Even a white-flight argument may be found in this statement. After pointing to declining white enrollments in some big city school systems, the president cautioned that too much desegregation would merely accelerate white loss to the point of resegregation. Then minority pupils would look upon integration as something other than an "unmixed blessing."[34]

Finally, President Nixon proclaimed that an open and pluralistic society did not require complete racial integration. In words that would be repeated in South Boston and other defended neighborhoods, he concluded:

> . . . . [I]t is natural that people with a common heritage retain special ties; it is natural and right that we have Italian or Irish or Negro or Norwegian neighborhoods; it is natural and right that members of these communities feel a sense of group identity and group pride. In terms of an open society, what matters is mobility: the right and the ability of each person to decide for himself where and how he wants to live, whether as part of the ethnic enclave or as part of the larger society—or, as many do, share the life of both.[35]

Every explicit reference to busing in Nixon's 1970 message was negative. In one passage the president maintained that limited funds were better spent on improving schools, curriculum, and faculty than wasted in purchases of tires, gasoline, and more buses "to transport young children miles away from their neighborhoods."[36] Elsewhere he characterized busing as "taking children out of the schools they would normally attend, and forcing them instead to attend others more distant, often in strange or even hostile neighborhoods."[37]

The administration's sharp disagreement with judicial busing policy was again evident when President Nixon urged passage of the Student Transportation Moratorium Act of 1972 and a companion measure allocating $2.5 million for special programs to serve disadvantaged students. Busing had become a major issue in the 1972 Democratic presidential primaries, and George Wallace's success with it in Florida unquestionably influenced Nixon's determination to make another strong antibusing statement. This he did immediately after the Florida primary in a televised address to the nation, and almost two years to the day of his 1970 message. Nixon sent Congress a slightly longer written statement the next day.[38]

In a direct challenge to judicial authority Nixon requested congressional enactment of a ban against any further federal-court orders requiring busing for desegregation. During the year in which this moratorium was to be in effect Congress would devise other methods of school desegregation. Thereafter busing could be used only in extraordinary circumstances. Citing the need for "action now," Nixon called for legislation instead of a constitutional amendment. Certain lower-court rulings, he claimed, had created "confusion and contradiction in the law; anger, fear, and turmoil in local communities; and, worst of all, agonized concern among hundreds of thousands of parents for the education and safety of their children . . ."[39] Continuing in this vein, the president said:

> They want their children educated in their own neighborhoods. Many have invested their life's savings in a home in a neighborhood they chose because it had good schools. They do not want their children bused across the city to an inferior school just to meet some social planner's concept of what is considered to be the correct racial balance . . .[40]

He also spurned the claim that white racism explained opposition to court-ordered busing as "dangerous nonsense" and "vicious libel."[41]

The moratorium bill expired in committee, and the shooting of George Wallace left the president unchallenged as the nation's foremost opponent of busing. Senator George McGovern's nomination further reoriented the issues in 1972, and busing was infrequently mentioned during the fall campaign. Nonetheless, Nixon's view of busing was known to most voters. One 1972 election study found only 18 percent of the electorate unable to pinpoint Nixon's antibusing position, as compared to 32 percent who were unfamiliar with McGovern's views. The same sample saw Nixon as more conservative on busing than on any of thirteen other issues put to them.[42] Another study revealed busing to be the least important of eleven issues mentioned by voters in 1972, but 86 percent still described the Nixon posture correctly.[43]

Of course, the Watergate scandal diverted attention from busing, as it did from almost every other problem, and an increasingly preoccupied Nixon made few mentions of busing during his abbreviated second term. His most substantive reference appeared in the 1974 State of the Union address, in which he said busing should be used only as a last resort, "tightly circumscribed even then."[44]

In summary, presidential policy openly conflicted with that formulated by the federal courts. By 1972 President Nixon was urging Congress to join in defiance of judicial authority to prescribe busing even as a remedy for *de jure* segregation. However, even a Congress cowed by antibusing furor in Detroit and other cities was unwilling to set out on so certain a collision course with the courts. Had Watergate not driven him from office, Nixon almost certainly would have sided with antibusing forces in Boston. In any case, his successor, Gerald Ford, was equally opposed, having endorsed a constitutional amendment to end busing. Such important resistance to judicial policy significantly reduced its legitimacy and isolated the lower federal courts. Nowhere was this more apparent than in public opinion.

Public Opinion on Busing, 1970-1978

Leading samplers of public opinion evidently did not regard busing as an issue significant enough to warrant specific questions before 1970. Once the problem emerged from its southern context, however, national opinion on busing was surveyed extensively.

Unfortunately, most questions asked about busing have been deficient in some important respect. Ambiguity has always been one of these shortcomings, as few surveys in the last decade specified what type of busing was at issue—voluntary or compulsory, one- or two-way, citywide or metropolitan. A phrase like "busing across district lines" was applicable equally to neighborhoods and to cities within an urbanized area.

These irksome limitations notwithstanding, remarkably consistent patterns are apparent in the mass of available data on public reaction to court-ordered busing. The most striking pattern is the overwhelming and unrelenting disapproval of whites. However worded, a question asked about busing during the 1970s rarely failed to elicit 75 percent or more opposition from whites. This result is all the more interesting because it was obtained while white acceptance of school desegregation as a general principle increased sharply.[45] Black opinion was less fixed, as most surveys revealed a bimodal distribution in which blacks opposed to busing sometimes outnumbered those in favor.

These trends turned up in early soundings by the Louis Harris poll. In a March 1970 survey, Harris asked the following question:

> As you know, many children are bused to school now. It has been pointed out that one way to integrate the schools is to bus children from one area to another. Suppose it could be worked out that there was no more busing of school children than there is now in each community and in each state—would you favor or oppose busing to achieve integrated schools?[46]

Among whites answering this meandering question, 16 percent favored busing, 7 percent were undecided, and 77 percent opposed it. Blacks divided into 47 percent in favor, 13 percent undecided, and 40 percent opposed.

The same poll contained two questions about segregated schools. One described *de jure* circumstances, further labeled them to be southern, and requested "right" or "wrong" conclusions from respondents. The second identified *de facto* conditions, associated them with northern cities, and asked, "do you think this system in the North of separate white and black schools, due to the neighborhoods being that way, is right or wrong?[47] Responding to these loaded queries, more than half the whites disapproved of *de jure* southern segregation, but only 16 percent felt all-white schools in urban northern neighborhoods were wrong. Over half the blacks said *de jure* segregation was evil, but only 40 percent held this view of northern *de facto* segregation. Almost two-thirds of the whites and one-third of the blacks endorsed *de facto* school segregation in the North.

Two years later, Harris asked if people were willing "to see children bused" in compliance with court orders. Evidently this reference to judicial authority had little influence on whites, 75 percent of whom replied negatively. Among blacks, however, 60 percent favored busing, 8 percent were unsure, and 29 percent opposed it.[48] Harris also used questions worded to include "busing school children to achieve racial balance" in three 1972 polls. White opposition varied from 78 percent to 85 percent, while black support remained steady between 50 percent and 52 percent.[49]

The Gallup Poll and the National Opinion Research Center (NORC) used the same question consistently throughout the 1970s: "In general, do you favor or oppose the busing of white and black school children from one school district to another?"[50] Thus exists a nine-year time series in which white opposition fluctuated from 76 to 85 percent, and black opinion varied from less than 40 percent supportive to more than 60 percent.

A final confirmation of these distributions is found in the 1972, 1974, and 1976 American national-election surveys conducted by the Center for Political Studies (CPS). The CPS question offered respondents polar extremes—"achieving racial integration of the schools is so important that it justifies busing children out of their own neighborhood" as compared to "letting children go to their neighborhood schools [is important enough to] oppose busing"—and asked them to locate themselves on a seven-point continuum. At one end was "bus to achieve integration" while "keep children in neighborhood schools" represented the polar opposite. Figure 2-1 shows how whites and blacks positioned themselves in each survey. Enormous white majorities stacked up at the "neighborhood schools" end, while blacks split into probusing and antibusing groupings of comparable size.

Although an extensive analysis of the factors underlying such massive white disapproval of busing would take us off course, a few observations are worth noting. First, socioeconomic variables had generally little consequence in explaining white opposition. Although increased income and education correlated with support for school desegregation, more money and schooling generally correlated inversely with probusing attitudes in the Harris and Gallup polls cited above. The same inverse relationship often obtained in NORC and CPS data as well. Secondary analysis of nine NORC and CPS datasets produced no noteworthy associations between busing opinion and such variables as gender, subjective social class identification, party identification, residence, presence of schoolchildren in the household, and whether children in the family had been bused for nondesegregation purposes.

What about the relationship between racial prejudice and busing opinion? One measure of this connection is shown in table 2-1, where white busing positions are cross-tabulated with general preferences in race relations in 1972 and 1976. In both surveys CPS asked respondents if they preferred "desegregation," "strict segregation," or "something in-between" by way of general interaction with blacks. The table reveals a strong and highly significant association between busing opinion and desired type of race relations, with probusing whites more than twice as likely to want desegregation than antibusing respondents. Yet the data fail to disclose a desire for apartheid among antibusing whites, most of whom endorsed "something in-between." The disproportionate numbers of pro- and antibusing whites should also be noted; in 1972, 76 percent of all whites preferring desegregation *opposed* busing, while in 1976 this figure was 73 percent. In the final analysis, however, a probusing view translated much more readily into a desire for racial integration generally.

When the object of desegregation was narrowed to schools, however, these differences narrowed substantially. Three NORC general social surveys asked respondents how they felt about black and white students attending the same schools. As would be expected, probusing whites favored school desegregation almost to a person. But an overwhelming number of

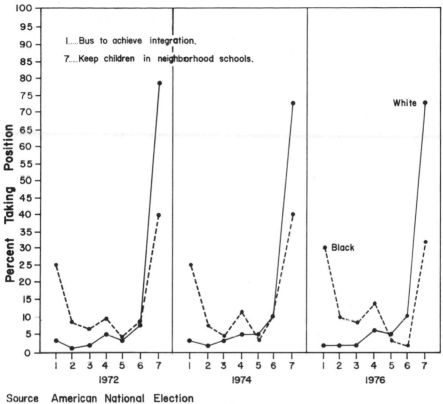

Source: American National Election Studies, Center for Political Studies, ICPSR.
Figure 2-1. White and Black Positions on School Busing Continuum, 1972, 1974, and 1976

antibusing whites also held this preference. In 1977, for example, fully 96 percent of the probusing whites wanted integrated schools, but so did 83 percent of their antibusing counterparts.[51]

NORC asked an especially interesting series of questions in five general social surveys conducted between 1972 and 1978. Evidently, the objective was to probe white willingness to enroll children in schools with growing numbers of blacks. Any respondent who expressed no opposition to enrolling children in a school where only "a few" of the other students were black was then asked about a school where "half" of the others would be black. No objection to this mix then produced a final query about a school in which "most" other pupils would be black.

Table 2-1

White Positions on Busing and Most-Preferred Type of Race Relations, 1972 and 1976

	Busing Position			Favor-Oppose
	Favor	*Ambivalent*	*Oppose*	*Difference*
Type of race relations preferred in 1972				
"Desegregation"	77%	60%	35%	+42%
"Something in-between"	16	36	49	−33%
"Strict segregation"	7	3	16	− 9%
Totals	100%	100%	100%	
*N*s	89	212	1,850	
Tau beta = .210; X^2 = 118.501, *df* = 4, *p* < .0001				
Type of race relations preferred in 1976				
"Desegregation"	65%	51%	32%	+33%
"Something in-between"	29	48	56	−27%
"Strict segregation"	6	1	12	− 6%
Totals	100%	100%	100%	
*N*s	91	291	1,776	
Tau beta = .187; X^2 = 92.280, *df* = 4, *p* < .0001				

Source: 1972 and 1976 Center for Political Studies (CPS) American National Election Studies, Inter-University Consortium of Political and Social Research (ICPSR) University of Michigan.

Notes: The first two positions on the seven-point busing continuum in each study were collapsed to form the "favor" busing category; the third, fourth, and fifth positions were combined to form the "ambivalent" category; and the last two were collapsed to form the "oppose" category.

Table 2-2 reports the rather interesting results obtained from cross-tabulating busing views with reaction to rising black enrollments. Of course, the whites who favored busing proved most willing to enroll children in desegregated schools, whatever their racial composition. But this commitment was not dramatically greater than that of antibusing whites, as the feeble tau betas demonstrate. Moreover, support for desegregation fell off among *all* whites when black proportions increased. In 1978, for instance, 98 percent of the probusing whites expressed no objection to placing their children in schools where blacks were a small minority, but only 57 percent were prepared to do so when integration meant a black majority. In short, busing attitude had some influence on readiness to desegregate, but so did the racial composition of schools.

If the connection between busing opinion and racial prejudice is as tenuous or complex as these findings imply, on what other grounds have whites so steadfastly opposed busing? An open-ended question asking respondents in the 1976 CPS election survey to explain their support for, or opposition to, busing yielded a rare inventory of rationales.[52]

Some sort of commitment to neighborhood schools constituted the most often mentioned reason for busing opposition; 27 percent of all antibusing justifications fit into this category. Another 21 percent pertained to

Table 2-2
Willingness of Whites to Send Children to Schools with Growing Proportions of Black Pupils, by Busing Position, 1972, 1974, 1975, 1977, and 1978.

Whites Who:	1972	1974	1975	1977	1978	Average
Percentage having no objection when "a few" of the children are black						
Favored busing	98	96	95	96	98	97
Were undecided	87	93	83	97	96	91
Opposed busing	91	94	92	91	93	92
Tau betas	.06	.02	− .02	.06	.07	.04
Percentage having no objection when "half" of the children are black						
Favored busing	90	82	82	85	85	85
Were undecided	80	74	71	75	76	75
Opposed busing	78	71	73	79	76	75
Tau betas	.10	.09	− .07	.05	.07	.07
Percentage having no objection when "most" of the children are black						
Favored busing	67	63	58	59	57	61
Were undecided	32	47	50	42	51	44
Opposed busing	54	46	50	50	54	51
Tau betas	.05	.12	− .06	.05	.01	.03

Source: National Opinion Research Center (NORC) General Social Surveys for years noted.

fears of unhappiness and tension for students. One could add to this another 9 percent, consisting of claims that pupils would be psychologically or educationally harmed. Fifteen percent of all reasons given for antibusing opinions were economic in nature, chiefly claims of wasted taxes. Preferences for some other method of desegregation made up another 11 percent. Parental choice and claims of personal freedom constituted a surprisingly low 7 percent of all antibusing rationales, but it is likely that such assertions were expressed in connection with support of neighborhood schools. Only 4 percent of all reasons given for busing opposition amounted to segregationist preference for separate schools, and barely 1 percent opposed busing because they thought bus transportation was unsafe for pupils.

The enormous majorities documented above, and additional questions about public awareness leave no doubt that nearly every adult in the United States had some type of opinion about busing in the 1970s. In three Gallup polls taken in 1970 and 1971, for example, the average proportion of respondents having heard or read about the problem was 94 percent.[53]

It is therefore paradoxical to note the relatively low intensity of public attitudes on busing in most surveys. One indication of the relatively slight importance most Americans attached to busing in the 1970s is found in the 1974 CPS election study, where respondents were asked to sort cards listing national issues and designate the most important in rank order. Almost a quarter of the sample immediately eliminated "race and busing," and only 4 percent of those who did not throw out this unfortunately combined category ranked it first or second in national importance among ten issues selected. More than one-third of those who kept busing in the top ten ranked it ninth or last.

In summary, President Nixon overestimated the intensity with which most Americans opposed busing, but he was correct in his perception that the vast majority did not want busing. He also appears to have been right in his assertion that racial bigotry was not the primary source of this opposition. In any case, it is small wonder that Boston antibusing activists often claimed to be more representative of mainstream American opinion than "limousine liberals" and other busing proponents.

Conclusion: A National Context

In this chapter we have endeavored to demonstrate a sharp divergence between judicial busing policy and popular opinion as often led by the White House. Judge Garrity ordered implementation of a busing program in Boston at a point when lower federal courts were aggressively using their equity powers to transform segregated school systems across the nation. They had come to this juncture after a long and difficult struggle with southern defenses of *de jure* segregation. "Freedom of choice" and "neighborhood schools" were two concepts ill-served by this recalcitrance; when the Supreme Court threw out the former in *Green* and expanded busing in Charlotte-Mecklenburg, it eliminated policy options for the North as well. The momentous Denver decision, handed down in the middle of Boston's federal litigation, established system-wide remedies for northern areas where *de jure* conditions could be proved only in some instances and under relaxed standards. But such an approach clashed with executive policy and popular opinion, thus limiting an affirmative role to an isolated judiciary compelled to move piecemeal on a case-by-case basis.

Notes

1. As estimated by the National Institute of Education and cited in U.S. Commission on Civil Rights, *Statement on Metropolitan School Desegregation* (Washington, D.C.: U.S. Government Printing Office, 1977), note 33, p. 70.

2. Cited by William Bagley in "Busing," Issue Brief IB-74106, Congressional Research Service of the Library of Congress, 10 October 1975, p. 5.

3. See especially Gary Orfield, "Congress, the President and Anti-Busing Legislation, 1966-1974," *Journal of Law and Education,* 4 (January 1975):81-143. An updated account is found in Orfield, *Must We Bus? Segregated Schools and National Policy* (Washington, D.C.: Brookings Institution, 1978), pp. 233-278.

4. On equity powers of federal courts see note 2, chapter 7. This account relies mainly on the following sources: Harrell Rodgers, Jr., "The Supreme Court and School Desegregation: Twenty Years Later," *Political Science Quarterly,* 89 (Winter 1974-1975):751-776; Frank T. Read, "Judicial Evolution of the Law of School Integration Since Brown v. Board of Education," *Law and Contemporary Problems,* 39 (Winter 1975):7-49; and, J. Harvie Wilkinson, III, *From Brown to Bakke: The Supreme Court and School Integration, 1954-1978* (New York: Oxford University Press, 1979).

5. 347 U.S. 483 (1954).

6. 349 U.S. 294 (1955).

7. See *Stell* v. *Savannah-Chatham Board of Education,* 220 F. Supp. 667 (S.D. Ga. 1963); *Briggs* v. *Elliot,* 132 F. Supp. 776 (E.D.S.C. 1955).

8. See Jack W. Peltason, *Fifty-Eight Lonely Men: Southern Federal Judges and School Desegregation* (New York: Harcourt, Brace and World, 1961).

9. 391 U.S. 430, 439 (1968).

10. *Plaquemines Parish School Board* v. *U.S.,* 291 F. Supp. 841 (E.D. La. 1968).

11. *U.S.* v. *Montgomery County Board of Education,* 289 F. Supp. 647 (M.D. Ala. 1968).

12. *Swann* v. *Charlotte-Mecklenburg Board of Education,* 311 F. Supp. 265 (W.D.N.C. 1970).

13. 431 F. 2d 138 (4th Cir. 1970).

14. 402 U.S. 1 (1971).

15. 402 U.S. 1, 28.

16. 402 U.S. 1, 25-27.

17. 402 U.S. 1, 31-32.

18. For an eloquent argument against treating the two forms of segregation differently see *U.S.* v. *Jefferson County Board of Education,* 380 F. 2d 385, 397-398 (Gewin J. dissenting) (5th Cir. 1967).

19. *Taylor* v. *Board of Education,* City of New Rochelle, 191 F. Supp. 181 (S.D.N.Y. 1961).

20. *Hobson* v. *Hanson,* 269 F. Supp. 401, 418 (D.D.C. 1967).

21. *Bell* v. *School Board of Gary,* 213 F. Supp. 819 (M.D. Ind. 1963) cert. denied 297 U.S. 294 (1964); *Deal* v. *Cincinnati Board of Education,* 369 F. 2d 55 (6th Cir. 1966) cert. denied 389 U.S. 847 (1967); *Downs* v.

Board of Education of Kansas City, 336 F. 2d 988 (8th Cir. 1964) cert. denied 380 U.S. 914 (1965).

22. *U.S.* v. *School District 151 of Cook County,* 404 F. 2d 1125 (7th Cir. 1968); *U.S.* v. *Board of School Commissioners,* 322 F. Supp. 655 (N.D. Ind. 1972) cert. denied 297 U.S. 924 (1973).

23. 303 F. Supp. 279 (D. Colo. 1969).

24. 313 F. Supp. 61 (D. Colo. 1969); 445 F. 2d 990 (10th Cir. 1971).

25. *Keyes* v. *School District,* No. 1, 413 U.S. 189, 208 (1973).

26. "Statement About Desegregation of Elementary and Secondary Schools," 24 March 1970, *Public Papers of the President: Richard M. Nixon, 1970* (Washington, D.C.: U.S. Government Printing Office, 1971), pp. 304-320.

27. Raymond Price, *With Nixon* (New York: Viking, 1977), p. 212.

28. "Statement," p. 305.

29. Ibid., pp. 309 and 315.

30. Ibid., p. 316.

31. Ibid., p. 319.

32. Ibid., p. 312.

33. Ibid., p. 312.

34. Ibid., p. 310.

35. Ibid., p. 318.

36. Ibid., p. 309.

37. Ibid., p. 314.

38. See "Address to the Nation on Equal Educational Opportunities and School Busing," 16 March 1972, *Public Papers of the President, 1972* (Washington, D.C.: U.S. Government Printing Office, 1974), pp. 425-429; and, in the same volume, "Special Message to the Congress on Equal Educational Opportunities and School Busing," 17 March 1972, pp. 429-443.

39. "Address," p. 426.

40. Ibid., p. 428.

41. Ibid., p. 427.

42. Benjamin I. Page, *Choices and Echoes in Presidential Elections* (Chicago: University of Chicago Press, 1978), p. 94.

43. Kenneth J. Meier and James E. Campbell, "Issue Voting: An Empirical Examination of Individually Necessary and Jointly Sufficient Conditions," *American Politics Quarterly,* 7 (January 1979):21-50.

44. "Address on the State of the Union Delivered Before A Joint Session of Congress," 30 January 1974, *Public Papers of the President, 1974* (Washington, D.C.: U.S. Government Printing Office, 1975), p. 72.

45. On this point, see D. Garth Taylor, et al., "Attitudes Toward Racial Integration," *Scientific American,* 238 (June 1978):42-49; and, Andrew M. Greeley, *Building Coalitions: American Politics in the 1970s* (New York: New Viewpoints, 1974), pp. 296-361.

46. *The Harris Survey Yearbook of Public Opinion 1970* (New York: Louis Harris and Associates, 1971), p. 229.

47. Ibid., pp. 225-226.

48. *The Harris Survey Yearbook 1972,* (New York: Harris and Associates, 1976), p. 292.

49. Ibid., p. 293. See also p. 286.

50. Thanks go to Clifford Sethness for calling attention to use of the same question by Gallup and NORC. See *Gallup Opinion Index* 58 (April 1970):8; *Gallup Opinion Index* 75 (September 1971):19; *Gallup Opinion Index* 77 (November 1971):23; and the cumulative codebook for *General Social Surveys, 1972-78* (Chicago: NORC, 1978), var. 104, p. 98.

51. In 1972, 96 percent of probusing whites thought black and white students should attend the same schools, but so did 84 percent of antibusing whites. Similar results obtained in the 1976 general social survey.

52. See *The CPS 1976 American National Election Study Codebook* (Ann Arbor, Michigan: Inter-University Consortium of Political and Social Research (ICPSR, 1977), var. 3205, pp. 95-97. For other analyses of public opinion on busing, see Jonathan Kelley, "The Politics of School Busing," *Public Opinion Quarterly,* 38 (Spring 1974):23-29; and David O. Sears, et al., "Whites' Opposition to 'Busing': Self-Interest or Symbolic Politics?" *American Political Science Review,* 73 (June 1979):369-384.

53. See *Gallup Opinion Indexes* 58, 75, and 77.

3 Judicial Implementation and Defended Neighborhoods

"Not Another Boston"

Despite the powerful opposition to busing described in the previous chapter, one city after another started court-ordered busing in the 1970s without serious incident. Calm prevailed even in Detroit and Cleveland, where some feared that ethnic enclaves might erupt in protest.

Surely one factor behind this compliance was a determination by public officials and ordinary citizens alike to avoid "another Boston."[1] In the early 1970s Boston replaced Little Rock as a symbol of white opposition to school desegregation. This study seeks to explicate the main reasons why Boston school desegregation was the most difficult in American history.

As is made clear later, much of the explanation is found in Boston's unique history of conflict over race and schools. Racially imbalanced schools dominated the Boston political agenda for an entire decade before the federal district court's busing orders, and this long and rancorous process unquestionably conditioned attitudes toward federal judicial policy.

Yet historical factors alone cannot fully account for the ferocity with which some Bostonians fought "forced busing" in the 1970s. Moreover, public consciousness has been so dominated by the passion and violence of Boston's antibusing movement that the far more typical instances of compliance with the court's orders have been overlooked. Even though 80 percent or more of the city's white population probably objected to compulsory busing at any point in the decade, and tens of thousands rallied against Judge Garrity's decrees in the early days of antibusing protest, only a tiny minority condoned violent resistance to judicial orders, and not so many more demonstrated the will or capacity to engage in repeated acts of civil disobedience.

Why, then, did a few neighborhoods explode in reaction against busing while elsewhere in Boston school desegregation proceeded quietly? Why has some neighborhood resistance lasted into the 1980s? Part of the answer to both questions surely resides in the type of community characteristic of the most defiant districts. This chapter sets out the chief features of the "defended neighborhood," and thereby constructs a framework for comprehending Boston's fierce but highly structured opposition to busing. To put so refractory a compliance environment in perspective, compliance itself and the process of judicial implementation must be discussed first.

Understanding Judicial Implementation
and Compliance

The study of public policy in recent years has been redirected by analysis of implementation and compliance. Jeffrey Pressman and Aaron Wildavsky's pioneering case study described policymaking primarily as the capacity to accomplish hypothetical goals in the face of agency conflicts, overlapping jurisdictions, multiple decision points, inertia, time lags, and numerous other impediments arising out of the "complexity of joint action."[2] If the results diverge significantly from what policy initially intended, this approach directs analysis to specific problems frustrating implementation.

Others have endorsed this view of implementation as a problematic but absolutely critical phase of the policy process. For example, Charles Johnson relied heavily on Pressman and Wildavsky in constructing a heuristic model of judicial implementation.[3] The complex and problematic nature of carrying out court rulings is elucidated by focusing on four populations having some part to play in judicial implementation. An "interpreting" population consists mainly of judges, but can include other legal actors and the press. More diverse is the "implementing" population, consisting of all actors charged with carrying out some aspect of the judicial program to be effected. A policy calling for unpopular social change cannot avoid inclusion of unsympathetic and even bitterly opposed administrators in the implementing population; unless co-opted or coerced, such officials may undermine implementation. Greater cohesion usually obtains in the "consumer" population, or those in whose name the policy has been decided. In school desegregation disputes, for example, the consumer population consists of nonwhite plaintiffs and all others in the disadvantaged class. Finally, the "secondary" population is comprised of all other persons "indirectly" affected by judicial policy.

Although useful in some respects, the Johnson model slights secondary populations confronted with redistributive judicial decisions. Christine Rossell correctly points up the redistributive aspects of judicial school-desegregation policy, especially when involuntary two-way busing is a principal remedy.[4] Some, but not all, whites in the secondary population are compelled to participate if they desire further education in the public schools, while others of different social classes, municipalities, or neighborhoods in the same metropolitan area are exempted. Hence selectivity of coercion further dramatizes the redistributive character of "forced busing," awakens class antagonisms among whites, and shows that some in the secondary population are no less affected by busing than any in the consumer population.[5]

The framework recently devised by Paul Sabatier and Daniel Mazmanian offers important correctives for analysis of redistributive policy implementation.[6] One such improvement is their reference to "target" rather than "secondary" populations. Another is a strong emphasis on the tractability of a problem addressed by judicial policy. Tractability variables conditioning the implementation process include the depth and extent of change required of a target population, that group's size and diversity, and the theory and technology available to administrators obliged to carry out policy goals. Statutory variables also bear on implementation, for example, policy content and clarity, the degree policy is informed by causal theory, financial resources, and integration between and among implementing institutions. Finally, implementation is much affected by such nonstatutory factors as public support of the policy, the skill and commitment of implementing and enforcement officials, and the cohesion and resources of target and consumer populations.

Attention to problem tractability and target-group behavior inevitably leads to analysis of compliance, the degree of overt conformity with policy directives. Hence compliance and implementation studies investigate many of the same variables, for example, policy content and clarity, enforcer commitment to policy, and cohesion and resources of target and consumer populations.[7] Harrell Rodgers and Charles Bullock developed a compliance framework most useful to the present study; their list of variables has been revised to make certain Sabatier and Mazmanian factors more explicit:[8]

1. Substance of the judicial policy:
   a. How redistributive is the required change, that is, what is required of public officials, target and consumer populations?
   b. How large and diverse is the target population? How large and diverse is the consumer population? How many public officials are required to implement and enforce judicial policy? How important are their positions?
   c. Does the judicial policy set out a causal theory relating specific remedies to particular wrongs?
   d. How clear are standards for determining compliance, and are data available for comparing performance with standards?
   e. Does the law set out specific sanctions for noncompliance?
   f. Are specific individuals made responsible for enforcing and complying with court orders?
2. Implementor and enforcer variables:
   a. Do oficials required to implement and enforce judicial policy directives regard them as legitimate?
   b. Do such officials fear conflict or adverse political consequences of compliance to the point that they will not comply?
   c. Are judicial sanctions realistic and severe enough to offset the benefits of noncompliance?

    d. Do officials with a previous history of defiance of policy in this area now feel obliged to oppose the policy at issue?

    e. Is there an agency with viable enforcement powers to carry out the policy?

3. Characteristics of the compliance environment:

    a. Does the target population feel threatened by the policy?

    b. Is the policy in conflict with target population values and norms?

    c. What other characteristics of the target population affect the compliance environment?

    d. How is noncompliance manifested, and who is mobilized against judicial policy?

    e. How successful is target-group opposition to implementation?

Questions listed under items 1 and 2 above are addressed in chapters 5, 6, and 7, while chapters 4 and 8 take up the items listed under 3. Chapter 10 summarizes the analysis for all questions.

Of course, this list does not add up to a framework for analysis of every aspect of the complex Boston busing controversy. Such a massive undertaking is simply beyond the scope of this study. Hence many legal and administrative details of implementation have been deleted in order to render a streamlined account instrumental to analysis of defended-neighborhood defiance of judicial policy. Black involvement is discussed only enough to add to the perspective on white busing opposition; the full story of black participation awaits another book. This study is concerned primarily with understanding the reactions of the white target population, especially those elements living in defended neighborhoods. It is to the defended neighborhood as an unusually obdurate compliance environment that our attention now shifts.

The Defended Neighborhood

"Neighborhood" defies easy definition in the social sciences. One approach is to make areal designations on the basis of correlations between physical, social, and economic characteristics. However precise, such definitions often fail to correlate with subjective designations by area residents. Although imperfect in its own way, the subjective approach is not without value:

> While the research data are thin . . . there does seem to be some reason to believe that man's . . . affiliation to his "place" includes a commitment not only to a segment of geography but also to the interaction network and the institutions which fill up that geographic space. . . .

To a large segment of American society no explanation is necessary for the concept of a neighborhood. . . . [Residents] may be hard put to define in formal terms what a neighborhood is, but they know one when they see one. They understand the differences between their neighborhood and other neighborhoods and . . . are astonished to find out there are people . . . who have never lived in a neighborhood and do not understand what it is. They are even more astonished to find that these same people cannot understand the need to defend one's neighborhood, and that they dismiss loyalty to one's neighborhood as immoral or racist. There may well be an element of racism . . . in much of the defense of one's neighborhood, though a fear of any . . . outsider "who will not be like us" is probably more important. . . . [T]here is far more involved in a neighborhood and affection for it than fear or bigotry.[9]

Of course, it is important to distinguish defended from other neighborhood types. Because most of the characteristics of a defended neighborhood are found elsewhere, the difference is one of degree rather than kind. It is the combination of relationships and their emergent influences on attitudes and behavior that create the defended neighborhood.

The defended neighborhood can be understood only partly as an urban village. Urbanization and industrialization have not yet rendered exchanges between inhabitants "impersonal, transitory, and segmental." Rather, a defended neighborhood is a "community saved" from the forces of abrupt change.[10] Life revolves around the familiar and routine, and is predicated on intimate relationships among fellow residents.

For additional variables defining the defended neighborhood we turn to Gerald Suttles, who has refurbished the concept for urban sociology.[11] All but the last of the following features have been taken from Suttles's formulation:

First, almost all inhabitants of the defended neighborhood are acutely aware of commonly understood territorial boundaries setting their area apart from others.

Second, most residents share the same conception of a common plight.

Third, most residents share the same notions of community and personal safety when inside the neighboorhood.

Fourth, most residents are linked to each other through mutual aid, insiders' networks, extended families, and other intimate relationships.

Fifth, at least some residents are prepared to employ violence to defend the neighborhood against unwanted social change.

Each characteristic warrants additional discussion.

Territoriality

Defended neighborhood residents share common conceptions of where the enclave begins and ends. Such boundaries are among the most important features of each inhabitant's "cognitive map," however physically indistinct the neighborhood may appear to outsiders. A defended neighborhood's social isolation does not depend on physical barriers to unimpeded traffic flow to and from the rest of the city, but "defended boundaries" in the form of canals, freeways, railroad tracks, or grass strips can underscore subjective notion of separation.[12] Residents also give special social meaning to territory inside the enclave—street corners, playgrounds, schoolyards, parks, monuments, and other landmarks. In some neighborhoods, a common sight on warm spring evenings is middle-aged men "hanging out" on traditional street corners. Yet another territorial imperative is the staking out of parking space by placing a chair, sawhorse, or garbage can in the street outside one's apartment; this practice is common in neighborhoods where housing stock predates the automobile age and garages are rare.

Common Plight

Urban dwellers typically share street crime, poor services, pollution, and other problems, but the foundation of the defended neighborhood's common plight is its unfavorable reputation. "Above all," Milton Kotler writes, "the neighborhood has a name."[13] To live in a notorious community is to share associated stigmas. Hence residents of "tough" or "racist" districts sometimes feel obligated to demonstrate they are not thugs or bigots; others feel impelled to live up to the image. In any event, "neighborhood identity remains a stable, judgmental reference against which people are assessed."[14]

Neighborhood reputation can be much more than merely a source of embarassment in dealings with strangers. Business or governmental elites may seize upon an unsavory image to justify schemes for urban renewal, gentrification, or some other change. After all, a "bad" part of town will be "diversified." In the same vein, school desegregation in a defended neighborhood can be justified in part as a way of ending the "parochialism" and "provincialism" of local youth.

When confronted by the prospect of change accompanied by such rationales, residents of a defended neighborhood likely will mobilize in reaction. Organized protest reinforces both community solidarity and general reputation, but does *not* create an already flourishing defended neighborhood. The territorial designation and community stigma necessary to the defended neighborhood probably existed long before the protest and probably will survive it. Suttles is emphatic on this point, noting that short-lived protests lend an "ephemeral and transient appearance" to the defended neighborhood.[15] A particularly artificial aspect of protest is its involvement of peripheral or poorly integrated residents, a point addressed at length in chapter 8.

The "Good Community"

The sine qua non of a defended neighborhood is the physical safety enjoyed by most of its inhabitants. It simply is not possible to imagine a defended neighborhood where most residents fear for their personal safety while inside their own enclave. The absence of such apprehension contributes to a "good community" syndrome, in which the typical inhabitant "does not fear standing an arm's length from his neighbor."[16]

An acid test of the good community is the environment created for small children in the neighborhood. Adults regard small children as innocents to be protected from the dangers of urban life. When outsiders propose policies that seem to threaten the well-being of local youth, such as busing them to distant and "dangerous" areas, childless couples and even single adults will rally to the side of parents in defense of "our kids."

Of course, the good community is sustained by nostalgia and selective recollection of what life was like before outsiders so unfairly menaced the neighborhood. Hence idyllic accounts figure importantly in the rhetoric of defended-neighborhood protest. Some of this rhetoric is intended to arouse sympathy for the underdogs, or perhaps gauge the gullibility of reporters and social scientists, but not all of it is conscious fabrication. As the conflict endures, protesters find it increasingly difficult to separate fact and myth. After a time, the good-community notion becomes impervious to contrary logic or evidence. Outsiders can be summarily dismissed with the rejoinder, "you just don't know what it means to live here."

Supplemental Social Bonds

At least three supportive social structures should be present in a defended neighborhood: mutual aid, insiders' networks, and extended families. Although these institutions exist in other neighborhoods, all must be present in particularly robust form in a defended neighborhood.

Mutual aid is no less than basic to "neighboring" in the defended enclave. When catastrophe befalls a family, neighbors aid the unfortunate in myriad ways. In communities where housing stock is primarily turn-of-the-century multiple-occupancy wooden dwellings, fires often test the generosity of neighbors. In defended neighborhoods the compassion of inhabitants for their own is legendary, thereby adding a favorable element to community reputation.

Newcomers to such a neighborhood are soon struck by the wariness and watchfulness of residents. More is at work here than merely the "eyes on the street" phenomenon described by Jane Jacobs.[17] The scrutiny of strangers goes along with restricted admission to inner circles or insiders' networks. No doubt the defended neighborhood is a congeries of such networks with varying degrees of exclusivity. Suttles insightfully describes these networks in a passage worth quoting at length:

> Perhaps the most subtle structural feature of the defended neighborhood is its shared knowledge or what might be called its underlife. People who share a residential identity are privy to a variety of secrets which range from the assured truths of gossip to the collective myths of rumor. These bits and pieces of knowledge touch intimately on the lives of those who share a residential area because they add to the collective guilt or pride of coresidents. But they are also some of the surest markers which separate insiders from outsiders. And at the same time these local half-truths are much valued because they provide at least an omen of what one's neighbors are really like. Thus, while persons who share a common residential identity may collude at impression management, they are also more apt to pry into one another's business and jointly move farther and farther away from an official version of what people are supposed to be like. Taken to their full extreme, these local truths may add up to a sort of subculture where a private existential world takes hold and overshadows that provided by equally unreliable versions of truth available through official sources.[18]

The social scientist taking up residence in a defended neighborhood soon discovers the importance of such networks to his own research. Inability to win what amounts to sponsorship from an established resident and network member dooms future interaction with most inhabitants. Even when accorded a modicum of acceptance, the newcomer is fed a heavy diet of official truths. Some residents may even plant deliberate falsehoods with the newcomer and then wait to see if such distortions get back to them; in this way residents can test the propensity of the researcher to discuss respondents with other residents.

The community's already pervasive insularity is further strengthened by extended family ties that stitch together large segments of the local population, thereby enhancing the tribal character of the neighborhood. It is not uncommon to find two, or even three, generations of the same family living in the same multiple-occupancy dwelling. Of course, such ties reinforce mutual aid and insiders' networks.

Literal Defense

Vigilantes are only the most obvious manifestation of literal neighborhood defense. As the "long hot summers" of the 1960s demonstrated, vigilantes mobilize to meet a crisis and then disband after tensions attenuate. Other forms of literal defense do not require a crisis; nor, as Donald Warren's study of black neighborhoods in Detroit demonstrates, need they be limited to defended neighborhoods.[19] "Selective expulsion" and "selective recruitment" nonetheless figure importantly in defended-neighborhood life.

The point of selective expulsion is to drive established but no longer desirable residents out of the community. Methods vary from social ostracism to physical assault, with property destruction probably most commonly used. Targeted families having small children in neighborhood schools are most vulnerable to such campaigns, for youngsters are easy to harass. While small-scale expulsion campaigns are common, more extensive efforts against dissidents or renegades can become functional to organized protest.

Selective recruitment is a type of "quality control" through which newcomers are screened and possibly discouraged from moving in. Sponsorship by established residents is but one form of selective recruitment; formation of local "improvement associations" to pressure realtors into selective renting or selling is another.

Implementation, Compliance, and Defended Neighborhoods

Most of the policy literature portrays implementation as complicated and problematic even under favorable conditions. Lack of administrative commitment, unclear directives, and simple inertia are among the problems that can derail goal achievement. Seemingly the implementation of unpopular and redistributive policies would become near impossible, particularly in the face of defiance of the type represented by Boston's defended neighborhoods. Virtually any change is unwelcome in the defended neighborhood, but compulsory two-way busing is bound to arouse sharp protest. If no small part of neighborhood defense is against ghetto encroachment, then antibusing protest will indeed be sharp. Is there some aspect of judicial implementation to mitigate such difficulties? This issue will be taken up in chapter 10, after the details of Boston's struggle over busing have been examined. At this point, however, our attention moves to South Boston, the archetypical defended neighborhood.

Notes

1. For example, a Dayton school official spoke precisely these words in explaining his city's peaceful school desegregation. Remarks at the 12 March 1977 Ohio Conference of Economists and Political Scientists annual meeting; Columbus, Ohio.

2. Jeffrey Pressman and Aaron Wildavsky, *Implementation* (Berkeley: University of California Press, 1973).

3. Charles A. Johnson, "The Implementation and Impact of Judicial Policies: A Heuristic Model," in *Public Law and Public Policy,* John A. Gardiner, ed. (New York: Praeger, 1977), pp. 107-126.

4. Christine Rossell, "School Desegregation and Community Social Change," *Law and Contemporary Problems* 42 (Summer 1978):133-183.

5. On this point see Lillian B. Rubin, *Busing and Backlash* (Berkeley: University of California Press, 1972), esp. pp. 39-76.

6. Paul Sabatier and Daniel Mazmanian, "The Implementation of Public Policy: A Framework for Analysis," *Policy Studies Journal,* 8 (Special Issue #2: 1980):538-560.

7. For example, see Frederick M. Wirt, *Politics of Southern Equality* (Chicago: Aldine, 1970).

8. Based on the list provided in Rodgers and Bullock, in *Coercion to Compliance* (Lexington, Mass.: Lexington Books, D.C. Heath and Company, 1976), pp. 6-7.

9. Andrew M. Greeley, *Why Can't They Be Like Us?* (New York: Dutton, 1975), pp. 96-97.

10. See Barry Welleman, "The Community Question: The Intimate Network of East Yorkers," *American Journal of Sociology* 84 (March 1979):1201-1231.

11. Gerald R. Suttles, *The Social Construction of Communities* (Chicago: University of Chicago Press, 1972).

12. On this point see Suzanne Keller, *The Urban Neighborhood* (New York: Random House, 1968), p. 121.

13. Milton Kotler, *Neighborhood Government* (Indianapolis: Bobbs-Merrill, 1969), p. 65.

14. Suttles, *Social Construction,* p. 35.

15. Ibid., p. 36.

16. Ibid., p. 234.

17. Jane Jacobs, *The Life and Death of Great American Cities* (New York: Random House, 1961), passim.

18. Suttles, *Social Construction,* p. 36.

19. See Donald I. Warren, *Black Neighborhoods* (Ann Arbor: University of Michigan Press, 1975), pp. 50-65. Of course, a predominantly black district can become a defended neighborhood. Race might well contribute to the neighborhood's stigma. Until the present day, however, housing discrimination has forced middle-class and working-class blacks to share the same ghettoes with lower-class elements, thereby undermining formation of the "good community" and associated feelings of personal safety. Quite possibly some of the older suburbs consolidated by middle-class blacks in recent years will become enclaves defended against other, less affluent, blacks who seek to follow.

4

Development of a Defended Neighborhood

Tough and Close in Southie

In a city noted for tough and colorful neighborhoods, South Boston still stands out. It was reputed to be a "spawning ground of politicians and prize-fighters, policemen and plug-uglies" well before the turn of the century.[1] If anything, the busing turmoil enhanced this fearsome reputation. Although all residents share a common stigma for living in a "clannish" and "bigoted" neighborhood, many relish being part of such a community and counter with expressions of "Southie pride." For example, a leading foe of busing said: "You have to be here and be a part of this community to really feel it. We're close, and we know we're close. We stick together . . . we're the toughest, the best-looking, and the smartest in the city. Maybe that's being conceited, but so what?"[2] Much the same claim was made by an antibusing writer for the South Boston *Tribune:* "We're a different breed of people in South Boston. We're unique in the nation. There isn't another community like this one in America. The closeness we feel towards one another can't be found in most other places. I like everybody here. I feel like we're all part of one big family."[3]

It is unwise to dismiss such contentions as nothing more than "impression management," to use Suttles's term, for they reveal commitments essential to the defended-neighborhood concept. This chapter describes how South Boston became the archetypical defended neighborhood.

The Ecology of Separation

Isolation from Boston proper has always figured importantly in South Boston history. Both natural and social obstacles have long impeded the brief journey from Perkins Square in South Boston to the Boston Common. South Bostonians still refer to their "town," even though South Boston never was an independent municipality.

After discovery in 1630, the South Boston peninsula was left uninhabited for almost a century. Used primarily as common pasture land for Dorchester farmers, South Boston was home to no more than twelve families when the American Revolution began.[4] Inaccessibility mostly explained the lack of settlers. Embraced by ocean, harbor, channel, and the

122929

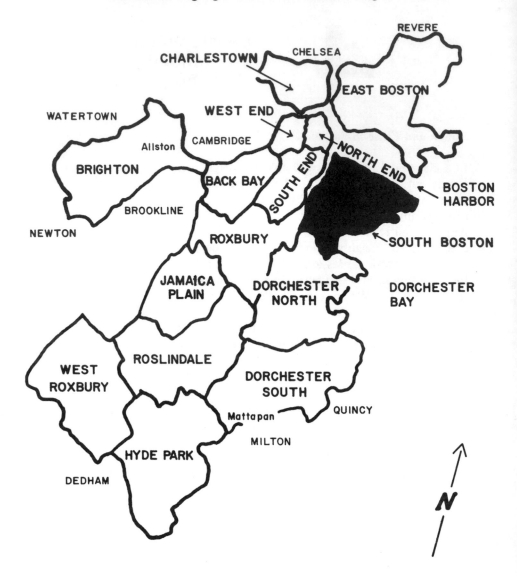

Figure 4-1. South Boston in Relation to Other Boston Neighborhoods

now-filled South Bay, South Boston's tenuous land link with Dorchester was inundated at high tide.

A new era began in 1803, when speculators quietly bought up most of the peninsula and then persuaded the Boston city legislature to annex South Boston the next year. Enough people had settled on the peninsula by the

1820s to justify bridging the Fort Point Channel, a narrow but deep channel severing South Boston from the city proper. Completion of this bridge in 1828 stimulated investment, and soon the South Boston side sprouted wharves, warehouses, and various works. A congested workingmen's district grew up nearby, while more-affluent newcomers pushed farther into the peninsula and built fine homes atop the heights overlooking the open sea.

Like other peripheral wards before the Civil War, South Boston grew faster than Boston proper.[5] Table 4-1 shows that South Boston's population more than doubled between 1840 and 1850, and matched city growth for the next several decades despite Boston's annexations. The South Boston population peaked at 67,913 in 1895.

Rapid growth was accompanied by a building sense of pride in what South Boston was becoming. In 1847 prominent residents called attention to the peninsula's "eight Churches, two Grammar and seventeen Primary schools, besides Private Seminaries; a Lyceum, Bank, and Insurance Office; also Wharves, Ship Yards, Factories, &c."[6] Moreover, the immigrants living in South Boston were said to be "only of that better class who will not live in cellars."[7] Some local boosters predicted a population of one-hundred thousand before 1900.

Table 4-1
Growth of South Boston and City of Boston, 1805-1895

| Year | South Boston | | City of Boston | |
	Population	Increase over Previous Period (%)	Population	Increase over Previous Period (%)
1805	60	—	—	—
1810	354	490.0	33,787	—
1825	1,986	461.0	58,277	72.5
1835	5,595	181.7	78,603	34.9
1845	10,020	79.1	114,366	45.5
1855	16,912	68.8	160,490	40.3
1865	29,363	73.6	192,318	19.8
1875	54,147	84.4	341,919	77.8
1885	61,534	13.6	390,393	14.2
1895	67,913	10.4	496,290	27.1

Sources: Thomas C. Simonds, *History of South Boston,* 1857 reprinted. (New York: Arno Press, 1974), p. 229; *Census of the Commonwealth of Massachusetts, 1895,* I, *Population and Social Statistics* (Boston: Wright & Potter, 1896), pp. 220-221.

Notes: The city of Boston data include Boston proper and annexations. The 1805 figure for South Boston is Simond's estimate. The 1810 data came from the federal census, all other data were taken from state censuses. The 1875 South Boston population was slightly exaggerated owing to inclusion of part of Dorchester in one South Boston ward. According to the 1885 Massachusetts census, however, the 1875 estimate was "very nearly correct."

Yet life in South Boston was not without its discontents, and resentment of treatment at the hands of city authorities sparked strong separatist feelings. In 1847, for example, a South Boston group complained to Boston's mayor and city council about the workhouse, asylum, and cholera facility placed in their ward. The group accused city officials of regarding South Boston as "the Botany Bay of the City, into which could be thrust those establishments which the City Fathers would consider nuisances in the neighborhood of their own private dwellings." After reminding officials that a "deep and navigable channel" separated South Boston from Boston proper, the complainants warned they could prosper as an independent city if need be. Their petition demanded "reciprocity of advantages" in all future relations.[8]

Development of an Irish Tribal Domain

Once opened to industrial development and settlement, South Boston did not immediately become predominantly Irish. Few Irish immigrants moved here in the 1820s and 1830s, and even the famine immigration of the next decade did not produce an Irish majority on the peninsula. Most of the Irish probably thought it too distant from available work or found lodging too costly. But increasing numbers of the Irish came into the ward because of additional industry, extended horse- and streetcar service, the razing of the Fort Hill slum, and the fire of 1875.

Erratic changes in census categories make it impossible to say precisely when South Boston became preponderantly Irish, but no doubt this was accomplished by the early 1870s. In 1880 we know that just over half of all inhabitants were either foreign-born Irish or born of Irish parents.[9] Eight of every ten residents were of foreign stock. Fifteen years later, about the same proportion of foreign-stock residents held, and the Irish were 62 percent of all foreign-stock residents of South Boston.[10]

Although predominantly Irish at the turn of the century, each South Boston ward was home to other ethnic groups as well. Lithuanian and Polish immigrants were concentrated in congested Ward 13, while a mix of Swedes, Germans, and Britons inhabited wards 14 and 15. About the same number of Italians and British Canadians could be found in each ward.[11] Such heterogeneity accompanied by Irish domination comports with Andrew Greeley's finding that few American cities after the Civil War had single-ethnic group enclaves, but mixed districts dominated by a single group were common.[12] Much the same heterogeneity is found in the contemporary neighborhood foreign-stock population; at 35.8 percent of all foreign-stock inhabitants, the Irish were still twice as numerous as any other ethnic group (see table 4-2).

Table 4-2
Foreign-Stock Population of South Boston, 1970

Ethnic Group	Number	Percentage of all Foreign Stock	Percentage of Total Population
Irish			
Foreign-born	965	6.7	2.5
First generation	4,168	29.1	10.8
All Canadians	2,366	16.5	6.1
Italians			
Foreign-born	432	3.0	1.1
First generation	1,268	8.9	3.3
Lithuanians			
Foreign-born	532	3.7	1.4
First generation	861	6.0	2.2
Polish			
Foreign-born	290	2.0	0.8
First generation	607	4.2	1.6
Other Europeans	2,078	14.5	5.4
Asians	319	2.2	0.8
Latin Americans	85	0.6	0.2
Others	49	0.3	0.1
Not asceraind	309	2.2	0.8
Totals	14,329	99.9[a]	37.2

Source: Fourth Count 1970 Census of Population and Housing tape.

[a]Does not total 100 percent due to rounding.

Signs of ethnic diversity are visible throughout contemporary South Boston. Numerous street intersections, or squares in local parlance, have been given such non-Celtic labels as "Louis Graceffa" and "Joseph Fasano." A statue of Father Joseph Laporte near the L Street Bathhouse commemorates a Catholic priest who devoted his tragically short life to helping wayward neighborhood youth. Not far from this monument is the "Lt. Charles Baszanotti" park.

Diversity abounds in the spiritual domain too. Irish Catholics attend St. Augustine's or the Gate of Heaven, while Polish Catholics go to Our Lady of Czestochowa, and Lithuanians gather at St. Peter's. Albanian Orthodox worship at St. George's Cathedral, while nearby Our Lady of Kazan ministers to a small Russian congregation. St. Matthew the Redeemer remains an Anglican outpost in a Catholic hinterland.

Ethnic diversity also is woven into the fabric of organized social life. Just as the Irish of earlier generations maintained the Ancient Order of Hibernians, Fenian societies, political clubs, and so on, the Lithuanians of the 1970s belonged to the Knights of Lithuania, the Lithuanian Citizens Association, the Lithuanian Veterans Association, and perhaps a dozen other groups. No local hall today is more used than the Lithuanian Social

Club, and Lithuanian Independence Day gets major publicity every year in South Boston's weekly *Tribune.*

Diversity does not appear in politics. The Irish still control neighborhoood power structures and speak for the community to the outside world. An unbroken string of ethnic Irish continues to represent South Boston in city, state, and national government. Unquestionably the neighborhood's most important social event is St. Patrick's Day, observed simultaneously with Evacuation Day commemorating the British departure from Boston in 1776. Before busing tensions made their reception uncertain, leading Massachusetts politicians marched in the St. Patrick's Day parade; the likes of Senator Edward Kennedy and Governor Michael Dukakis were replaced by Irish Republican Army (IRA) representatives in the late 1970s.

Irish symbols predominate in other ways as well. Charter flights to Ireland are pushed by the neighborhood travel agency, and Aer Lingus posters provide welcome color for the drab Broadway subway and bus station. South Boston's main newsstand sells a dozen Irish and Ulster newspapers; musical and athletic groups from Ireland often are in the neighborhood; small children learn Irish folk dances at the neighborhood library; and an Irish brogue is overheard in street conversation. Small wonder the neighborhood antibusing center sold cloth shamrocks to raise money, or that so many outsiders think South Boston is completely Irish. "All we ever heard," said a former police official of South Boston in the 1970s, "was Irish, Irish, Irish."[13]

It is easy to make either too much or too little of Irish ethnicity in analyzing South Boston's development into a defended neighborhood. Even though impressionistic, the subcultural argument of Irish insularity is unquestionably valuable to understanding the way in which South Boston and several other enclaves gained their identity. The struggle against nativist bigotry and crushing poverty certainly reinforced whatever cultural predispositions the Irish immigrants brought with them. Early movement out of the notorious Fort Hill slum sparked conflict and Yankee flight; having invaded and conquered most of the city by the late 1880s, the perennially factionalized Irish defined their loyalties according to enclave and political boss. Inside each enclave the village life of Erin was reconstructed.[14] No community better fit this model than South Boston, where an Irish-Catholic majority still thought of itself as an oppressed minority.

However crucial Irish subculture was in making South Boston a defended neighborhood both physically and socially separated from Boston proper, one must not overlook the concomitant development of a predominantly proletarian class structure and the overwhelming Catholicism of the neighborhood. Rather than simply "Irish, Irish, Irish," then, the roots of South Boston's defended neighborhood are better described as "Irish, Catholic, and working class."

A Footnote to Ethnic Diversity: Blacks in South Boston

European immigration was crucial to South Boston history, but no corresponding importance can be attached to nonwhite migration. In 1847 South Boston residents incorrectly boasted "not a single colored family" lived on their peninsula.[15] Three years later, the federal census turned up a handful of "free colored" inhabitants; the state census of 1855 reported five of fifteen residents of color to be mulattoes.[16] In any case, blacks were less than a percent of South Boston's total population until 1970. Between 1960 and 1970 the number of blacks jumped from 61 to 388 owing to public housing-project assignments. Forty-four percent of all 1970 black South Boston residents lived in a single project, the D Street complex.

Rising school-desegregation tensions made life increasingly difficult for black residents during the late 1960s and early 1970s. Blacks in the D Street project suffered physical assaults and property destruction on a routine basis and at a rate significantly higher than an already astonishing record of vandalism and mayhem.[17] Racial harassment climaxed with the 1973 shooting death of a black D Street project youth. Almost no blacks remained in South Boston when involuntary busing began in 1974.

At the same time selective expulsion campaigns started against black D Street tenants, the sprawling Columbia Point project in adjacent North Dorchester was shifting from a racially mixed to a black and "problem family" clientele. Violent crime rose sharply inside the project and at a nearby shopping center. An elderly white was murdered while fishing from rocks close to the project. Living units inside Columbia Point were left unoccupied as the project's unfavorable reputation grew. South Bostonians no longer ventured into the now largely abandoned shopping center. Carson Beach, located inside South Boston but extending nearly to the project, was soon to become a battlefield where white residents confronted black "invasions."

In sum, blacks were never significantly part of South Boston's cultural diversity. Although antibusing activists argued that they had enjoyed greater contact with blacks as coworkers than had "limousine liberals" in the suburbs, few South Bostonians had ever known blacks as neighbors. Reportedly blacks had once been welcome to fish and swim in South Boston, and heavy black use of one beach sector had prompted its designation as "Coon Lagoon." Perhaps the name reveals more than was intended in this illustration of alleged local racial tolerance, but, in any case, the controversies of the 1960s and 1970s ended free access to South Boston's inviting beachfront. After 1974 few blacks tested the water.

Enclaves within the Enclave

Despite the seemingly solid facade of antibusing protest, South Boston always has been characterized by substantial social and economic differences. Considerable variation in housing stock and lifestyle is found when one explores different sections of the neighborhood. Settlement patterns of the early 1800s established basic distinctions lasting into the present. South Boston's poorest inhabitants have always lived in the Lower End, the congested quarter that grew up around wharves and warehouses along the Fort Point Channel, whereas more affluent residents have always populated the higher elevations overlooking Boston Harbor and Dorchester Bay. A description of South Boston written near the turn of the century is still remarkably accurate today:

> The district . . . naturally divides . . . into two general parts. That nearest the city which is on the level ground we shall speak of as the lower section. The two hills and the intervening space together with the City Point area we shall refer to as the upper section. It is the lower part which forms the congested quarter, and the upper part which gives to South Boston its unusual advantages.
>
> The main thoroughfare, Broadway, runs from one end to the other of the peninsula dividing each section. . . . The first impression of unexampled unattractiveness which the lower section makes upon the visitor is accentuated by the monotony of its numbered and lettered streets. The hand of man has indeed dealt unkindly with the promised grandeur of the first speculators. The lower part of Broadway is a dreary array of structures devoted partly to dwellings but in large measure to small stores and saloons. . . .
>
> As one reaches the higher level, prosperous looking stores suggestive of an independent city mitigate the earlier impression. With the ascent of the first hill the spirits rise and when the Avenue has topped the second the visitor feels that he has discovered a part of Boston not hitherto known and deserving greater fame. The whole of Boston Harbor lies open to the view. . . . Below at the foot of the hill the City Point park forms the terminus of one of Massachusetts' beautiful parkway systems. Following a car route around the hill the familiar L Street Bathhouse is to be found and when at last at Q Street the alphabet is finally vanquished by the sea one remembers its beginning at A and B Streets like an unpleasant dream.[18]

Today the neighborhood consists of six primarily residential districts and a seventh industrial area claiming half or more of South Boston's total land mass. City Point and Telegraph Hill border one another, take in the remaining hills, and display the neighborhood's most-attractive housing stock. Much of City Point consists of tree-lined streets with well-maintained three deckers; the district is also favored by lovely beaches and park strips overlooking the bay and, in summer, its small craft. Telegraph Hill is centered around Dorchester Heights, where Washington's troops once placed the cannon that drove the British out of Boston. South Boston High School shares the hill with fine old homes comparable to those on Beacon Hill. The tree-shaded three deckers lend an impression of false prosperity to Columbus Park and certainly convey a more favorable image than the nondescript frame dwellings, seedy taprooms, and assorted commercial buildings cluttering up Andrew Square, a drab crossroads dominated by its bus barn and subway station. Adjacent to Andrew Square is the Lower End, not greatly different from its description in the early 1900s. Lower Broadway is still characterized by "a dreary array" of multipurpose wooden structures—saloon or store at ground level and living quarters atop. Behind this facade are back streets of visibly deteriorating wooden housing, many structures wholly or partly abandoned owing to fires or vandalism. Empty lots typically are overgrown by weeds high enough to hide foundations of razed or burned dwellings. On warm days the Lower End's architectural distress is supplemented the the appearance of drunks who congregate on sidewalks and panhandle passers-by. In the midst of such decline is the infamous D Street project, a complex of twenty-seven two-story brick residential units, an administration building, and an elementary school. All are situated on an asphalt plain generally strewn with broken glass and other debris. Perhaps a fifth of the D Street apartments were empty at any point during the late 1970s, their boarded windows testimony to the methodical vandalism associated with the place. Increasingly, the D Street population of about three thousand came to consist of elderly singles or large, female-headed families living beneath the poverty line. Extraordinary turnover long has characterized D Street's population.[19]

Table 4-3 offers a more systematic comparison of City Point, Telegraph Hill, Columbus Park, Andrew Square, D Street, and the Lower End on selected census characteristics. Although every section lost some population during the period observed, the magnitude of decline varied greatly by section. Columbus Park's decline was particularly noteworthy, and further deterioration may be seen in educational and income data. D Street conditions worsened progressively, as the table shows, and its 1970 median family income barely exceeded the 1960 median. In almost every comparison, City Point and Telegraph Hill approximated the general condition determined for the entire city.[20]

Less diversity was obtained in the jobs and careers of South Boston workers when examined according to residence. City Point and Telegraph Hill had the smallest blue-collar proportions, while D Street and Andrew Square reported the highest, but these differences were insignificant.

Table 4-3
Socioeconomic Comparison of South Boston Sections, 1940-1970

Year	City Point	Telegraph Hill	Columbus Park	Andrew Square	Lower End	D Street	South Boston	Boston
Population changes, 1940-1970								
1940	15,691	13,586	6,150	3,153	15,424	—	54,363	770,816
1950	15,302	12,959	9,691	2,902	10,694	4,123	55,670	801,444
1960	12,316	10,985	7,368	2,149	7,414	3,727	43,959	697,197
1970	11,378	10,144	5,750	2,222	5,455	3,539	38,488	641,071
Percentage change over previous decade								
1950	−2.5	−4.6	a	−17.4	−3.9	b	+2.4	+4.0
1960	−19.5	−15.3	−24.0	−25.9	−30.7	−9.6	−21.0	−13.0
1970	−7.6	−7.7	−22.0	+3.4	−26.4	−5.0	−12.4	−8.3
Percentage of adults with less than high school education								
1940	60.7	82.0	46.9	76.3	72.5	b	68.0	51.7
1950	39.7	42.2	33.2	52.0	66.4	12.7	42.0	35.5
1960	37.8	37.0	38.6	65.1	50.4	33.1	41.0	34.6
1970	26.0	28.0	32.1	39.1	40.4	40.6	31.3	26.1
Median family income, 1940-1970								
1960	$5,988	$5,867	$4,252	$5,560	$4,942	$4,372	$5,319	$5,747
1970	$9,464	$10,757	$6,407	$7,614	$8,072	$4,594	$8,704	$9,133
Percentage of families below poverty line								
1970	9.7	4.7	20.8	15.3	15.0	38.0	13.5	11.7

Sources: *Statistics for Census Tracts: Boston,* 1940 Census of Population and Housing, Table 1, pp. 4, 13-14; Table 3, pp. 26, 36-37; *Census Tract Statistics: Boston and Adjacent Area,* 1950 Census of Population, PD-6, Table 1, pp. 7, 11; Table 2, pp. 34, 40-41; *Census Tracts for Boston SMSA,* 1960 Census of Population and Housing, PHC(1)-18, Table P-1, pp. 14, 21-23; Table P-3, pp. 127, 134-135; *Census Tracts for Boston SMSA,* 1970 Census of Population and Housing, PHC(1)-29, Table P-1, pp. P-3, P-31; Table P-2, pp. P-43, P-71; Table P-3, pp. P-83, P-111.

aThe 1940 Columbus Park subtotal is low because some dwellings in this section were included in Dorchester tract.

bD Street project was not built until 1949; hence the sharp drop in Lower End population for 1940-1950 is somewhat misleading, as the D Street tract (M-3) was included in the 1940 Lower End subtotal; accordingly, D Street tenants were added to residents of the Lower End in 1950 to compute percentage change from 1940.

In sum, the physical facade of South Boston exaggerates other distinctions in a predominantly working- and lower-middle class population. Almost every section had some lower-middle class inhabitants, although South Boston's most affluent residents were located in City Point and Telegraph Hill. Lower-class people lived primarily in D Street and the surrounding Lower End. Perhaps unknown to outsiders, these locational distinctions no doubt proved crucial to social relations among defended-neighborhood residents before the busing protest. Reportedly, one of the few institutions mixing people from all parts of the neighborhood was South Boston High.

Drawing such distinctions does no violence to the concept of a defended neighborhood. First, the participation of each and every inhabitant is not required to create a defended neighborhood. Indeed, it seems many South Bostonians did not consider D Street to be part of their neighborhood. Second, according to Suttles, a defended neighborhood divides into levels ranging from "egocentric" to "sociocentric" frames of reference:

> When a person speaks of "my neighborhood," he may be referring to a small area which centers on himself and is different for any two individuals. "Our neighborhood," on the other hand, tends to refer to some localized group . . . also . . . identified by other structural boundaries such as ethnicity or income. "The neighborhood," however, has a more fixed referent and usually possesses a name and some sort of reputation known to persons other than the residents.[21]

Crime inside the Defended Neighborhood

Like other big-city neighborhoods, South Boston has a long history of crime and gang conflict. Organized underworld activities in the neighborhood may have been less important in the 1970s than in the previous decade, when several shootings attracted press notice. More is known about South Boston's youth gangs, especially numerous in the 1920s and 1930s.[22]

Gang violence reached serious proportions in the summer of 1966. Gang conflict presumably explained two murders and several hospitalizations in only four days; a victim of one beating refused to name the assailants who had cut his throat.[23] Newspaper reports identified three heavily armed juvenile gangs operating in different parts of South Boston; the press also blamed youth gangs for breaking over a hundred plate-glass windows in six months of terrorism against local merchants.[24] A gang may also have slaughtered animals in a pet shop six years later.[25]

No section of the neighborhood escaped this violence completely, but the incidence of stabbings, beatings, and vandalism was highest in the Lower End and D Street. Drawn to South Boston because of its "crime spree" in 1966, some reporters stayed to recount hellish conditions inside the D Street project. One wrote of residents barricading apartment doors at night while juveniles rampaged in the corridors.[26] Another noted D Street tenant complaints about the way in which young offenders were treated by the South Boston district court. One irate tenant blamed the court for undermining police efforts by adhering to local norms:

And even when they do get a kid, and bring him down to court, do you know what happens? The kid gets this: "How are you Johnny? How's your mother and father, and what are you doing here anyway?" So the cop is likely to end up the villain. They shouldn't have people from Southie down at that courthouse. They should have people from the outside.[27]

A city investigation four years later uncovered additional evidence of Hobbesian conditions inside D Street. Multiple victimization was common, especially in cases of property destruction. In only one year, 598 residents of the project had been the victims of 1,900 personal and property crimes. Most offenders were teenage males living in or near the project and hence known at least by sight to their victims.[28]

Drug problems also attracted the press, but the extent of this "crisis" was sharply debated. A 1972 claim that drug abuse had attained epidemic proportions was denied strenuously by probation and police officers. According to the police spokesman: "The situation here isn't as bad as in other places because people still look out their windows and call us when they see something wrong. They have a pride in their neighborhood, and they want to do something about it."[29]

Fear of Crime

The problems just described might raise doubts about designation of South Boston as a defended neighborhood. No neighborhood can be so described if significant numbers of residents fear for their personal safety while on their own turf. This section addresses two questions: First, how does South Boston compare to other Boston neighborhoods with respect to crime rates, and, second, how safe do South Bostonians feel in their neighborhood compared to residents of other neighborhoods in the city?

In the 1970s, at least, South Boston's crime rate compared favorably to that of other Boston neighborhoods. A 1970 study reported South Boston had the city's lowest burglary rate and one of the lowest robbery rates. On the other hand, the incidence of assault and battery in the Lower End and D Street combined was one of the city's highest.[30]

A 1977 citywide poll included numerous questions relating to crime victimization and feelings of personal safety. In this survey, South Bostonians viewed their own enclave as a safe haven, whereas respondents living in nearby neighborhoods were fearful of being raped, mugged, or assaulted. Table 4-4 ranks seventeen Boston neighborhoods according to victimization reports and respondent perceptions of neighborhood safety. South Boston tied with Chinatown for the lowest victimization figure, and was second highest in the percentage of respondents feeling "almost totally safe" in one's own neighborhood. Only 5 percent of the South Boston respondents

Table 4-4
South Boston Compared with Other Boston Neighborhoods on 1977 Crime Questions

Neighborhood and Sample N[a]	1976 Crime Victimization Rate[b] (%)	Neighborhood Rank	Percentage of Residents Saying Neighborhood "Almost Totally Safe"	Neighborhood Rank
Allston-Brighton (448)	21	4.5	29	8
Back Bay-Beacon Hill (284)	26	1.0	30	7
Charlestown (207)	13	10.5	49	3
Chinatown (107)	6	16.5	14	17
N. Dorchester (262)	25	2.0	18	14
S. Dorchester (444)	19	6.0	23	11
East Boston (303)	7	15.0	47	4
Fenway (364)	21	4.5	17	15
Franklin Field-Mattapan (351)	17	7.5	22	12
Hyde Park (286)	10	12.5	37	6
Jamaica Plain-Mission Hill (371)	14	9.0	27	10
North End (245)	8	14.0	66	1
Roslindale (262)	13	10.5	28	9
Roxbury (307)	24	3.0	15	16
South Boston (293)	6	16.5	59	2
South End (276)	17	7.5	21	13
West Roxbury (309)	10	12.5	40	5

Source: Calculated from A Survey of Attitudes Toward the City of Boston and its Neighborhoods, Peter D. Hart Research Associates, (May 1977), Table 70 and 71.

[a] Sample Ns are weighted.

[b] Percentage saying they had been a victim of a crime committed inside their own neighborhood in 1976.

described their enclave as "very unsafe." When asked to state specific fears about living in their neighborhood, 47 percent of the South Bostonians said they had no such fears. Only one other neighborhood received a stronger endorsement from its residents in this question. Among South Bostonians noting particular apprehensions, most (10 percent) were afraid of fire.[31] On the other hand, as would be expected, fully one-fourth said their neighborhood had a "weakness" because of "vandalism," "delinquents," or "uncontrolled" youth. Only East Boston and Charlestown, both defended neighborhoods, had higher proportions of concern about the same problems.

In summary, most residents of South Boston felt quite safe inside their neighborhood. Unlike immediately surrounding districts, where large percentages of residents feared for their personal safety, the foundation of the good community did exist in most parts of South Boston. The "spree" of 1966 had not recurred, and, possibly, knowing youths who belonged to gangs allayed adult concerns about physical violence. Property destruction remained a serious problem, however, and it appears unruly youth were blamed for it.

Ties that Bind

Up to this point, every effort has been made to take seriously the central point expressed in a South Boston letter to the *Herald-American*:

> . . . Do not clump us all together in one neat little package. It is not fair. People are different. We have our fighters and our lovers. We have hard-working men and those who loaf. . . . Do not, in all fairness, try to take any one geographical location and say the same thing about all of its people.[32]

All of the problems described above notwithstanding, South Boston presents a remarkably solid front to the outside world. Extended families, mutual aid, and insiders' networks help make this unusual cohesion more than myth.

Unable to document the full extent to which residents are actually related to one another, we are still convinced of the importance of extended families to maintaining solidarity in South Boston. Several respondents emphasized kinship in their accounts of why South Boston was so tightly knit. "In Southie," said one, "you are always somebody's uncle, or their cousin, or maybe their godfather."[33] Another respondent estimated that 25 percent of the neighborhood population had at least one South Boston relative through either marriage or blood.[34]

South Boston's generosity and compassion for its own in times of catastrophe is legendary. Every year fires injure and make homeless a score or more of residents; neighbors typically respond immediately by providing food, shelter, clothing, money, and so on. A Hyde Park antibusing activist spoke admiringly of this tradition:

> If somebody's in trouble over there, everybody tries to help them. I've seen them take collections up and raise thousands of dollars to help somebody put their house back together, and get some furniture in their house because they don't have insurance, or they've got too many kids, or they don't have the money . . .[35]

Finally, the existence of insiders' networks became obvious while interviewing in South Boston. An interview frequently began with the respondent recounting what had been said by an earlier respondent or by revealing enough other details to demonstrate that antibusing activists kept in close communication. Insiders' networks provided an efficient communication network in times of protest against busing. Some respondents boasted of the ability to turn out several hundred demonstrators in only two or three hours of telephone calling.

Conclusion: South Boston and the Defended Neighborhood

This chapter described how South Boston became a defended neighborhood. Although landfills eliminated the South Bay, railroad lines and the Southeastern Expressway replaced the bay as obstacles to unimpeded movement to and from South Boston. One must still cross a bridge to enter South Boston. Neal Peirce characterizes South Boston as "perhaps the most isolated ethnic community in any American city," and, after describing community norms conducive to cohesion, concludes "the other side of the close-community coin is the parochialism, the narrow-mindedness, the fierce suspicion of outsiders."[36]

In 1970 only 43 percent of all South Bostonians twenty-five and older were high-school graduates.[37] Not all of them had attended South Boston High, some going to parochial or other public schools in the city. Nonetheless the symbolic importance of South Boston High to the neighborhood should not be discounted. South Boston High's football and hockey teams were cheered on by perhaps the city's most passionate and rowdy fans. For most young people in the neighborhood, South Boston High was the end of their formal education. It was also a place to meet youngsters from other parts of the neighborhood, to form relationships leading to marriage or deep friendship. Although whites from other sections of Boston had been admitted to fill the seats, it was very much a neighborhood school. With the busing controversy South Boston High gained a notoriety previously reserved for Little Rock, Arkansas's Central High.

Although this chapter focused wholly on South Boston, there were other defended neighborhoods in Boston when busing started. Striking parallels may be observed in Charlestown and East Boston, and, to a lesser degree, in Hyde Park.[38] The North End might qualify as well. In any case, the foundation of vigorous defense against unwanted social change had been laid in such places long before the busing controversy. The following chapter describes the conflict over racial imbalance that eventually ended with busing.

Notes

1. Francis Russell, *A City in Terror: 1919, The Boston Police Strike* (New York: Viking Press, 1975), p. 124.

2. Interview by Buell, 14 June 1977.

3. Interview by Buell, 14 June 1977.

4. Thomas C. Simonds, *History of South Boston,* 1857 reprint ed. (New York: Arno Press, 1974), p. 229.

5. See Peter R. Knights, *The Plain People of Boston, 1830-1860: A Study in City Growth* (New York: Oxford University Press, 1971).

6. Simonds, *History,* p. 300.

7. Quoted in Oscar Handlin, *Boston's Immigrants: A Study in Acculturation,* rev. and enl. ed. (New York: Atheneum, 1974), p. 98.

8. Quoted in Simonds, *History,* p. 301.

9. *The Census of Massachusetts: 1880* (Boston: Wright & Potter, 1883), pp. 185-186. South Boston wards 13, 14, and 15.

10. *Census of the Commonwealth of Massachusetts: 1895,* vol. I, *Population and Social Statistics* (Boston: Wright & Potter, 1896), pp. 220-221.

11. See *Census of the United States: 1910, Population: Reports by States, Alabama-Montana* (Washington, D.C.: U.S. Government Printing Office, 1913), Table V, p. 890.

12. Andrew M. Greeley, *The American Catholic* (New York: Basic Books, 1977), p. 236.

13. Interview by Buell, 2 September 1977.

14. For standard accounts of Irish political culture transplanted to American cities, see William V. Shannon, *The American Irish: A Political and Social Portrait* (New York: Collier-Macmillan, 1974); Nathan Glazer and Daniel P. Moynihan, *Beyond the Melting Pot,* 2nd ed. (Cambridge: MIT Press, 1970); and, Edward M. Levine, *The Irish and Irish Politicians* (Notre Dame, Ind.: Notre Dame University Press, 1966).

15. Quoted in Handlin, *Boston's Immigrants*, p. 98.

16. See *The Seventh Census of the United States, 1850* (Washington, D.C.: Robert Armstrong, 1853), Table II, p. 52.

17. See Deborah Blumlin, *Victims: A Study of Crime in A Boston Housing Project,* (Mayor's Safe Streets Act Advisory Committee, Boston: 1973), p. 47.

18. Eleanor H. Woods, "South Boston," in *The Zone of Emergence,* 2nd ed. abr., Robert A. Woods and Albert J. Kennedy, eds., (Cambridge, Mass.: MIT Press, 1969), pp. 168-169.

19. As computed from census tract data, the turnover in D Street residents for 1950-1970 was 96 percent; see *Census Tracts: Boston SMSA,* PHC(1)-29, 1970 Census of Population and Housing, Table H-w, p. H-71. D Street was all of tract 607 in this census. The sectional breakdown of South Boston used here has been taken from *South Boston: Background Information, Planning Issues and Preliminary Neighborhood Strategies,* Boston Redevelopment Authority (June 1975), with a change of "West Broadway" to "the Lower End." Census tracts were combined in the following manner to aggregate sectional characteristics: City Point, 601-602 and 605 (in earlier censuses N-1, N-2, N-3); Telegraph Hill, 603-604 (earlier N-4 and O-1); Columbus Park, 610-611 (earlier O-2 and P1B); Andrew Square, 612-613 (earlier O-4 and P1A); and the Lower End, 606 and 608-609, 614 (earlier M-1, M-2, M-4, and O-3).

20. City Point and Telegraph Hill compare favorably to the city on population losses when white decline is examined. Boston's drop in white population was substantially higher than suggested by overall rates of change shown in table 4-3.

21. Gerald D. Suttles, *The Social Construction of Communities* (Chicago: University of Chicago Press, 1972), p. 37.

22. A study of juvenile delinquency records fifty years ago found one of Boston's highest male arrest rates in the Lower End; it was twice that of City Point and six times that of Telegraph Hill. See Clifford R. Shaw and Henry D. McKay, *Juvenile Delinquency and Urban Areas,* rev. ed. (Chicago: University of Chicago Press, 1969), pp. 233-235.

23. *Boston Herald,* 7 July 1966, p. 1.

24. *Boston Globe,* 7 July 1966.

25. "Thieves, Sadistic Vandals Leave 4 So. Boston Shopkeepers 'Scared,' " *Boston Herald,* 6 March 1972, p. 3.

26. *Boston Record-American,* 8 July 1966, p. 3.

27. "Just What's The Matter in Southie?," *Boston Advertiser,* 10 July 1966, p. 18.

28. Blumlin, *Victims,* p. 33.

29. "Pot, Booze Prevail in Southie," *Boston Record-American,* 20 April 1972, p. 53.

30. See Albert P. Cardarelli, *Crime in Boston: An Analysis of Serious Crime Patterns in 81 Boston Neighborhoods,* Mayor's Office of Justice Administration (1970), p. 6.

31. *A Survey of Attitudes Toward the City of Boston and its Neighborhoods*, Peter D. Hart Research Associates (May 1977), table 73.

32. Letter to the editor, *Boston Herald-American,* 8 July 1976, p. 10.

33. Interview by Buell, 14 June 1977.

34. Interview by Buell, 10 May 1976.

35. Interview by Buell, 11 July 1977.

36. Neal Peirce, *The New England States* (New York: Norton; 1976), p. 123.

37. *Census Tracts: Boston SMSA* (1970) PHC(1)-29, Table P-2, p. P-71.

38. For an excellent account of Charlestown as a defended neighborhood, see Langley C. Keyes, Jr., *The Rehabilitation Game: A Study in Neighborhood Diversity* (Cambridge, Mass.: MIT Press, 1969), pp. 92-94.

5 The Politics of
Racial Imbalance

A Decade of Controversy

Conflict over race and schools dominated Boston's political agenda for a full decade before black parents finally took their case to federal court. Rancor growing out of the racial imbalance dispute unquestionably heightened resistance to any form of busing in South Boston and other defended neighborhoods. This chapter describes how the imbalance-controversy developed. Much of what follows features Louise Day Hicks, daughter of the defended neighborhood, champion of the antibusing cause, and perennial office seeker.[1] Hardly the only public official to oppose busing and the state imbalance law, Mrs. Hicks was nonetheless unmatched in her ability to mobilize defended-neighborhood protest and represent such reaction in the councils of government. Certainly no other public figure gained anything like the notoriety and media attention given Mrs. Hicks, and no other local politician had a more important role in shaping the race and schools debate before 1974.

Race and Schools in Boston: An Overview

The episodes of the 1960s and early 1970s are better understood if placed in historical context. Bostonians take pride in their city's "firsts," including the nation's first public school, instruction by grade, and, fittingly, educational bureaucracy.[2] Boston also was one of the first American cities to hear black complaints about inferior schooling.

Apparently the first expression of such discontent was made in 1781, when black Bostonians petitioned the Massachusetts Great and General Court for a separate school. State and city legislatures rebuffed this and subsequent appeals until 1806, when the city finally agreed to accept and support an already struggling school in the African Meetinghouse. By the time a new Abiel Smith School was built on the same site in 1835, racial segregation had become firmly and formally established in Boston.

But black preference for segregation did not mean corresponding satisfaction with the Smith School's faculty, curriculum, or physical condition. As the building steadily deteriorated and the content and quality of instruction came increasingly under criticism, the black community divided over the desirability of maintaining separate schools. Boston abolitionists recognized the rising disenchantment of some black parents and made the Smith School an object of a local campaign. Their various appeals to city authorities were rejected, however, as officials reportedly feared that mixing the races would stampede the whites and promote violence between Irish immigrant and black children.[3] After years of agitation over the school, the abolitionists pinned their hopes on a lawsuit brought by Benjamin Roberts, a black printer, who sought to enroll his daughter Sarah in an all-white school much closer to their home. The case was argued in the Massachusetts Supreme Judicial Court in December 1849. A unanimous decision read by Chief Justice Lemuel Shaw upheld the plenary power of the Boston School Committee to "arrange, classify, and distribute pupils" in accordance with "experience and judgment."[4]

Defeat in court did not deter further abolitionist attempts to enact legislation in the Great and General Court. These efforts finally bore fruit in 1855, when the legislature passed a bill disallowing racial and religious distinctions in admitting students to public schools. The governor's signature doomed Boston's segregation.[5]

Certain demographic facts of the time surely helped city fathers comply with the new law. A common finding of contemporary desegregation research is that white fears are less pronounced when the number of black students involved is small.[6] Certainly whites in nineteenth-century Boston had little basis for anxiety on this score, as black pupils were but a tiny portion of the total student population. In 1870, for example, only 348 were counted in the entire school system, and, two decades later, only 1.5 percent of the 68,798 students in Boston schools were black.[7] Even in 1940, which saw an increase in the number of black students to 3,735, whites still enjoyed a 97 percent majority in public and private schools combined.[8]

An additional fact probably allaying white fears was the concentration of Boston's small black population in a handful of wards. In 1850, for instance, 79 percent of the city's black residents lived in an area of no more than two square miles.[9] By 1910 fully 85 percent resided in the South End and Roxbury districts, but in neither neighborhood did blacks exceed 23 percent of a ward's population.[10] Under the circumstances, then, it is most likely that a majority of Boston's black students attended schools that were integrated in the late nineteenth and early twentieth centuries.

Whatever the racial composition of city schools during this period, the proportion of school-age black youngsters actually enrolled compared favorably to whites, particularly when the latter were classified by nativity. In 1900, for example, 51 percent of all black youths aged five to twenty were in school. Among whites the figure varied by nativity: 66 percent of the native-born with native-born parents, 64 percent of the native-born of foreign or mixed parentage, and 38 percent of the foreign-born.[11] Each group's school proportion increased steadily over the next four decades, and differences between groups diminished greatly. Nonetheless, in 1940 a slightly larger proportion of black children was enrolled than was true of foreign-born whites.[12]

The end of *de jure* segregation did not lead to integration of Boston teachers. In complying with the 1855 law the school committee discharged all black instructors at the Smith School, and very few blacks were hired to teach in city schools for the remainder of the century. The 1890 census counted only one among 1,380 public- and private-school teachers.[13] Despite increases in the first half of the present century, no more than 1 percent of all public and private school teachers in 1960 were black.[14]

This background sketch would be incomplete without noting two simultaneous changes in Boston's population after World War II. Between 1950 and 1970 the city lost 31 percent of its white residents, an exodus partly set in motion by the completion of Route 128 and accompanying suburbanization. Between 1940 and 1970 Boston's black population increased by 342 percent, a jump that brought blacks from 3 percent to 16.3 percent of the total city population.[15]

Traditional ghetto boundaries were soon strained by this flood of black migrants, and, by 1970, virtually all of the South End and Roxbury had been consolidated. The number of census tracts with at least 250 black inhabitants rose from twenty-two in 1940-1950, to 37 in 1950-1960, and to 58 in 1960-1970. In 1970 such tracts could be found in Jamaica Plain, Roslindale, Mattapan, Hyde Park, North and South Dorchester, the Back Bay, and Brighton as well as in Roxbury and the South End. Analysis of the speed with which these tracts changed color reveals that the pace picked up with each new decade. The rapidity with which some parts of the city underwent transition between 1960 and 1970 was astounding. This fact was hardly lost on the Boston School Committee, as later discussion of its school construction and pupil assignment policies would reveal.

Louise Day Hicks and the *De Facto* Segregation Dispute

No controversy clouded the 27 June 1961 announcement by Louise Day Hicks that she would run for a position on the five-member Boston School Committee. The only daughter of Judge William Day of the South Boston district court, she had grown up in comfortable surroundings and represented the affluent extreme of South Boston's socioeconomic spectrum. After graduation from Wheelock College in 1938 she had briefly taught first grade before clerking in her father's office. In 1942 she had married a New York electrical engineer named John Hicks, who had promptly entered wartime naval service. The couple moved into the Day family home in South Boston after his discharge. Two sons were born in 1945 and 1946. Mrs. Hicks had continued to clerk for Judge Day while becoming active in school, civic, and religious affairs. When her father died in 1950, Mrs. Hicks enrolled at Boston University and earned a B.S. in education and a law degree. The 1961 bid for school committee was the first political campaign for the forty-three-year-old Mrs. Hicks. Endorsed by the League for Better Schools and the Boston Teachers' Alliance, she campaigned on mildly reformist themes and voiced stock criticisms of patronage politics in school-committee affairs.[16] A fourth-place showing in the September preliminary election allowed her to compete with the nine other top vote getters in November for the five-member committee.[17] In the general election she ran third with 40,559 votes.[18]

Near the end of her first term she was able to win the chair of the school committee by combining the votes of committee members Arthur Gartland and William O'Connor with her own. In making her acceptance speech Mrs. Hicks urged greater emphasis on remedial programs, a more sustained effort to reduce dropout rates, and continued involvement in the Action for Boston Community Development (ABCD) program.[19]

While Louise Day Hicks was beginning her political career, outspoken members of the black community such as Ruth Batson and Paul Parks were starting to mobilize opinion against the school committee. Black discontent with physical conditions in ghetto schools, teacher attitudes toward black students, and other problems coincided with the massive population growth noted earlier and the advent of the civil-rights movement.[20] By 1960 a liberal and biracial group named Citizens for Boston Public Schools had begun publicizing the dilapidated state of ghetto schools and calling attention to racial isolation of pupils.

The latter concern was pressed by representatives of the city's NAACP chapter before the Massachusetts Commission Against Discrimination (MCAD) in June 1961. MCAD was a quasi-judicial body established to investigate discrimination in housing and other areas and was empowered to issue cease-and-desist orders upon proof of wrongdoing. The commissioners now replied to NAACP charges of deliberate school segregation by insisting on evidence. In order to obtain data on the race and location of students in the public schools, the NAACP turned to the Boston School Department. The reply was that such statistics were not collected by local officials. Demands arose for a racial census of public-school pupils, a task undertaken by state authorities in 1964.

Unwilling to await results of this census, the NAACP approached the Massachusetts State Advisory Committee of the U.S. Commission on Civil Rights. This body took testimony on *de facto* segregation in March 1963 and again a year later. Eventually the advisory committee released reports upholding claims of segregated schools and housing in Boston.[21]

The NAACP also requested hearings by the Boston School Committee. On 11 June 1963, during an eight-hour executive session, Mrs. Hicks and fellow members listened to criticism of pupil-assignment policies, deterioration of ghetto school buildings, lack of new school construction, teacher mistreatment of minority children, and insufficient special programs. Headmasters of schools named in this testimony appeared three days later and disputed many of the allegations. The school committee and the NAACP met again on 15 June amid calls for a citywide student boycott of the public schools. Nothing was accomplished, however, as the committee refused to grant the NAACP's contention that *de facto* segregation existed in the Boston system. The NAACP insisted on this concession as a necessary basis to continue discussion.

In retrospect, it seems likely that neither side fully understood the difference between *de facto* and *de jure* segregation. Press reports of the time contain language by spokespersons of both parties more appropriate to intentional or *de jure* segregation. Indeed, at one point most members of the committee were supposedly willing to concede some "racially imbalanced, predominantly Negro schools" in Boston, but would not countenance use of the term *de facto* segregation to explain their presence.[22]

In any event, the term soon became a symbol impossible for the school committee to embrace or the NAACP to abandon. Acrimony over what had become a principle pushed the two groups into adversary roles and led to frequent charges of bad faith on both sides.

Just how wide this gulf had become was apparent on 15 August, when the NAACP and school committee next met. Once again, NAACP representatives demanded that *de facto* segregation be addressed first. Mrs. Hicks promptly adjourned the session. Outraged blacks and white supporters picketed school committee headquarters; police started around-the-clock surveillance of the Hicks home on 16 August.

The *de facto* segregation struggle clearly altered the political career of Louise Day Hicks. As late as the previous May, she had responded sympathetically to parental complaints about ghetto schools at a Roxbury meeting. Her Roxbury performance impressed enough members of the Citizens for Boston Public Schools to make their endorsement of her reelection bid in September a serious prospect. This possibility was still alive after the 11 June meeting with the NAACP when Mrs. Hicks reportedly drafted a compromise proclamation acknowledging the "unique" educational problems of ghetto youth, endorsing the civil-rights movement, and urging city officials to adopt "cooperative" and "sympathetic" approaches to racial problems. Reportedly the NAACP was willing to accept this statement in place of an explicit concession on *de facto* segregation, pending certain word changes. The NAACP supposedly gave the revised version to the newspapers without first clearing it with Mrs. Hicks, however, and she is said to have angrily retracted it upon learning of its impending publication from a newspaper editor.[23]

Whatever the true account, she showed no willingness to compromise in September, when Governor Endicott Peabody intervened in the dispute and implored the school committee to underwrite a declaration admitting that in "predominantly Negro schools the children receive an inferior education." Accounts of the time implied an agreement by the NAACP to accept this concession in place of contrition on *de facto* segregation, but Mrs. Hicks would have none of it. Immediately after meeting with Peabody she told reporters that the claim of inferior education for black students was false, maintaining that some blacks actually enjoyed an advantage over whites because of higher expenditures on remedial programs. She also disclosed having told the governor that the *de facto* segregation quarrel was an "educational matter" rather than a "civil rights" issue.[24]

Even at this early juncture, Louise Day Hicks had formulated various positions on race and schools that would be reiterated tirelessly throughout her political career. One such stance was to reassure audiences that "school district lines in Boston have always been drawn according to the neighborhood school concept without any consideration of race, creed, or color of the pupils."[25] Another was that racial discrimination could not account for the shortcomings of ghetto children in school: "Our teachers tell us that it is not a problem of discrimination; it is a problem of the child who comes to school hungry and cold and not motivated to learn . . . . I do not believe the colored child will learn from the white child by osmosis."[26]

Louise Day Hicks emerged from the *de facto* segregation clash as the "gutsy" defender of white neighborhoods and local values, and she developed this image against the NAACP with telling effect. On 24 September 1963 she topped the list of school-committee candidates in the preliminary election by winning 78,665 votes. Boston newspapers and political observers were quick to note that her tally exceeded Mayor Collins's vote by 21,000. In her victory speech Mrs. Hicks asserted that most black parents actually supported her rather than the NAACP, and branded the NAACP leaders as unrepresentative and destructive:

> The NAACP officials here are not the true leaders of the Negro community. They are not speaking for the community in the sit-ins they staged . . . the demonstrations they fostered . . . and the boycott of classes they called last June. The real harm done by the NAACP was to the very children they said they were aiding. They drew a color line where none had existed before.[27]

A coalition of liberal, civil-rights, and black organizations in the Boston area worked to unseat Hicks in the November election. Fifty-eight Boston College professors (including seventeen Jesuits) issued a declaration shortly before election day condemning conditions in predominantly black city schools and calling on the school committee to "break the current pattern of segregation" by redistricting.[28] In response, Mrs. Hicks sought to discredit the academics by contending they knew too little to discuss the situation in the Boston schools intelligently, a tactic she would often use again against critics. After reiterating that race had nothing to do with determining school district lines, she invited the professors to "come into the schools, see what we are doing, and then issue a statement."[29]

Mrs. Hicks definitely had the last word on election day, when she again led all school-committee candidates, garnering 128,358 votes from nearly 69 percent of those who turned out. "The people of Boston have given their answer to the *de facto* segregation question," she exulted at her victory celebration.[30]

It is instructive to examine the returns at this high point in her political fortunes. Merely a third of all registered voters had gone to the polls in the 1961 general election, but almost 61 percent had voted in 1963. Since a reelected Collins trailed the Hicks total by almost twenty-thousand votes, the 1963 electoral surge can hardly be explained by interest in the mayoral race. Examination of the ward returns for the 1961 and 1963 November runoffs reveals remarkable growth in the proportion of voters supporting Hicks. The average gain in her voting strength across twenty-two wards was 28.6 percent. Table 5-1 shows doubling or better of her support in eight wards and improvement by 20 percent or more in ten others. More than 80 percent of all voters in seven wards supported her in 1963, and she fell below 50 percent in only three wards. Only in Roxbury's black Twelfth Ward did her 1963 level dip below the 1961 figure.

Soundly beaten at the polls, the anti-Hicks coalition again threatened a student boycott and pressed its case with the Commonwealth. Another meeting between the school committee and representatives of the NAACP did not resolve differences, and the boycott was set for 26 February 1964. During a televised debate with the chairman of Boston's Congress of Racial Equality (CORE) chapter on 14 February, Mrs. Hicks claimed black children were being coerced to join the upcoming boycott. Brushing aside her opponent's denial, she also asserted that the boycott was an irresponsible undertaking that would teach black youngsters how to "flaunt" the law. "These children need more, not less, education," she concluded.[31] Despite pleas by Governor Peabody and other public officials, about one-fifth of the city's black students boycotted classes on 26 February. Some attended alternative "freedom schools," while others joined about 1,500 protestors at city hall.

The Commonwealth Intervenes

Governor Peabody and state education officials had watched the *de facto* segregation controversy escalate with growing dismay. After the failure of

Table 5-1
Percentage of Voters Supporting Louise Day Hicks in 1961 and 1963
General Elections for Boston School Committee, by Wards

Ward	Neighborhood(s)	Percentage Voting for Hicks 1961	1963	Percentage Change in Hicks Support 1961-1963
1	East Boston	31.1	55.5	+24.4
2	Charlestown	40.3	80.9	+40.6
3	North End/			
	West End	26.0	56.1	+30.1
4	Back Bay	29.9	49.1	+19.2
5	Back Bay/			
	Beacon Hill	29.3	52.7	+23.4
6	South Boston	71.8	83.1	+11.3
7	South Boston	65.0	85.4	+18.4
8	South End	33.4	56.9	+23.5
9	South End/			
	Roxbury	22.9	26.3	+ 3.4
10	Mission Hill	31.4	74.9	+43.5
11	Jamaica Plain	32.9	69.5	+36.6
12	Roxbury	23.9	16.3	− 7.6
13	Savin Hill-			
	Dorchester	42.7	74.0	+31.3
14	Blue Hill Ave.-			
	Dorchester	30.3	54.1	+23.8
15	Meeting Hse. Hill-			
	Dorchester	44.8	82.8	+38.0
16	Neponset-			
	Dorchester	46.6	84.5	+37.9
17	Mattapan	44.3	80.7	+36.4
18	Hyde Park	35.9	77.1	+41.2
19	Roslindale	35.8	78.2	+42.4
20	West Roxbury	35.0	81.2	+46.2
21	Allston	35.5	64.8	+29.3
22	Brighton	34.8	75.1	+36.7
	Citywide	38.4	68.8	+30.4

Sources: *Public Document 10: 1961*, p. 154; *Public Document 10: 1963*, p. 150.

his mediation efforts, Peabody and Owen Kiernan, commissioner of education, met with black leaders in Boston and denounced segregated schools. Early in 1964 Commissioner Kiernan assembled the Advisory Committee on Racial Imbalance and Education (quickly dubbed the "Kiernan Committee") for the purposes of conducting a racial census of all public schools in Massachusetts and identifying any that were racially imbalanced. The Kiernan Committee defined any school with 50 percent or more nonwhite enrollment as "racially imbalanced."

Although New Bedford school authorities attempted to block the census with a suit on behalf of certain Cape Verdean constituents who objected to racial classifications, the Kiernan Committee was able to complete its survey quickly and release preliminary findings in July 1964.[32] Its interim report revealed that forty-five of the fifty-five racially imbalanced schools in Massachusetts were in Boston. The Boston School Committee chose not to respond until the release of the final version.

That document became available in April 1965.[33] A less-biased account probably would have served the Kiernan Committee's policy objectives better. In any case, no one reading the opening "conclusions" about the pernicious effects of racial imbalance was left in doubt about the report's obvious perspective. Equally evident was the scant support these declarations received from the main body of the report, a series of simple tabulations by race of enrollment in each school system in the state. Perhaps in an effort to bridge this discrepancy, those compiling the final version had commissioned special essays addressing various aspects of segregated education. Although most of these contributions were well reasoned and empirically supported, one in particular must have provoked a reaction from Mrs. Hicks and her supporters. The piece in question denied any valid educational purpose for neighborhood schools in contemporary urban society, and argued that white ethnics of Celtic and other non-Anglo Saxon origins would readily swap neighborhood schools for more cosmopolitan settings where children would gain "an enlarged view of the world."[34]

A hint of bias also was present in the discussion of how badly school buildings in predominantly black sections had deteriorated. Relying primarily on a 1962 inventory of every school building in Boston, the report correctly pointed out that "the worst school buildings are often the most seriously racially imbalanced."[35] A fuller account would also have acknowledged that Boston school committees in the early part of the century had cut corners on essential maintenance with shocking results. After 1930 it was time to pay the piper for misplaced frugality: Between thirty and fifty school buildings had to be closed every ten years. These abandonments were seldom replaced with new facilities. New construction between 1940 and 1950, for example, had added space for only 150 students.[36] Therefore, sad physical conditions were a critical problem in Charlestown and other mainly white school districts, as well as in the schools of Roxbury, North Dorchester, and the South End. Small wonder that the 1962 Sargent report had recommended closing eighty-one schools in the near future: twenty-seven by 1965, thirty-five by 1970, and nineteen by 1975.[37] Twenty-two of these were defined as racially imbalanced by the Kiernan Committee.

The final report of the Kiernan Committee was more successful in spelling out the extent of racial imbalance in the Boston system. Table 5-2 recapitulates the 1964 findings, showing that almost three-fourths of all nonwhite students attended racially imbalanced schools and that more than half were enrolled in schools 71 percent or more nonwhite. Nearly all such schools were located in black or rapidly changing sections of the city.

Table 5-2
Distribution of Nonwhite Pupils in Boston Public Schools, 1964

| | Racially Imbalanced Schools by Percentage Nonwhite Enrollment | | | | | |
	91-100%	81-90%	71-80%	61-70%	51-60%	Total
Number of schools	20	8	4	8	5	45
Percentage of all nonwhite public school pupils	37.6	11.7	7.6	10.3	5.4	72.6

| | Remaining Schools by Percentage Nonwhite Enrollment | | | | | |
	41-50%	31-40%	21-30%	11-20%	1-10%	<1%	Total
Number of schools	3	7	13	11	52	70	156

Source: *Because It Is Right—Educationally,* Report of the Advisory Committee on Racial Imbalance and Education, Massachusetts State Board of Education (April 1965), Table IX-B, p. 61; list, pp. 63-64.

A steadily escalating war of press releases was in progress when the final version of the Kiernan Committee report appeared. Earlier in April, Mayor Collins had again asked the school committee to concede the existence of some racial imbalance and open a dialogue with black leaders. Mrs. Hicks had responded that no dialogue was needed, as black leaders seemed to have nothing to discuss with the school committee. She also accused Collins of setting up the school committee for trial in the press.[38]

On 14 April she ferociously attacked the Kiernan Committee's final product. Scoring the report's authors and supporters as hypocrites who placed their own children in all-white private schools, Mrs. Hicks ridiculed the conclusions about the harmful effects of racial imbalance and sought to turn them against her foes: "If their theory has any validity at all," she taunted, "then it should follow that the education provided by the private schools of Boston is inferior." She added that "keen interest" would follow whatever enrollment adjustments were made by the private schools.

Much animosity was reserved for the authors of the report, whom Mrs. Hicks castigated as "a small band of racial agitators, non-native to Boston, and a few college radicals" who had instigated "a conspiracy to tell the people of Boston how to run their schools, their city, and their lives."

She seemed especially outraged by the report's recommendation that approximately three-thousand black and white pupils be reassigned to different schools in order to start a modest racial-balancing program. This idea was denounced as "undemocratic, un-American, absurdly expensive, unworkable, and diametrically opposed to the wishes of the parents of this city." Putting an obvious challenge to the mayor, she proposed a citywide referendum to discover popular preferences regarding neighborhood schools and racial imbalance. Any suggestion "that this school committee remove children from their local schools and forcibly transfer them to schools in other neighborhoods," was "incomprehensible" to her.

Mrs. Hicks elaborated an already familiar thesis about how best the "environmental disadvantages" of ghetto students could be ameliorated: The educational and cultural deficiencies of this group required compensatory and remedial programs, and, to be most effective, such training had to be concentrated where the need was greatest—in the ghetto schools. Busing "culturally deprived" and ill-prepared black children to predominantly white schools, where special programs were unavailable, only worsened matters for all concerned.

After her customary excoriation of "self-appointed experts" who lacked accurate information for their criticisms, she concluded on a theme to be used again in future campaigns:

> It is indeed sad . . . that those who disagree with any proposal of the NAACP are declared bigots, criticized by the press, and subjected to continual villification. Courage is something we all admire. . . . Genuine courage is demonstrated by those who dare to disagree with the pompous proclamations of the uninformed.[39]

Given this stir, the racial-imbalance caldron bubbled for the rest of the year. Mrs. Hicks claimed to have received about twenty-five hundred supportive letters and telegrams in the week following her salvo at the Kiernan Committee. Mayor Collins declined her referendum challenge, terming it "nonsense" and "government by post card."[40] When plans were announced for Dr. Martin Luther King, Jr., to visit Boston, tour ghetto schools, and lead a march to city hall, speculation arose about a Hicks-King confrontation. Mrs. Hicks promptly laid down her rules for such a meeting: King was to come alone to her office, prepared to hear of the accomplishments of the school system. The civil-rights leader did not stop at 15 Beacon Street during his brief stay. In late May, Mrs. Hicks applied for a gun permit after receiving threatening phone calls, and after three strangers attempted unsuccessfully to gain entry to her home. While taking part in Charlestown's annual Bunker Hill Day parade on 17 June, she was struck in the right eye by an apple hurled from the crowd; medical examination revealed a torn and detached retina. Three days later, Senator Edward M. Kennedy criticized the school committee for dismissing teacher-activist Jonathan Kozol, and compared Boston segregation to Mississippi's during a commencement address at Northeastern University. Mrs. Hicks, in turn, accused Kennedy of meddling in school-department affairs without reliable information. On 2 July, she filed for another school-committee term, informing reporters that her decision to run came only because of intense pressure from her supporters. Her petitions submitted on 28 July contained

16,000 more signatures of registered voters than required by law.[41] Meanwhile, efforts to push a racial-imbalance law through the state legislature were bearing fruit, a crucial development with both short- and long-term consequences for Boston.

Enactment of the Racial Imbalance Law

The Racial Imbalance Act passed by the state legislature in early August represented a victory of sorts for the coalition that had grown up in opposition to the school committee, but it also contained compromises that would constrain implementation.[42] A key provision allowing reassignment of students as a means of overcoming racial imbalance was partly offset by granting parents the option of not allowing their children to be bused. Local school committees were required to report annual statistics on enrollments by race, but, thus armed, the state board of education could only deal with schools more than 50 percent nonwhite. The definition of a "reasonable" time for compliance remained unclear, and any school committee denied state funds because of noncompliance with the statute could obtain judicial review. Involving the courts, of course, would prolong implementation. Finally, symbolic policitics in this instance favored opponents as well as proponents. Only one white Boston legislator had voted for the act, and Mrs. Hicks and supporters were thus able to claim that the legislation represented but another case of outsiders meddling in the problems of Boston.

Passage of the act may also have unintentionally delayed the eventual desegregation of Boston schools. On 13 January 1965 the federal district court in Springfield found that city's neighborhood-school policy unconstitutional and ordered immediate remedies.[43] The NAACP in Boston had filed a federal suit shortly after the Springfield ruling, contending that racially imbalanced schools, new construction sites, and pupil-assignment violated *Brown*.[44] However, likely enactment of a racial-imbalance law and the rule that all state remedies should be exhausted before turning to the federal courts evidently led the NAACP attorneys to drop their case.

In any event, passage of the imbalance act hardly subdued Mrs. Hicks. Shortly before the governor affixed his signature, she announced her intention to vote against acceptance of state school aid if necessary to prevent compulsory busing in Boston. When Edward Logue of the Boston Redevelopment Authority (BRA) publicly reminded her that state funds belonged to taxpayers rather than to Louise Day Hicks, she retorted that he ought to handle urban renewal and keep out of school affairs unless prepared to run for the school committee.[45] This was not a propitious moment for Superintendent William Ohrenberger's proposal to bus 560 students from overcrowded and predominantly black North Dorchester schools to schools in other parts of the city. The Hicks majority quickly replaced his idea with a staggered class schedule for the schools in question.

Mrs. Hicks naturally drew encouragement from the 1965 preliminary election, in which she again ran well ahead of all other school-committee candidates. She attributed this impressive win to popular endorsement of her stand against the imbalance law and to reaction against Operation Exodus, a voluntary black busing program to be discussed later.

Racial imbalance dominated the fall school-committee campaigns. Endorsed by the Citizens for Boston Public Schools, George Parker denounced Mrs. Hicks as a demagogue whose defiance of the imbalance law had put Boston in the same league as Selma, Alabama.[46] Such attacks seemed not to disturb Mrs. Hicks, who confidently made her rounds of living rooms, neighborhood halls, and hotel ballrooms vowing unrelenting opposition to redistricting and involuntary busing. Her rallies featured bands playing spirited renditions of "Every Little Breeze Seems to Whisper Louise," the Hicks campaign song.

The November 1965 election saw another triumph for the Hicks camp. Perhaps its most consistent foe on the school committee, Arthur Gartland, was unseated by the seemingly more dependable John McDonough. The proimbalance-act candidates who had survived the preliminary election were crushed. Indeed, combining the votes given to George Parker and Melvin King, the act's two strongest supporters, yielded a figure still eleven thousand votes shy of the Hicks tally. Her 93,056 votes had come from 65 percent of the participating electorate. Immediately, speculation started about a 1967 Hicks mayoral bid.

Although based on ward aggregates rather than surveys with individual voters, figures 5-1 and 5-2 nonetheless imply that the 1961, 1963, and 1965 Hicks school-committee candidacies performed an educational function for the Boston electorate. The fishhook configuration produced by plotting her 1961 and 1963 percentages of the November vote in each ward was due, of course, to her much stronger showing in the latter contest. A distinctive linear pattern suggestive of stable and predictable ward support and opposition emerged in the 1963-1965 plot. As would be expected, Mrs. Hicks ran quite strongly in predominantly white areas, particularly in her native South Boston, equally insular Charlestown and East Boston, Irish sections of Dorchester, still preponderantly Jewish Mattapan, and middle-class neighborhoods distant from downtown such as Hyde Park and West Roxbury. Whether these lopsided majorities would materialize for her in a mayoral race remained to be seen. No one doubted she would continue to do poorly in heavily black wards, her frequent claims of black parental support notwithstanding.

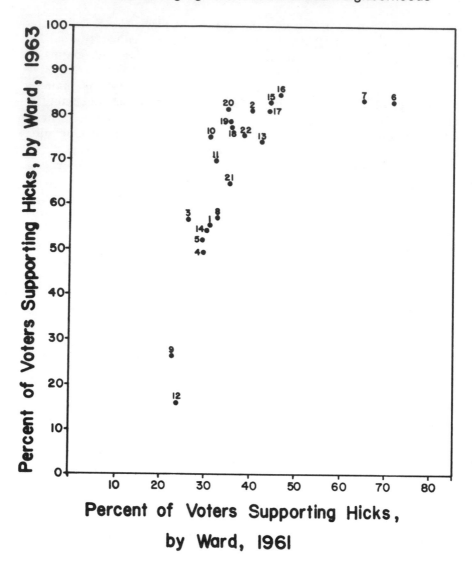

Figure 5-1. Percentage of Voters Supporting Hicks, by Ward, in School-
Committee General Elections, 1961-1963

A study of 317 white Boston voters interviewed before and after the
1965 school-committee elections produced additional information about
Hicks support and opposition.[47] In a subsequent analysis the sample was
sorted into pro-Hicks respondents (willing to vote for her in mayoral and
school-committee races), partial supporters (willing to vote for her in
school-committee but not mayoral elections), and anti-Hicks respondents
(unwilling to vote for her in any election). The anti-Hicks group was the

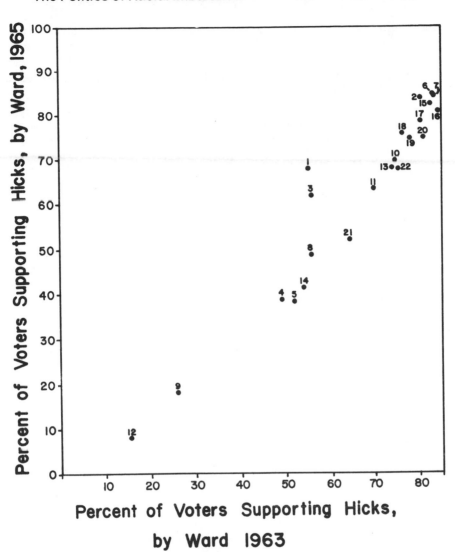

Figure 5-2. Percentage of Voters Supporting Hicks, by Ward, in School-Committee General Elections, 1963-1965

youngest, most affluent, most educated, and most likely to reside in racially mixed neighborhoods. It was also most supportive of school desegregation, although differences between the subsamples appeared surprisingly low to the researchers. Pro-Hicks respondents were most conservative in replying to several general questions and, when education was held constant, were most likely to agree that "white people have a right to keep Negroes out of their neighborhoods if they want to." The same held for subsample agreement with "Negroes certainly have their rights, but it is best to keep them in their own districts and schools and to prevent too much contact with whites."[48] According to the initial analysis, the pro-Hicks respondents were motivated by a complex combination of racial prejudice and resistance to neighborhood change:

> . . . . [O]ur study indicates strongly that behind the resistance to school desegregation lies the greater fear of neighborhood desegregation; and even beyond that, fear that the old, good ways of life will change if Negroes move in. This concern may be especially acute in a city so identified with Catholic immigrants, who have put such great emphasis on neighborhood life, church, and ethnic identity. To the extent that she seems to be a champion of the old, tight, "good" neighborhoods, Mrs. Hicks has tapped a responsive nerve.[49]

Exulting in victory and broadly hinting of her mayoral ambitions at every opportunity, Mrs. Hicks kept herself before the public with frequent and increasingly harsh speeches against the racial-imbalance act, "pseudo liberals," civil rights "agitators," Vietnam war opponents, and others who would "subvert" local schools.[50] She also began an annual ritual of filing bills to amend or repeal the imbalance law. In July 1967, for example, she showed up at the statehouse to offer the following amendment: "No child shall be excluded from, or assigned to, a public school of any town on account of race, color, or religion; nor shall a child be transported from the district school established for his neighborhood unless written consent is given by the parent or guardian of said child."[51] Meeting afterward with reporters, she said her amendment would surround parental choice with legal protection against "unproven sociological theory."[52] Later that summer she filed initiative petitions for a referendum on the imbalance act with Massachusetts Attorney General Elliot Richardson. Richardson had helped draft the act. Mrs. Hicks declared in her subsequent statement to the press:

> Our purpose is to bring this matter before the highest court—that of public opinion—and let the people speak on this issue through the ballot box. The racial imbalance law is unworkable and undemocratic. It is strangling the education of Boston's children.[53]

Attempts to Implement the Imbalance Law in Boston

In the fall of 1965 the state board of education, as required by the new imbalance law, requested a school committee plan to end racial imbalance in the Boston public schools. The outgoing committee voted three to two for a plan entailing construction of fifteen schools, renovation or expansion of seven existing schools, a uniform grade structure for the entire school system, and an "open enrollment" policy.[54] Under this last proposal, students would purportedly be allowed to take vacant seats in neighborhood schools other than their own after local children had been accommodated; parents of the transferring students were to pay all extra transportation expenses.

After analyzing this plan for two months, a special task force created by the state board concluded that up to that time, nothing proposed by the school committee would have reduced imbalance significantly. The state board then directed its task force to prepare a substitute plan for school-committee consideration. Meanwhile, the state board suspended Boston's school funding.

A task force plan calling for two-way busing was quickly rejected by the new school committee, again chaired by Mrs. Hicks, and a slightly revised version of the school committee's original plan was sent back to the state board. It was soon returned as unacceptable. Back went an almost identical plan that met with the same result. This administrative ping pong continued until August 1966, when both sides turned to the state courts.

Evidence of the 1966 fund suspension's impact on Mrs. Hicks's constituents could be found in South Boston's Norcross elementary school district. A 1965 fire had destroyed the old building, thus requiring Norcross pupils to attend the Hoar School in South Boston's Lower End. Staggered class schedules and long delayed delivery of portable classrooms alleviated overcrowding of the Hoar somewhat, but Norcross parents and Mrs. Hicks demanded a new school. They were equally adamant that the new school not be racially balanced. When the state board indicated its determination that any new school be racially balanced, some Norcross parents reportedly vowed to go to jail before allowing their children to be bused.[55] State officials were not impressed by Mrs. Hicks's repeated argument that the racial imbalance law did not apply to predominantly white areas.[56] Arguments over who was to be served by a new Norcross school were still going on in 1969, when press reports disclosed active participation by Mrs. Hicks in discussions of a proposed school's seating capacity. A plan apparently acceptable to the state board called for a structure large enough to accommodate 700 neighborhood and 300 black children, the latter bused in to provide racial balance. Under this plan, the state would pay nearly two-thirds of all construction costs. Mrs. Hicks advocated a 700-pupil school for local pupils only. Conceding at a public meeting that her plan would sacrifice state funding, she countered that the city eventually would save money by eliminating busing costs. She also argued that a smaller school better suited South Boston's declining population.[57]

Mrs. Hicks and fellow school committee members enjoyed greater initial success in Suffolk County Superior Court, where Judge Donald Macauley ruled in favor of the school committee's challenge to the state board's impoundment of Boston school aid. He decided against the school committee's challenge to the racial imbalance law. On appeal, his impoundment ruling was overturned, and, once again, the school committee had to submit a racial balance plan to the state board.[58]

The new school-committee plan was submitted on 28 February 1967 and was accepted by the state board on 15 March. Eventually labeled a "first stage" plan for Boston school desegregation, it proposed closing two schools, expanding construction, continuing open enrollment, providing more special education courses, and reassigning 3,456 students to alleviate racial imbalance. The plan's preface insisted that Boston schools were "desegregated," if racially imbalanced at the same time, a distinction fast losing revelance to this complicated dispute.[59]

Although Mrs. Hicks continued to assail the racial imbalance law, state and city educational relations now entered upon a comparatively cooperative period. Two subsequent school-committee plans were accepted with only minor changes. The "second stage" plan for 1968-1969 recommended various school closings and construction projects to facilitate reassigning 3,170 students, and a "third stage" plan for 1969-1970 proposed nine new construction projects plus the reassignment of another 1,390 pupils.[60] This progress notwithstanding, racial imbalance in the Boston public schools continued to grow. Table 5-3 shows that the number of imbalanced schools and proportions of nonwhite students enrolled in them increased well into the next decade.

Changes in leadership positions can prove extremely important to the success of implementation, and this factor definitely operated in the Boston case. Once a new commissioner, Neal Sullivan, took office, the state began to deal more aggressively with Boston. Sullivan's determination to force the pace of compliance was evidenced by his appointment of Charles Glenn to head the newly established Bureau of Equal Educational Opportunity (EEO). Glenn set out to enforce a 1970 directive that Boston's open-enrollment policy be changed as part of a "fourth stage" school committee plan. The school committee refused to make this change, and Boston's state aid was again suspended on 25 May 1971.

On 15 June the school committee submitted a plan listing steps to assure racially mixed enrollments at four newly built elementary schools (Trotter, Curley, Marshall, and Lee). This plan also recommended additional construction, modifications of open enrollment policy, and busing of 1,170 students. It put forth an idea first suggested by Model Cities, that selected schools be matched with libraries, museums, and other cultural institutions in programs designed to make students aware of their city's many educa-

Table 5-3
Increase of Racial Imbalance in Boston Public Schools, 1965-1973

Academic Year	Nonwhites as Percentage of All Pupils	Nonwhite Percentage in Imbalanced Schools	Number of Imbalanced Schools
1965-1966	25.7	68.2	46
1966-1967	26.1	69.7	49
1967-1968	27.6	69.7	52
1968-1969	29.3	71.7	57
1969-1970	30.8	73.5	62
1970-1971	32.5	76.4	63
1971-1972	34.4	78.6	65-67
1972-1973	40.4	78.9	75

Sources: For the 1965-1972 period, the data were taken from "A Study of the Racial Imbalance Act," Center for Law and Education of Harvard University, Publication No. 6109 (1972): p. 167. This report was based on racial censuses required under the imbalance act. For 1972-1973 the data were taken from *Distribution of Students by Racial/Ethnic Composition of Schools, 1970-1976,* Northeast Region, Office of Civil Rights of the Department of Health, Education and Welfare (Washington, D.C.: USGPO, 1978), p. 211.

Notes: The 1972 row is based on the OCR "minority" categories. When only blacks are examined for this year, a different picture results. According to OCR data, 73 percent of all black students attended 59 schools with 50 percent or more black enrollments.

tional resources. Finally, with suburban discomfiture surely the objective, the school committee pointed out the extent of *de facto* segregation in suburban schools and recommended examination of possible metropolitan desegregation programs.[61]

In further negotiations the school committee agreed by a three-to-two majority to change Boston's open enrollment policy so that students would be allowed to transfer only when their transfer would reduce racial imbalance in their new schools. The school committee majority also agreed to prepare a comprehensive balancing plan and to change the school-district lines in Dorchester so that white elementary-school students would be assigned to the Lee and Marshall schools, rather than to all-white facilities equally distant from their homes. In response to these concessions, the state board restored Boston's school funding.

Hopes for an end to conflict were promptly shattered, as enraged white Dorchester parents demanded a return to the old assignment pattern. Few black or white pupils showed up at the Lee School when classes began on 8 September, and scattered violence accompanied demonstrations outside several Dorchester schools. Tensions were high when a sobered school committee met with perhaps four hundred people in the O'Hearn School's tiny auditorium on 21 September, and heard a drumfire of criticism against its concessions in Dorchester. Compaigning a second time for mayor, Mrs. Hicks joined in the audience's reaction against the new assignments. When the harried school committee voted, near the end of this session, a new majority formed and rescinded the Lee School part of the fourth-stage plan.[62]

Angered state officials again suspended Boston funds. Lawsuits followed, and soon the school committee and the state board were entangled in a web of legal difficulties that would take two years to resolve. MCAD joined the fray by suing the school committee for failing to enforce a 1971 cease-and-desist order against continuing racial discrimination. Investigators from the Department of Health Education and Welfare (HEW's) Office of Civil Rights came to town looking for possible Title VI violations. And a group of black parents started to plan a class-action suit against the school committee in federal district court.

Near the end of its complex legal struggle with the school committee, the state board was directed to conduct hearings on a new and comprehensive plan to reduce racial imbalance in the Boston public schools. The basis for such hearings had been established by several court decisions too complicated to recount here, and the plan under review as the result of two years of research and exhibit preparation intended for court battles with the school committee. A task force led by John Finger, special consultant to the state board, had divided Boston into "geocodes," or tiny geographical units, in order to calculate how pupils could be reassigned to nearby schools, thus minimizing distances traveled while reducing imbalance. The task force had also devised a uniform grade structure: K-5, 6-8, 9-12. Finger estimated the number of imbalanced schools in Boston would be reduced to twenty-one by implementation of his plan.[63]

The state board appointed Professor Louis Jaffee, an administrative law expert, to conduct the hearings. Jaffee heard testimony from all parties and analyzed the data during the spring of 1973. On 28 May he announced his findings, declaring that the Finger plan had been properly derived from the racial imbalance law and subsequent interpretations. He also revealed reservations about several particulars of this plan.

One such concern was a proposed reassignment of high school students in Roxbury, North Dorchester, and South Boston. By 1973, Roxbury was almost completely black, North Dorchester was becoming so rapidly, and South Boston had grown even more defensive because of the imbalance controversy. The Finger plan "paired" Roxbury Girls High (to be renamed Roxbury High and made coeducational) with South Boston High. At the time, Girls High was 100 percent nonwhite and 593 pupils under capacity; South Boston High was 99.6 percent white and 630 pupils over capacity. It was left to Boston school department administrators to decide the precise details. Sensing real trouble here, Jaffee warned that South Boston reputedly was "intensely hostile to blacks."[64] In similar vein, he recommended a review of a proposed busing exchange between the Gavin and Hurley middle schools in South Boston and the South End.

On 25 June the state board accepted Jaffee's findings, but not his reservations. It then directed the school committee to implement the Finger plan in 1974-1975. School committee attorneys unsucessfully appealed to the Supreme Judicial Court, which subsequently issued an order compelling school committee compliance.[65]

Seven months of haggling over the particulars of what became known as the "revised short term plan" followed. For the most part, the school committee cooperated only when members perceived an opportunity to limit the plan. State board officials often had to obtain court orders to keep discussions on track, as the school committee was unmoved by pleas from the new commissioner, Gregory Anrig, and Mayer Kevin White. Despite the school committee's dilatory tactics, most of a judicially dictated timetable had been met by 15 May 1974. The most important unresolved issue was funding of the busing required by the Finger plan when the federal district court intervened.

Racial Imbalance and the 1967 Mayoral Election

In certain crucial respects, the mayoral campaigns of Mrs. Hicks were but larger versions of her school committee races. Antioutsider, antisuburban, and antiestablishmentarian themes dominated both her successful preliminary election campaign and her unsuccessful runoff against Kevin White in November. Racial imbalance figured more importantly in the first contest, but, by no means, was neglected by Mrs. Hicks in the second. This section will show the extent to which the imbalance issue was joined with her other themes.

A most revealing indicator of the Hicks perspective was her "Boston for the Bostonians" campaign slogan. Under this banner, Mrs. Hicks proposed to storm Washington, if necessary, to get millions of federal dollars for Boston with no strings attached. These funds, rather than higher property taxes, were to pay her promised raises to city police and firefighters. But perhaps the most candid explanation of what the slogan meant was given by Mrs. Hicks in mid-October:

> I have used the expression "Boston for the Bostonians" to instill pride in
> the people who live here. I am not concerned with those who live outside
> the city. I am not interested in the state as such. I feel the top priority
> should be for the interests and welfare of Boston itself.[66]

White quickly reminded the electorate of Boston's dependence on federal and state resources, and warned against thinking of the city as "an island by itself."[67]

An example of how Mrs. Hicks joined attacks against the imbalance law and suburban duplicity under her "Boston for Bostonians" notion was her response to criticisms of school committee "token" compliance with the imbalance law by Beryl Cohen, a Brookline senator in the state legislature. Mrs. Hicks acidly suggested Cohen demonstrate his concern for Boston blacks by sponsoring legislation to build integrated, low-income housing in Brookline and other suburbs. Referring to his complaint as "one more example of suburban interference in Boston's affairs," she concluded: "The racial imbalance law does not affect Brookline, so he smugly tells the elected officials of Boston what they should do. I, for one, am tired of nonresidents telling the people of Boston what they should do."[68]

A few days earlier, she had dealt with suburbia and racial imbalance in more sarcastic fashion:

> Those of you in suburbia who honestly believe that this type of education is socially and educationally harmful, help the poor city correct the situation. Take the Negro families into your suburbs and build housing for them and let them go to school with your children.[69]

When White branded her the fear and false-promises candidate, Mrs. Hicks retorted that he was the establishment puppet.[70] Her remarks about "the establishment" grew more biting once it became clear that Governor John Volpe, Senator Kennedy, Edward Logue, and many other luminaries were actively helping White. Near the end of this bitter struggle, she claimed the "suburban based establishment" was behind a "diabolical plot" to destroy her through lies.[71]

Another of her slogans, "You know where I stand," had been employed as shorthand for the racial imbalance issue throughout the preliminary election campaign. Most likely, the voters knew exactly where she stood, as argued above, but to know her evidently was to sense her limitations. Eight months before the voters chose White over her, Thomas Pettigrew had predicted a rational electorate acting out of economic self-interest would reject Mrs. Hicks if she got into the runoff. "They don't want her as mayor," the Harvard sociologist had explained, "they want her standing guard at the school committee."[72].

The Pettigrew thesis appeared plausible enough when the 1967 Hicks ward vote was contrasted to her support in the 1965 school-committee general election. Mrs. Hicks suffered an average 17 percent loss of supporters citywide, but fell most sharply in her traditional strongholds. She still carried Charlestown, for example, but by 59 percent rather than the 84 percent given her two years before. Afterwards, Mrs. Hicks expressed disappointment over having won only 51 percent of the East Boston vote, and attributed her unexpectedly poor showing there to Governor Volpe's effective appeals to fellow ethnics.[73] Three of every four voters in Hyde Park had supported her in 1965, but two years later she got the barest of majorities in Ward Eighteen. Roslindale fell short in identical fashion, and even larger defections cut into her Dorchester base. Had her earlier proportions obtained in South Boston and any two of the bigger Dorchester wards, other things being equal, Mrs. Hicks would have been elected. But in no ward, including her own, did voters support her for mayor as they had for school committee.

Mrs. Hicks and the Imbalance
Issue, 1968-1974

Defeat did not remove Louise Day Hicks from the forefront of opposition to the racial imbalance law. Her offensive resumed with testimony on 19 February 1968 to the state legislature's joint education committee in which she repeated familiar arguments for repeal. Evidently pursuing a minimax strategy, she also endorsed amendments proposed by Mayor White and the school committee's John Kerrigan to exempt some or all primary-school grades.

Mayor White sought the middle ground, as he often would do in the conflictual years ahead. As presented by Herbert Gleason, counsel for the city of Boston, the White argument proffered symbolic endorsement but asked tacitly for a substantive response:

> Everyone here knows that Mayor White supported enactment of the Racial Imbalance Act in 1965 and that he remains committed to its principles. He believes that all school committees should be encouraged to eliminate racial imbalance in the public schools.
>
> But, as a candidate and now as Mayor of Boston, he is concerned lest the Commonwealth withhold funds for the operation and construction of schools which Boston desperately needs because the city has been unable to eliminate racial imbalance in all the schools which today have a predominantly white population.[74]

Edward Logue, defeated mayoral candidate and no longer director of the BRA, chided officials for failing to take note of rapidly changing white-black proportions in the Boston public schools and predicted a black majority by 1973. According to Logue, the problem demanded a metropolitan solution involving at least 20 suburbs. He proposed a metropolitan voluntary busing plan in which no participating school's enrollment would exceed 10 percent minority.

Among the other proposals put to the joint committee was a plan explained by Deputy Commissioner of Education Thomas Curtain which extended school construction grants to any school district willing to accept enough nonwhite students to constitute 5 percent of total enrollments. Still another bill called for 100 percent state reimbursement to any school system having to fund busing for racial balance.[75]

Although the year had begun with new ideas, no alternative to outright repeal or partial exemption seems to have impressed Mrs. Hicks. She returned to the statehouse in December to propose more bills repealing or amending the imbalance law. Senator William Bulger, an articulate spokesman for South Boston, cosponsored her stock repeal measure. She produced the familiar parental-consent amendment and a companion provision changing "nonwhite" to "Negro" in the existing statute.[76] The Hicks testimony in favor of these bills one month later consisted mainly of complaints about suburban duplicity and the law's strangulation of city schools.[77].

Two reasons additional to a perennial candidate's appetite for publicity apparently explained her legislative efforts. First, Mrs. Hicks wished to remove an impediment to implementation of a Model Cities plan to build several schools in Roxbury and North Dorchester. Intended to upgrade educational opportunities in impoverished neighborhoods, the plan had become ensnared in Boston's imbalance conflict. Mrs. Hicks wanted to cleave this Gordian knot with the sharp blade of repeal. Otherwise, she claimed, the program would "never reach fruition under the undemocratic, discriminatory, unworkable, [and] costly racial imbalance law." Also in this connection, she offered a most curious interpretation of recent history: "We have given it [the imbalance law] a chance to work and we have seen that it does not work."[78] Second, she wanted the law repealed in order to "disarm" the newly appointed Neil Sullivan, who had helped design the Berkeley, California busing program before becoming commissioner of education. Sullivan's desegregation views and outsider status made him especially objectionable to Mrs. Hicks:

> It is unfortunate that Massachusetts had to go so far for a man of this caliber, this philosophy. He bows completely to the demands of the black minority. He forgets that mothers all over the city, including black mothers, believe in neighborhood schools and want them for their children.[79]

Sullivan's actions soon confirmed her worst fears. His impact on state board-school committee negotiations has already been noted. In March 1969 he raised hackles in Boston by urging HEW's Robert Finch to endorse busing.

An outraged Mrs. Hicks charged that Sullivan had been "imported" by "a small influential group" intent on forcing implementation of the imbalance law.[80] Ostensibly to shore up local defenses, she asked the school committee to adopt a special order prohibiting the transportation of any pupil beyond the appropriate neighborhood school without written parental permission. Possibly angered by her preemption of the school committee's domain in an election year, Chairman John Kerrigan ruled the request out of order and, adding insult to injury, further dismissed it as a "non-issue" to a body already unanimous in its opposition to busing. Mrs. Hicks professed dismay, implied that the school committee's failure to act had heightened citizen anxiety, and, in her capacity as an obvious but undeclared candidate, hinted her return might be required to keep the school committee on track.[81]

But coming back to the school committee after running for mayor must have seemed to her a return to political square one. In any case, Mrs. Hicks declared for city council, a nine member body given almost no power by the city charter, lacking in patronage, and saddled with a reputation for political histrionics.[82] But it would provide her a public forum until the next mayoral election.

Law and order, frequently laced with race and schools, were the chief issues in her successful 1969 bid for a seat on the council. An early sampling of her perspective on these problems was given to a gathering of police and county prosecutors in suburban Quincy on 21 November 1968. Mrs. Hicks assailed "pseudo intellectuals" for criticizing the police, telling her audience, "You and I know that to them justice means special privileges for the black man and the criminal."[83]

In the same speech she blamed adult troublemakers for recent violence at the King and Gibson elementary schools in Roxbury. The fighting and destruction at the Gibson were serious enough to require police intervention and temporary closing of the school. Purportedly, it was with this episode in mind that Mrs. Hicks, one month later proposed legislation prescribing stiff penalties for anyone attempting to induce a minor "to absent himself unlawfully from school."[84] In view of what her supporters would soon be doing in South Boston and other defended neighborhoods, this proved to be in retrospect one of the most ironic moments in Boston's desegregation controversy. Equally ironic was her campaign message on civil disobedience: Society would break apart if individuals were allowed to decide which laws to obey.[85]

Old ward patterns reappeared in the 1969 voting. Mrs. Hicks easily topped the list in both elections, winning the support of 65 percent of the voters in November. She promised celebrants at her victory bash they never again would be defeated, and she avowed that it was time to return Boston to Bostonians.[86]

When Representative John McCormack announced plans to retire after forty-five years in the Congress, Mrs. Hicks declared her candidacy for the Ninth Congressional District on 28 June 1970. Her victory in November was assured after defeating Joseph Moakley, South Boston state senator, and David Nelson, a black attorney, in the Democratic primary. Following an inevitable November victory, however, she toyed with the notion of retaining her council seat, to be occupied on Mondays when council was in session, and representing her district in Washington for the rest of the week. Her mayoral ambitions made this scheme seem more credible, and she did not relinquish the council position until three days after the congressional session began.[87] In the meantime, she proposed more bills to repeal the imbalance act and again testified that the law was "unenforceable" despite Boston's attempts to make it work.[88]

In 1971 she again declared her mayoral candidacy, but ran second to White in the preliminary election. A drubbing in the runoff, in which she got only 38 percent, ended talk of Louise Day Hicks as mayoral timber. Her reelection to Congress was imperiled by redistricting, and Moakley shrewdly passed up the Democratic primary to run against her in November as an independent. In the general election Moakley won a 44 percent plurality compared to 42 percent for Mrs. Hicks and 14 percent for the Republican candidate. An embittered Mrs. Hicks offered no customary congratulations and later complained that Moakley had misrepresented her antibusing stand to black voters.[89] In April 1973 a "people's lobby," Louise Day Hicks Associates, was incorporated with Rita Graul and Virginia Sheehy among its list of officers; both would play key leadership roles in the citywide antibusing coalition formed in reaction to Judge Garrity's desegregation decision. Mrs. Hicks got back on the city council in 1973 with a diminished but still impressive 54 percent of the vote in November. She was serving in this capacity when the federal district court decided Boston's public schools had been unlawfully segregated.

Operation Exodus and METCO

One final development requires brief discussion before this background sketch may be regarded as reasonably complete. Both Operation Exodus and the METCO program were voluntary busing projects begun to provide better educational opportunities for black students.

Operation Exodus started as a response to the school committee's 1965 refusal to reduce overcrowding in North Dorchester schools through busing. Its aim was to test the open enrollment policy by the voluntary busing of black children to predominantly white schools in Hyde Park and other neighborhoods where vacant seats were available. Appeals for donations were quickly answered by religious, labor, business, and civil rights groups.

The first day of Operation Exodus, 9 September 1965, saw a visit by Mrs. Hicks and her police escort to project headquarters. Chairwoman Hicks maintained she had come to make sure parents had obtained the necessary authorizations for student transfers, but an irate Operation Exodus parent told her, "We know why you're here, so the press will follow you around."[90] Unsure of her reception, the police advised her to leave. The buses delivered black students to their new schools without major incident.

At its peak Operation Exodus transported over six hundred children, mostly in grades K-6, and boasted an elaborate organizational structure consisting of operating staff, committees, and a board of directors. Parents were in command at every level and took some pride in the absence of professional educators. Eventually the program offered recreation, tutoring, vocational education, and cultural enrichment opportunities as well as busing. Perhaps $150,000 had been raised in the initial year of operation, but, by 1968-1969, participation had fallen off. In part this was due to private schools started as offshoots of Operation Exodus.

A second reason for Operation Exodus's decline was the rise of another busing program under the auspices of the Metropolitan Council for Educational Opportunity (METCO) in 1966-1967. Unlike Operation Exodus, METCO's purpose was to bus black children to better educational opportunities in suburbia. Started as a largely private program, METCO became increasingly state supported.

At first Mrs. Hicks opposed METCO. At a February 1966 meeting between officials from five suburban school systems and the Boston School Committee, she wanted to know why the suburbs were not prepared to build subsidized housing for blacks and she insisted that her stand against busing black children inside Boston prevented her from endorsing busing them outside Boston. What traumatic effects would follow being transported such long distances, she wanted to know, and what difficult adjustments to new schools and classmates would be required? "These little children need the compensatory education programs that only Boston has," she concluded.[91] Thomas Eisenstadt of the school committee disagreed: "Although I would hesitate to think that the suburbs can provide better education than Boston, I think the different climate because of the different racial composition in the suburbs would be beneficial."[92] By 1973, however, she was willing to accept METCO so long as it remained voluntary.[93]

In 1966-1967 METCO bused 220 black pupils to schools in seven suburban school districts. The number of participating districts more than doubled in the following academic year, and 395 black children were bused. By 1974-1975 nearly twenty-five hundred students were being transported to thirty-five suburban districts, and the program also offered numerous educational opportunities.[94] Later in the decade, however, suburban districts withdrew from the program—ostensibly for financial reasons—and the educational benefits of METCO for black students became the subject of a ferocious academic dispute.[95]

The Stage Is Set

Ordinarily, most white Bostonians in 1974 would have disapproved of balancing school enrollments through involuntary busing and redistricting, and this would have been truest of those living in the city's defended neighborhoods. But the decade of strife described in this chapter was not ordinary, and it left a profound imprint on implementation of federal desegregation programs, particularly in South Boston and several other enclaves, where already strong predispositions were reinforced by years of racially specific controversy. Anxiety and recalcitrance in these districts were further heightened by massive and rapid population turnover in adjacent neighborhoods.

The intervention of Louise Day Hicks in the *de facto* segregation squabble proved to be decisive for the racial-imbalance and school-desegregation struggles as well. One spilled over into another as the continually reelected Mrs. Hicks played a major role in transforming disputes into clashes between fundamental values, and hence into a zero-sum affair in which only one side could win and compromise was impossible. The mandate repeatedly given her at the polls made her assertions of the majority-rule principle nearly impossible to rebut, and none of her defeats could be interpreted as repudiations of her antibusing stands. Her tireless defense of neighborhood schools constantly reminded inhabitants of defended neighborhoods that their schools were imperiled. Her excoriation of suburban hypocrisy not only stirred latent class resentments but also denied liberals and integrationists a moral monopoly in appeals for egalitarianism. As battle lines were more sharply drawn, Mrs. Hicks became a public figure who seemed increasingly larger than life—a media event in her own right, a symbol of unflagging determination or revolting sophistry, depending on the beholder. Hardly the only principal in this lengthy struggle to exhibit such flaws, she seemed increasingly impervious to her own gross contradictions: Open enrollment was fine until exercised by blacks through Operation Exodus. Suburban liberals were rank hypocrites for making sure their children would never sit next to blacks in school, but METCO was opposed anyway. Civil disobedience portended social collapse when practiced by white liberals and black militants, but not when she and her supporters took it up. Anyone promoting student boycotts was to be fined severely—until boycotts became a stock tactic of her organization.

For the most part overshadowed by political drama, legal and administrative versions of the imbalance struggle moved painfully but inexorably toward formal resolution. The battle lines of Boston's conflict over race and schools were well defined long before Judge Garrity issued his ruling. Ironically, the forces of repeal finally succeeded in gutting the imbalance law, but at this point the impending federal court ruling made their victory of little consequence.[96] We turn now to the class action suit in federal district court and the rulings to follow.

Notes

1. Between 1961 and 1979 Louise Day Hicks ran in twenty-seven preliminary and general elections, winning twenty. During this time, she was a candidate for school committee, city council, mayor, state treasurer, county registrar of deeds, and U.S. representative.

2. See Stanley K. Schultz, *The Culture Factory* (New York: Oxford University Press, 1973).

3. Ibid., pp. 192-193. See also Leonard W. Levy and Douglas L. Jones, *Jim Crow in Boston* (New York: Da Capo Press, 1971), pp. vii-xxxviii.

4. *Roberts* v. *City of Boston,* 5 Cush. 198, 208 (1849).

5. Mass St. 1855, Chap. 254, Sec. 1-3.

6. See Harrell R. Rodgers, Jr., and Charles S. Bullock, III, *Coercion to Compliance* (Lexington, Mass.: Lexington Books, D.C. Heath and Company, 1976), pp. 47-67; Everett F. Cataldo, Michael W. Giles, and Douglas S. Gatlin, *School Desegregation Policy* (Lexington, Mass.: Lexington Books, D.C. Heath and Company, 1978); and, Franklin D. Wilson, "Patterns of White Avoidance," *Annals of the American Academy of Political and Social Science* 441 (January 1979): 132-141.

7. *Statistics of the Population of the United States,* Ninth Census (Wasington, D.C.: U.S. Government Printing Office, 1872), table XI, p.

8. See *Population,* II:3, *Kansas-Michigan,* Sixteenth Census, 1940 (Washington, D.C.: U.S. Government Printing Office, 1872), table XI, p. 440. p. 672.

9. See *The Seventh Census of the United States: 1850, An Appendix* (Washington, D.C.: Robert Armstrong, 1853), table II, p. 52.

10. See *Population,* II, *Alabama-Montana,* Thirteenth Census: 1910 (Washington, D.C.: U.S. Government Printing Office, 1913) table V, p. 890. A useful account of Boston's black community from 1865 to 1900 is Elizabeth H. Pleck, *Black Migration and Poverty* (New York: Academic, 1979).

11. See *Population,* II, Twelfth Census: 1900 (Washington, D.C.: U.S. Government Printing Office, 1902), tables 50-51, pp. 383-390.

12. *Population,* II, (1940), table A 38, p. 672.

13. *Compendium of the Eleventh Census: 1890,* II, *Vital and Social Statistics* (Washington, D.C.: U.S. Government Printing Office, 1894), table II, p. 255.

14. *Characteristics of the Population,* I:23, Massachusetts, Census of Population: 1960 (Washington, D.C.: U.S. Government Printing Office, 1963), table 20, p. P-23-388.

15. See *Statistics for Census Tracts: Boston, Mass., 1940* Census of Population and Housing, table 1, pp. 4-5; *Census Tract Statistics: Boston, Mass. and Adjacent Area,* 1950 Census of Population, PD-6, table 1, pp. 7-16; *Census Tracts: Boston, Mass. SMSA,* 1960 Census of Population and Housing, PHC(1)-18, table P-1, pp. 17-28; *Census Tracts: Boston, Mass. SMSA,* 1970 Census of Population and Housing, PHC(1)-29, table P-1, pp. 28-37.

16. *Boston Evening Globe,* 27 June 1961; *Boston Globe,* 28 June 1961; *Boston Traveler,* 28 June 1961; see also, Min S. Yee, "Mrs. Hicks Thrives on Controversy," *Boston Globe,* 6 August 1967.

17. Boston has a nonpartisan, at-large system of elections in which school-committee and city-council candidates run every two years. A September preliminary election reduces the field to the top ten school-committee and top eighteen city-council candidates. In November the general election selects five school committee and nine city-council members. A similar procedure is followed every four years to elect Boston's mayor; the September preliminary narrows the choice to the top two.

18. *Annual Report of the Election Department,* 1961, Public Document 10, City of Boston (1962), p. 154.

19. "School Committee Picks Mrs. Hicks As Chairman," *Boston Globe,* 8 January 1963, p. 1.

20. See Jonathan Kozol, *Death At An Early Age* (Boston: Houghton, Mifflin, 1967).

21. *Racial Imbalance in the Boston Public Schools,* Report of the Massachusetts State Advisory Committee to the U.S. Commission on Civil Rights (Washington, D.C.: U.S. Government Printing Office, 1965); and, by the same committee, *Discrimination in Housing in the Boston Metropolitan Area* (1965).

22. See Peggy Lamson, "The White Northerner's Choice: Mrs. Hicks of Boston," *Atlantic,* June 1966, pp. 58-62.

23. Ibid., p. 60.

24. All quotes in this paragraph were taken from "Mrs. Hicks Says Nix to Peabody Plea," *Boston Traveler,* 3 September 1963, p. 1.

25. "NAACP Line Plan Hit By Mrs. Hicks," *Boston Herald,* 14 September 1963.

26. Quoted in "Louise Hicks Offers 'Pat' to the NAACP," *Boston Record,* 25 October 1963.

27. Quoted in "Mrs. Hicks, Hub NAACP Clash On Vote's Meaning," *Boston Record,* 26 September 1963.

28. Quoted in "BC Panel Ignorant About Hub Schools—Mrs. Hicks," *Boston Record,* 1 November 1963.

29. Ibid.

30. Quoted in "Mrs. Hicks Sees Programs OKd," *Boston Record,* 7 November 1963; See also "Policies Endorsed, Mrs. Hicks States," *Boston Globe,* 6 November 1963.

31. Quoted in "Mrs. Hicks Sees Kids Pressured," *Boston Traveler,* 15 February 1964.

32. The Cape Verdean challenge was presented in *School Committee of New Bedford* v. *Commission on Education,* 208 N.E. 2d 819 (1965); vacated on other grounds, 348 F 2d. 261 (1st Cir. 1965).

33. *Because It Is Right—Educationally,* Report of the Advisory Committee on Racial Imbalance and Education, Massachusetts State Board of Education (April 1965).

34. Jean D. Grambs, "A Sociological View of the Neighborhood School Concept," in *Because It Is Right,* p. 76.

35. *Because It Is Right,* p. 25. See also Frank Levy, *Northern Schools and Civil Rights* (Chicago: Markham, 1971), table 5, p. 90.

36. See *A Report On The Schools Of Boston,* Boston Redevelopment Authority (May 1962), p. I-25; generally referred to as "the Sargent Report."

37. Ibid., p. I-28.

38. See "Mrs Hick Disputes Collins, Asks 'Who Leads Negroes?'" *Boston Evening Globe,* 9 April 1965; "Mrs. Hicks: 'Pupils Pawns in Negro Power Struggles,'" *Boston Record,* 10 April 1965, p.1.

39. All quotes in the several paragraphs describing the 14 April 1965 reaction of Mrs. Hicks to the Kiernan Committee's final report were taken from Frank Bucci, "Boston School Heads Attack Racial Report," *Boston Traveler,* 15 April 1965, p. 1.

40. "Flood of Mail Backs Stand of Mrs. Hicks," *Boston Record,* 19 April 1965.

41. "Mrs. Hicks Agrees to Talk to Dr. King," *Boston Herald,* 19 April 1965; "Waits in Vain to See Dr. King," *Boston Record,* 24 April 1965; "Mrs. Hicks Raps Ted on 'Imbalance,'" *Boston Evening Globe,* 21 June 1965; "Mrs. Hicks Files for Third Term." *Boston Record,* 3 July 1965; *Boston Record,* 28 July 1965.

42. General Laws, Chap. 71, Sec. 37C-37D; Chap. 15, Sec. 1-I to 1-K (1965). For accounts of passage of the imbalance statute, see James Bolner with Robert A. Shanley, *Civil Rights In The Political Process* (Amherst, Mass.: University of Massachusetts Bureau of Government Research, 1967); and, Lawrence W. O'Connell, "The Reform Group in Central City School Politics" Ph.D. diss., Syracuse University, 1968.

43. *Barksdale* v. *Springfield School Committee,* 237 F. Supp. 543 (1965); vacated 348 F. 2d 261 (1965). See also *Balancing The Public Schools,* Massachusetts State Board of Education (1975), pp. 16-22.

44. *Blakely* v. *Boston School Committee,* Civ. No. 65-292-F, dismissed

for want of prosecution. See also "Suit By 81 Boston School Children Charges School Segregation," *The New York Times,* 21 April 1965, p. 29.

45. "Mrs. Hicks Raps Logue As Meddler," *Boston Record,* 17 August 1965.

46. "Mrs. Hicks Called 'Agitator' At 'Blitz,'" *Boston Herald,* 24 October 1965; see also Peter Schrag, *Village School Downtown* (Boston: Beacon Press, 1967), pp. 6-23.

47. J. Michael Ross, Thomas Crawford, and Thomas Pettigrew, "Negro Neighbors—Banned in Boston," *Trans-action,* 3 (September-October 1966): 13-18.

48. See Thomas F. Pettigrew, *Racially Separate Or Together?* (New York: McGraw-Hill, 1971), pp. 211-229.

49. Ross, Crawford, and Pettigrew, "Negro Neighbors," p. 16.

50. "Mrs. Hicks Backs Program, Lashes 'Insidious' Enemies," *Boston Globe,* 23 November 1965; "'Repeal State's Imbalance Law' Urges Mrs. Hicks," *Boston Record,* 23 November 1965, p. 2.

51. Quoted in "Hicks To File Bill On Pupil Assignments," *Boston Record,* 17 July 1967.

52. Ibid.

53. "Hicks Files Imbalance Repeal Bid," *Boston Record,* 3 August 1967.

54. See "Boston School Panel Calls For Free Transit To Ease Imbalance," *The New York Times,* 21 December 1965, p. 1.

55. See "Semantics Divide Mrs. Hicks, Kiernan," *Boston Sunday Globe,* 15 January, 1967.

56. See "Double Session Dealings in Hub Upset Mrs. Hicks," *Boston Record,* 16 January 1967. Her point was that suburbs without enough black children to have any 50 percent or more black schools were ignored by the imbalance law, hence all-white neighborhoods in Boston should be similarly treated. If imbalanced because of racial residential patterns, she argued, at least the Boston schools were desegregated.

57. See "Mrs. Hicks Joins Southie Residents Opposing School Sites," *Boston Record-American,* 13 June 1969; "Wants End To Law On Imbalance," *Boston Record-American,* 19 June 1969; and, "Mrs. Hicks Running But Silent As To Office," *Boston Herald,* 19 June 1969.

58. *School Committee of Boston v. Board of Education* Suffolk Sup. Ct. No. 85833 Eq.

59. *The 1966-67 Plan Toward Elimination of Racial Imabalance In The Public Schools.* Boston School Committee (February 1967). See note 56.

60. *Second Stage Plan Toward Elimination of Racial Imbalance In The Public Schools,* Boston School Committee (June 1968); *Third Stage Plan* (April 1969).

61. *Fourth Stage Plan* (June 1971).

62. "Hub Board Abandons Lee School Transfers," *Boston Globe,* 22 September 1971, p. 1.

63. *Revised Short Term Plan To Reduce Racial Imbalance In The Boston Public Schools,* Task Force on Racial Imbalance, Massachusetts State Board of Education (25 April 1973), pp. 11-16.

64. Report and Recommendations of Louis L. Jaffee, Esq., *School Committee of Boston* v. *Board of Education,* 292 N.E. 345 (1973).

65. *School Committee of Boston* v. *Board of Education,* 302 N.E. 2d 916, 923 (1973). See "Court Tells Hub: Comply By Dec. 11, " *Boston Globe,* 15 November 1973, p. 1. In April 1973 the school committee attempted to abrogate another understanding with the state board regarding location of English High School in a new building. On 16 July 1973 the Supreme Judicial Court of Massachusetts ordered school-committee compliance with the initial agreement; see *Bradshaw* v. *Tierney,* Sup. Jud. Ct. 73-91 (1973).

66. Quoted in "Mrs. Hicks 'Woman of Year,' " *Boston Record,* 18 October 1967.

67. See "Mrs. Hicks Backs Downtown Renewal," *Boston Herald,* 18 October 1967.

68. "Mrs. Hicks Blasts Cohen," *Boston Herald,* 24 October 1967.

69. "Hicks Would Hike Firemen's Pay," *Boston Herald,* 20 October 1967.

70. See "Mrs. Hicks, White Set For Head-On Tax Clash," *Boston Evening Globe,* 23 October 1967.

71. Quoted in "Mrs. Hicks Calls Foe Outsider, 'Puppet,' " *Boston, Record,* 6 November 1967, p. 2; see also "Hicks Bares Fund Backing," *Boston Record,* 28 October 1967, p. 5; and, "Mrs. Hicks Hits 'Establishment'"; Kevin White Raps Poor Housing," *Boston Sunday Globe,* 29 October 1967.

72. See "Survey Predicts Mrs. Hicks Defeat," *Boston Herald,* 30 April 1967.

73. See "Mrs. Hicks Hits 'Gang Up,' " *Boston Herald,* 14 November 1967, p. 1.

74. Quoted in "Imbalance Law Change Urged," *Boston Herald,* 20 February 1968, p. 1.

75. Ibid. See also "Anti-Bias Incentive Urged," *Boston Globe,* 20 February 1968, p. 1.

76. "Mrs. Hicks Raps Imbalance Law, Seeks Repeal," *Boston Record-American,* 4 December 1968, p. 2.

77. "Mrs. Hicks Urges Imbalance Repeal," *Boston Evening Globe,* 27 January 1969, p. 1.

78. Quoted in "Mrs. Hicks Raps Imbalance Law," p. 2.

79. *Boston Herald,* 4 December 1968.

80. Quoted in "Mrs. Hicks Scores Sullivan On Busing," *Boston Record-American,* 27 March 1969.

81. See "School Post Mrs. Hicks' Aim?" *Boston Herald,* 23 April 1969.

82. See Edward C. Banfield, *Big City Politics* (New York: Random House, 1965), pp. 37-50.

83. Quoted in "Mrs. Hicks Urges Spiritual Rebirth," *Boston Record,* 22 November 1968.

84. See "Mrs. Hicks Raps Imbalance Law," p. 2.

85. See "School Victim of Social Ills—Mrs. Hicks," *Boston Evening Globe,* 18 October 1968.

86. " 'Hicks For Mayor' Is Cry," *Boston Herald-Traveler,* 5 November 1969.

87. See "Two Hats For Hicks? She's Silent," *Boston Globe,* 5 November 1970; "Mrs. Hicks Not Leaving Council Now," *Boston Globe,* 11 November 1970; and, "Rep. Hicks Discovers One Hat Enough," *Boston Evening Globe,* 25 January 1971.

88. "Mrs. Hicks To Oppose Racial Law," *Boston Record-American,* 8 December 1970.

89. "Hicks Out, But Not Down, Readiness For '74 Rematch," *Boston Globe,* 8 January 1971, p. 1.

90. See "Mrs. Hicks Gets Murder Threat," *Boston Record,* 10 September 1965, p. 1; Schrag, *Village School,* pp. 118-125.

91. Quoted in "Mrs. Hicks Challenges Bus Plan," *Boston Herald,* 19 February 1966.

92. Ibid.

93. "Hicks, Private Citizen, Still Fights," *Boston Globe,* 4 March 1973.

94. *Schools and Programs Of Choice,* Bureau of Educational Opportunity, Massachusetts Department of Education (1977), pp. 31-32.

95. On declining suburban METCO involvement, see "Is METCO Effort Dying In The Suburbs?" *Boston Globe,* 27 September 1976, p. 14. For the academic dispute, see David J. Armor, "The Evidence On Busing," *Public Interest* 28 (Summer 1971):90-126; Thomas F. Pettigrew, et al., "Busing: A Review Of The Evidence," *Public Interest* 30 (Winter 1973):88-118, and, in same issue, Armor's response, "The Double Double Standard," pp. 119-134.

96. Repeal measures passed in the state legislature in 1973 and again in 1974. Governor Francis Sargent successfully vetoed the 1973 repeal, but had to accept 1974 amendments weakening state board authority in compliance enforcement. These amendments subsequently were overturned in *School Committee of Springfield* v. *Board of Education,* 319 N.E. 2d 427 (1974), cert. den. 421 U.S. 947 (1975). Governor Michael Dukakis vetoed another repeal bill passed by the legislature in 1975.

The Federal
District Court Ruling

Stages of Federal Judicial Involvement

The long struggle chronicled in chapter 5 generated issues bound to involve the federal courts. When the district court finally received a class-action suit against the school committee, the central legal emphasis shifted from racial imbalance to deliberate segregation. This change in focus and the active role taken by Judge W. Arthur Garrity in enforcing his orders proved decisive for events in Boston.

Judge Garrity's role during the second decade of Boston's school controversy may be divided into three reasonably distinct stages. In the first, he presided over a courtroom trial and related proceedings, weighing facts and deciding whether constitutional rights had been violated. After finding school officials guilty of having perpetuated unlawful segregation, he began the second stage by interpreting Supreme Court decisions in a manner that bolstered his authority to order major corrective changes. This stage ended with his formulation of remedial policy, the first link in the implementation chain. The third stage started when he found it necessary to take part in implementation, as events required his continuing interaction with members of the implementing, consumer, and secondary populations and further steps to enforce his orders. As of this writing, the third stage has not formally ended. In other words, Judge Garrity did not merely order change and await its implementation by others; instead he was as important to implementation as he was to policy formulation. This chapter focuses on the first two stages of the judge's involvement.[1]

Origins of a Federal Case

In 1977 the school committee may have mollified Mrs. Hicks and white Dorchester parents by retracting its Lee School agreement with the state board, but it also created enough outrage in the black community to prompt several groups into independent decisions to sue the committee in federal court. One such group was the biracial Dorchester Council for Community Schools, which hired the law firm of Foley, Hoag, and Elliot. Another group approached the Harvard Center for Law and Education, a federally supported public-interest law firm and research group. Unaware of the other's involvement, each firm assigned three attorneys to prepare a federal case.

When the two firms learned about one another, they met to discuss joint action. Several of the NAACP attorneys also attended in an advisory capacity.[2] The session led to agreement that a class-action suit was the best method of fighting the school committee and to the formation of a four-man team to prepare a single case. Headed by the Center's Harold Flannery, a former justice department attorney experienced in desegregation suits, the team could turn to the NAACP and the Lawyers Committee for Civil Rights Under Law for consultation.

In subsequent meetings the team decided to build its case on the denial of equal protection and the violation of civil rights laws, rather than on racial imbalance. It was also decided to make Commissioner Sullivan and the state board defendants along with the school committee, because of the board's failure to end segregation in its attempts to enforce the imbalance law. Finally, this was to be a class-action suit brought by selected black parents. The last decision was an important strategem intended to enjoy the legal advantage given members of a "suspect" category in federal lawsuits where deprivations of rights were alleged.

In keeping with federal practice, the complaint itself was a simple document charging violations of the Thirteenth and Fourteenth Amendments of the U.S. Constitution and infringements of the 1964 Civil Rights Act.[3] Mrs. Tallulah Morgan headed a list of fourteen black parents and forty-four minors designated as plaintiffs; James Hennigan, the school committee chairman, was listed as the main defendant.[4] The plaintiffs sought a declaratory judgment against "nine racially discriminatory policies, practices, customs, and usages" of the school committee; they also requested an injunction prohibiting further racial discrimination in the schools, a decree requiring a desegregation plan that met eight conditions, and the awarding of attorneys' fees and any other financial relief the court held to be "just and proper."[5] The school committee responded by denying all allegations, acknowledging its disbursement of Elementary and Secondary Education Act (ESEA) funds, noting correct listing of defendants, and granting the accuracy of certain data pertaining to enrollments and teachers by race.

Between 22 May 1972 and 5 February 1973 opposing attorneys met regularly in pretrial conferences presided over by Judge Garrity, who had been selected in an impartial process to take the case. Ordinarily attorneys in such a case would have at least explored a settlement before a trial, but the school-committee counsel had been instructed not to settle in this instance. So both sides used the nine months to collect evidence, present briefs to Judge Garrity, and argue motions on various types of evidence. Although these presentations were to prove crucial to the trial's outcome, this critical period was virtually ignored by the press.

The plaintiffs assumed they would have to bear the burden of proving *de jure* segregation. Without local laws prescribing segregation, segregative intent would have to be adduced from the words and actions of school-committee members.[6] A large staff of lawyers and secretaries searched for such incriminating evidence in the mass of memoranda, minutes, transcriptions, correspondence, and other documents extracted from the defendants.[7]

It was also assumed the defense would maintain that any segregation uncovered in the Boston system was *de facto* in origin and thus beyond federal action. Given the *de facto* segregation squabble of the previous decade, this was an ironic argument, but one that had prevailed in Gary, Indiana and Cincinnati, Ohio.[8] Therefore, much pretrial work consisted of constructing refutations of the *de facto* defense.

When the actual trial began, expert witnesses were called to rebut the *de facto* argument; among these was Karl Taeuber, a recognized authority on residential segregation and a staunch opponent of the view that housing segregation could be strictly *de facto* in origin.[9] Few witnesses testified about pupil assignments or segregated faculty, and those who did only reinforced points already documented in the pretrial record.

As anticipated, the defense argued that any segregation found in Boston schools was *de facto* rather than *de jure,* and denied that past school-committee inaction against racial isolation was proof of segregative intent. Documents pertaining to enrollments, pupil assignments, racial-balancing plans, faculty hiring, operation of particular schools, and related subjects were offered in evidence. Nearly all defense witnesses were school personnel. In sum, the defense held that the school committee could not be held accountable for conditions beyond its control.

Although joined with the school committee as defendants, the state board of education was hardly inclined to make common cause with its old adversary, and so moved to file a cross-claim against the school committee. Judge Garrity was unwilling to annul this shotgun marriage, however, and denied the motion. Nonetheless the state board made abundantly clear its agreement with the allegations against its codefendants, and confined its own defense to justifying its efforts during the imbalance controversy.

Scarcely more press notice was given the trial in February and March 1973 than to the pretrial proceedings. For the most part, the trial allowed counsel to refine or elaborate upon arguments and evidence introduced during the pretrial phase. The public was never informed about the extent to which Judge Garrity's decision was based on the pretrial record.

The judge permitted new evidence and arguments to be introduced after the trial ended. The plaintiffs used this opportunity to charge the school committee had intended further discrimination by attempting to prevent relocation of now substantially black English High School in a promised new building. Too, when the Supreme Court handed down its long-awaited Denver school decision, Judge Garrity permitted new arguments on its relevance to Boston.[10]

The Judge

A brief biographical sketch of the man behind the robes is in order before taking up his decision. Before 21 June 1974 "Garrity" was hardly a household name in Boston. After his Boston ruling, however, the judge became a symbol of the whole desegregation conflict. Civic associations praised his "courage" and "integrity" under fire. President Ford pointed to him as a prime example of federal judges who exceed their authority. Antibusing protestors in Boston inveighed against this "sick," "stupid," "hypocritical," "heartless," and "ignorant" "judicial tyrant," so unfeeling for the city's white neighborhoods.[11] An effigy of Garrity flapped grotesquely at South Boston antibusing functions in 1977. Extensive security protected his suburban Wellesley home and courtroom.

Probably some of the intense loathing expressed toward Judge Garrity in South Boston and Charlestown had to do with the special antipathy reserved for "renegades" by the Irish. Garrity's ancestors immigrated from County Sligo to Charlestown in 1835, and the judge's father was one of the generation who overcame Harvard's "no Irish need apply" rule. After taking a Harvard law degree, the elder Garrity became a commissioner in the federal judicial system.

Like so many middle-class Boston Irish, W. Arthur Garrity went to Holy Cross, where he received his B.A. degree cum laude in 1941. He was admitted to Harvard Law School when the United States entered World War II. After two years of law school, Garrity having persuaded army recruiters to overlook his poor eyesight, enlisted. He compiled a distinguished service record, winning five battle stars in France and Germany. After the war he returned to Harvard and obtained his law degree.

Garrity's legal career soon intertwined with Democratic politics. He briefly was an assistant federal attorney, and he helped in Senator John F. Kennedy's 1958 reelection campaign. Two years later Garrity was important to Kennedy's crucial Wisconsin primary win. In 1961, a grateful Kennedy administration appointed him U.S. Attorney for Massachusetts.

After his ill-fated nomination of Francis Morrissey for a newly created federal district judgeship in Boston, Senator Edward Kennedy turned to Garrity. Unlike Morrissey, Garrity had a recognized law degree, federal experience, and the approval of the American Bar Association. He was confirmed without difficulty in 1966.

At the time he was assigned the Boston desegregation case, Judge Garrity was regarded by his peers as an able and meticulous jurist who generally followed precedent. Various bar awards attested to his reputation.[12]

His desegregation opinion, when finally released, was extensive, consistently reasoned, and amply grounded in legal precedent. Judge Garrity's subsequent use of remedial powers in deciding school policy questions is more open to criticism, but it is noteworthy that neither his liability opinion nor later orders were overturned on appeal. He is fairly described as the instrument of federal judicial policy, however popular.

The Liability Decision

Judge Garrity announced his opinion on 21 June 1974. He held that the defendants had "knowingly carried out a systematic program of segregation affecting all of the city's students, teachers, and school facilities." Moving from this finding of deliberate intent, he concluded the entire school system was "unconstitutionally segregated."[13] He arrived at this conclusion by answering three questions: First, were the Boston schools segregated? Second, was there evidence of *de jure* segregation? And, third, if present, did unlawful segregation permit him to impose the remedies developed under federal policy?

By 1974 the answer to his first question was obvious and, in fact, undisputed by the defendants.[14] After reviewing the legal and administrative record, he turned to school statistics, pointing out that 84 percent of all white students attended schools more than 80 percent white and 62 percent of all black students were enrolled in schools over 70 percent black. Only seven schools had a racial composition within 10 percent of the entire system's student population ratio.[15]

Garrity came to an affirmative answer to his second question by examining findings related to six aspects of school operations: (1) utilization of facilities, (2) districting and redistricting, (3) feeder patterns, (4) open enrollments and controlled transfers, (5) recruitment and assignment of staff, and (6) vocational and examination schools.

Facilities

The judge noted that all schools in some areas of Boston were overcrowded, while the reverse problem existed in others. Analysis of enrollments suggested a strong correlation between racial composition and use of capacity, and Garrity found corroborative evidence of official intent in school-committee minutes, where school-department administrators were on record as expressing racial concerns in justifying their unwillingness to transfer students from overcrowded but overwhelmingly white schools. He also found the school committee had used portable classrooms to deal with the problem rather than transferring whites to nearby schools with identical grade structures, empty seats, and primarily black enrollments. These decisions were seen by the judge as additional evidence of segregative intent.

There could be no doubt about the purpose of a scheme designed to reduce overcrowding of South Dorchester's Cleveland Junior High. Students from this 91 percent white school were reassigned to all-white South Boston High, already overcrowded and more distant than three schools with black enrollments of 89 percent, 91 percent, and 94 percent. During the trial an assistant superintendent had admitted the importance of white parental pressure to this arrangement. Now Garrity fastened on it, and cited it again in a later section of the opinion.

Finally, the judge saw compelling evidence of segregative purpose in the assignment of pupils to newly built schools, especially with respect to the controversial Lee in Dorchester and the overwhelmingly black Weld in overwhelmingly white Roslindale. The abortive 1973 attempt of the school committee to deny a new high-rise building to predominantly black English High constituted yet another instance of intent in the judge's opinion.[16]

Districting

Districting is drawing of geographical boundaries to create attendance zones. Analysis of any relationship between districting and racial distribution was complicated greatly by Boston's varied procedures. A "pure" district scheme existed only at the elementary-school level. Intermediate schools depended on a mixed district and "feeder-pattern" arrangement for their students. After finishing at one school an entire group of students was "fed" to a more-advanced facility. All "area" high schools, such as South Boston High, depended on feeder patterns instead of geographically defined districts, but the correspondence was often close enough to confuse even school officials. Technically speaking, however, Boston did not have "neighborhood" high schools.

Yet another complication was the use of different grade structures within the same system. In 1962 the Sargent report identified seven three-year and nine four-year high schools plus the two six-year Latin schools.[17] Use of multi-school districts at the elementary level further compounded problems of analysis; some of these districts contained up to six different schools, all under the administration of a district principal. Open enrollment and controlled transfers left no district or feeder pattern sacrosanct, and, of course, the elite Latin examination and other special schools enrolled students from all parts of Boston.

It more or less followed that redistricting meant only redrawing boundaries for elementary and intermediate schools, rather than alteration of feeder patterns to intermediate or high schools. In Garrity's terminology it also excluded new districting required to incorporate a newly built school, or changing the level of an existing school.

Under these circumstances, any racial relationship was bound to be complicated, and the judge found it so. He did not accuse the school committee of having redistricted in such a way as to create segregation where none had previously existed. But he did find the defendants guilty of changing district boundaries to keep certain schools identifiably white or black. The judge included maps to illustrate some rather obvious educational gerrymandering in Dorchester and Mattapan. Garrity derived segregative intent from school-committee refusal to alter districts in order to reduce racial concentrations.

Feeder Patterns

Judge Garrity declared that feeder patterns had been "manipulated with segregative effect" since 1966.[18] This meant in part that certain patterns had been adjusted to allow continuing attendance at predominantly white intermediate and high schools. The judge concluded that varying grade structures and feeder patterns had been combined in the following manner:

> . . . . [A] dual system of secondary education was created, one for each race. Black students generally entered high school upon completion of the eighth grade, and white students upon completion of the ninth. High school education for black students was conducted by and large in citywide schools, and for white students in district [sic] schools. White students were generally given options enabling them to escape from predominantly black schools; black students were generally without such options.[19]

Open Enrollments and Controlled Transfers

Almost every antibusing respondent interviewed for this study argued that open enrollments had permitted both desegregation and exercise of free choice by students of all races. Judge Garrity saw the program in a different light. Although open enrollment allowed personal choice, it was the exercise of that option by large numbers of whites that disturbed him. In 1970-1971, of the 6,700 students availing themselves of this option, some 1,028 had made "segregative" choices. Included among such transfers, however, were 324 nonwhites who had moved from predominantly white to mainly nonwhite schools. More open acknowledgment of this datum might have enhanced the fairness of the Garrity decision.[20] In any case, after reviewing the history of how open enrollments had been replaced by controlled transfers in the face of state coercion, the judge found numerous subsequent exceptions to have been poorly concealed attempts to preserve white choice. Thus controlled transfers were found to be contaminated by segregative intent.

Faculty-Staff Recruitment and So Forth

Judge Garrity located additional instances of segregative intent in minority faculty and administrative recruitment, advancement, and school assignment. He accepted the plaintiffs' contention that use of the National Teacher Examination (NTE) discriminated against black applicants. In this connection Judge Garrity cited a precedent in which use of the NTE had been found discriminatory.[21]

Garrity further agreed that Boston's efforts to recruit black teachers had not been dedicated enough to attract an acceptable proportion of the total staff. Just what this proportion would have to be was not entirely clear, but Judge Garrity found significance in the fact that 5.4 percent of all permanent public-school faculty were black, whereas 33 percent of all students and 16 percent of all Bostonians were black.[22] The judge had little patience with counterclaims that qualified black applicants were scarce, and pointed up the school committee's unwillingness to adopt a quota policy as further proof of segregative intent. He also noted sharp reductions in the school department's minority-recruitment budget between 1970-1971 and 1971-1972.

As for school assignments, the judge saw an invidious racial policy in the placement of more than two-thirds of all black faculty inthe city's fifty-nine predominantly black schools. Testimony by a black administrator that assignments provided adult role models for black youth was scorned as "curbstone opinion" by the judge.

Finally, the judge saw discrimination in a promotion system that had disproportionate numbers of blacks in lower echelons. Since most black teachers had been hired in relatively recent years, and mostly in the provisional rank, a promotion system based on experience did concentrate black faculty in junior classifications.

Examination and Vocational Schools

The importance of the Supreme Court's Denver decision showed clearly in Judge Garrity's treatment of Boston's elite examination and vocational schools. Admission to the Latin and other examination schools was determined by competitive test scores, and enrollments were overwhelmingly white. The vocational schools were preponderantly black. The plaintiffs had been unable to prove discrimination by the examination schools, although they were held to be segregated. According to *Keyes,* however, a finding of intentional segregation in any part of a school system created the presumption that segregation in any other part was deliberate in origin. *Keyes* allowed Garrity to turn the tables on the defendants, forcing them to prove that the examination school enrollments were not in some manner *de jure.* He concluded that the school committee had not rebutted the presumption.

Several matters remained once the judge finished his analysis of school-system operations. First, the state board was absolved of liability for Boston's segregation, but was also kept on as a party in order to facilitate desegregation.

Second, Judge Garrity rejected housing patterns as a viable explanation for Boston's segregated schools. He pointed up a lack of correspondence between settlement and feeder patterns and reviewed already mentioned evidence that effectively demolished the claim. Moreover, additional evidence of segregative purpose was found in the school committee's location of schools near certain public housing projects.

Finally, Judge Garrity denied the existence of a genuine neighborhood-school system in Boston. He rejected the defendants' appeal to a rule in *Keyes* that different treatment might be accorded "a separate, identifiable and unrelated section of the school district."[23] The judge acknowledged Charlestown, East Boston, South Boston, and Brighton to be "fairly intact communities with somewhat restricted access to other parts of the city," but disputed that their schools were physically isolated from the rest of the system.[24] Rather they were part of a centrally administered system, the judge wrote, and thus were included in open enrollments, redistricting, altered feeder patterns, and other practices undercutting strictly neighborhood enrollments.

In this connection, the judge showed that 764 of South Boston High's students had been fed from Dorchester in 1972. Charlestown had received 369 students from other areas in the same year.[25] The forty-eight students from other parts of the city who attended East Boston High amounted to a less dramatic contradiction of neighborhood schools, but the judge's point was made.

Thus having established unlawful segregation in Boston, Judge Garrity took up his third question: Was he authorized to impose system-wide remedies made possible by Supreme Court decisions?

According to the judge's reading of *Keyes,* he was entitled to infer *de jure* segregation from "surrounding circumstances" as well as from explicit behavior by the defendants. Such circumstances could include "the absence

of valid educational, fiscal, administrative or other governmental justifications for decisions having clearly forseeable segregative consequences."[26]
Judge Garrity found a basis for such inferences in the school committee's
documentary record. "In the chronology and context in which the defendants would have decided upon choices open to them," Garrity
declared, "they took many actions in their official capacities with the purpose and intent to segregate the Boston public schools . . . "[27]

As for intentional action, the judge had little difficulty in concluding
that "substantial portions" of the system had been so segregated. This permitted application of system-wide remedies based on the *Keyes* reciprocal-
effects test, which holds that deliberate segregation in one school affects
enrollment by race in all others. Therefore, he ordered implementation of
the state board's revised short-term plan in 1974-1975, and directed the defendants "to begin forthwith the formulation and implementation of plans
which shall eliminate every form of racial segregation in the public schools
of Boston . . ."[28]

A Decisive Turn of Events

This chapter followed Judge Garrity's role in the trial and initial policy-
formulation stages of his involvement in the Boston controversy. Chapter 7
discusses his continual involvement in the actual implementation process.
Acting as an instrument of federal judicial policy, Judge Garrity had little
trouble in finding numerous instances of segregative purpose and action by
the defendants during Boston's history of conflict over racial imbalance.
The fortuitously announced *Keyes* decision greatly strengthened his basis
for findings of school-committee guilt and added significantly to the scope
of his remedies. After a decade of struggle, the whole controversy had been
dramatically transformed. The legal issue had changed, the state had
become a relatively minor party, and the authority of the federal government was now arrayed against local officials.

But there is more to implementation of controversial social change than
judicial commands that it shall be done. The same historical context that
provided Judge Garrity with ample evidence of school-committee misdeeds
had witnessed the rise of Louise Day Hicks and other antibusing politicians
and sharply defined issues outside the courtroom. Moreover, judicial policy
had to be implemented in the schools of now thoroughly aroused defended
neighborhoods. The battle of Boston had only just begun.

Notes

1. Judge Garrity was not the first federal official to find *de jure*
segregation in the Boston public schools. On 2 March 1973 a federal ad-

ministrative law judge reached this conclusion after hearing testimony in response to 1969 complaints about rapid racial turnover in the Solomon Lewenberg Junior High School and the results of a subsequent OCR investigation. Nearly all federal educational aid was suspended, thus adding to pressures against the school committee. See In re Boston Public Schools, Boston, Mass., Initial Decision (No. CR-982 72-1) (Adm. Proceedings: HEW, NSF, HUD, 2 March 1973); in re Boston Public Schools, Final Decision of the Reviewing Authority (19 April 1974); and Muriel Cohen, "The Boston Case," *Boston Globe,* 7 January 1973, p. A-49.

2. The attendance of the NAACP led th press to assume incorrectly that its attorneys were behind the suit. Actually the NAACP role was advisory.

3. 42 U.S. Code 1981, 1983, and 2000.

4. *Morgan* v. *Hennigan,* 379 F. Supp. 410 (D. Mass. 1974). After Judge Garrity's liability decision, Hennigan was replaced by John Kerrigan as chief defendant, as Kerrigan had become school-committee chairman. The suit was brought under rule 23 of federal civil procedure. Under this rule federal courts allow some members of a class to litigate on behalf of all members without their consent if the plaintiffs seek to protect the class against a common adversary.

5. Complaint at 6-8, *Morgan* v. *Hennigan,* Civ. Act. No. 72-911-G (D. Mass. 1974).

6. This was the approach taken in *Taylor* v. *Board of Education,* 191 F. Supp. 181 (S.D.N.Y. 1961), 294 F. 2d. 36 (2d. C. 1961); and in *Hobson* v. *Hansen,* 269 F. Supp. 401 (D.D.C. 1967).

7. Over 800 items were included in the plaintiffs' exhibit list, among them 170 statements taken from transcripts of school-committee meetings.

8. *Bell* v. *School Board of Gary,* 213 F. Supp. 819 (N.D. Ind. 1963), 324 2d. 209 (7th Cir. 1963); *Deal* v. *Cincinnati Board of Education,* 369 F. 2d. 55 (6th Cir. 1966).

9. Taeuber has frequently maintained that de facto segregation is invalidated by discrimination. See "Demographic Perspectives on Housing and School Segregation," *Wayne Law Review* 21 (March 1975):833-850; and "Housing, Schools and Incremental Segregative Effects," *Annals of the American Academy of Political and Social Sciences* 441 (January 1979): 157-167.

10. *Keyes* v. *School District No. 1, Denver,* 413 U.S. 189 (1973).

11. All comments made to Buell by South Boston respondents.

12. For information on Garrity see Harold Chase, et al., *Biographical Dictionary of the Federal Judiciary* (Detriot: Gale, 1977), p. 89; and Marguerite Del Giudice, "Man and Judge: W. Arthur Garrity, Jr.," *Boston Evening Globe,* 21 June 1976, p. 8.

13. *Morgan* v. *Hennigan,* 379 F. Supp. 410, 482 (1974).

14. Ibid, 425.

15. Ibid, 418-425.

16. Ibid., 424-432.

17. See *A Report on the Schools of Boston,* Boston Redevelopment Authority (May 1962): pp. 1-28.

18. *Morgan* v. *Hennigan,* 379 F. Supp. 410, 442 (1974).

19. Ibid., 448.

20. Ibid., 452-453. Some of these students likely were Hispanic or Asian, but data on this point were unavailable.

21. *Baker* v. *Columbus Municipal School Dist.,* 329 F. Supp. 706 (N.D. Miss. 1971).

22. For a criticism of this and other points in Garrity's opinion, see Nathan Glazer, *Affirmative Discrimination* (New York: Basic Books, 1975), p. 65.

23. *Keyes.* v. *Schools District No. 1, Denver,* 413 U.S. 189, 201-202 (1973).

24. *Morgan* v. *Hennigan,* 379 F. Supp. 410, 474 (1974).

25. Many of the Charlestown students were evidently Chinese. See Pamela Bullard and Judith Stoia, *The Hardest Lesson* (Boston: Little, Brown, 1980), pp. 90-110.

26. *Morgan* v. *Hennigan,* 379 F. Supp. 410, 478-479 (1974).

27. Ibid., 480. The definition of intent here is close to a later Supreme Court definition in *Washington* v. *Davis,* 426 U.S. 229 (1976).

28. *Morgan* v. *Hennigan,* 379. F. Supp. 410, 484 (1974).

**Implementation and
Resistance—The Role
of Judge Garrity**

Implementation and the Judicial Process

Having discovered unlawful segregation in Boston schools, Judge Garrity
now took steps to end it. Unlike some other lower federal judges, he was unwilling to play any but a dominant role in implementing desegregation.[1]
Tenacious opposition to his provisional decrees only deepened his resolve to
see enforcement of a more-comprehensive and permanent program. Before
long this commitment would involve him in deciding such routine school
operations as curriculum, teacher retraining and recruiting, discipline codes
and student rights.

His authority to order such changes derived from the power of federal
judges to decide matters in equity.[2] But the judicial process normally is not
the most rapid or systematic approach to dissolving complex social ills.
Rather, Judge Garrity often found it necessary to handle problems
piecemeal, responding to litigants more often than initiating action on his
own. He was often heavily dependent on the same parties for essential feedback on the impact of his orders. Under highly favorable conditions—a
policy accorded general legitimacy, willing compliance, and lack of
strife—he would have found it difficult to assess his impact completely and
objectively.[3] But resistance reminiscent of Little Rock made such evaluation
impossible. Thus Boston desegregation was a process of trial, error, and in-
ordinate complexity, throughout which Judge Garrity refused to alter his
course. His role in this process from 1974 until the present is described in
this chapter.

The "Phase 1" Plan

Chapter 5 briefly discussed use of "geocodes" by the Finger task force to
reconstruct the Boston school system. Pursuing twin goals of racial balance
and minimum busing distances, the task force had used redistricting, reassignments, and creation of a uniform grade structure in planning changes.
Because Judge Garrity adopted this plan as "Phase 1" of his desegregation
program, certain of its features must be reviewed at this point.

The patchwork Boston school system presented difficult challenges to
state planners. They found elementary schools easiest to handle, for it was

possible to make use of existing districts and expand boundaries when necessary to incorporate majority-black schools into predominantly white districts. The primary grades were uniformly set at K-5. Some elementary and all junior high schools were converted into middle schools to create an intermediate level with grades 6-8. Most middle schools were situated near enough both white and black populations to make racially mixed enrollments feasible. High schools posed the hardest problems because of their different ways of obtaining students, grade structures, curricula, and so on. The task force made 9-12 standard high school grades, with the Latin schools excepted. A distinction between area and citywide high schools was not eliminated, but several mainly black citywide schools were made into "district" schools and otherwise altered for desegregation purposes. The new term district made sense because the task force also drew up geographic districts for high schools. Generally, the approach was to add a nearby black section to a predominantly white area served by a "neighborhood" high school. Some gerrymandering was unavoidable, however, as in the long district established for English High, which ran through West Roxbury, Roslindale, Jamaica Plain, and Roxbury.

One combination state planners refused to avoid was putting Roxbury and South Boston high schools in the same district. Easily the most controversial feature of the plan, this district was carved out of South Boston, North Dorchester, Roxbury, and the South End, with Columbia Point housing project thrown in for good measure. After fashioning this explosive matrix, the Finger group left the details of pairing the two high schools to the Boston School Department. Much of this unwelcome burden fell upon Dr. William Reid, South Boston High's headmaster.[4] It was decided to transfer 535 white students, including the whole junior class, from South Boston High to Roxbury (formerly Girls High and now coeducational). If enrollments had held as projected, this arrangement would have made Roxbury High 51 percent white. South Boston High was to receive 797 black sophomores and seniors in return, a development that would have made the main building 24 percent black and the nearby Hart and Dean annexes 46 percent black. Some 158 "others," mostly Hispanic students, were assigned to Roxbury and South Boston as well.

Judicial Hearings and Inadequate Preparations

After issuing the necessary interlocutory orders to begin Phase 1, Judge Garrity held more hearings in July and August. After releasing his June ruling, he had challenged the school committee to produce an alternative desegregation plan, but it had chosen instead to appeal his decision.[5] Now its attorneys urged delaying desegregation in view of the brief time remaining before the start of school. The plaintiffs insisted that Phase 1 was not comprehensive enough.

Judge Garrity chose to stay with the state plan, which meant he would have to address various problems not resolved by the state board, for example, matters related to contracts for teachers and administrators. After the hearings, Judge Garrity ordered racial quotas for hiring teachers and an expanded minority faculty recruitment program.[6]

But more than judicial decrees were required to prepare for Phase 1. The Finger task force had not dealt with myriad specifics of transportation, student reassignments, and so on, leaving these for local school officials. After the Supreme Judicial Court ordered implementation of the state plan, the Educational Planning Center (EPC) of the Boston School Department had begun work, but not much progress had been achieved when Judge Garrity intervened with his ruling in June 1974. At this point, the EPC had yet to settle such difficulties as student-record transfers, teacher and staff reassignments, extra safety personnel, bus contracts and routing. An enormous task had to be completed in slightly over two months and, in the chaotic effort that followed, important facets of the new program were neglected. School department attempts to inform teachers were insufficient, and efforts to communicate with the general public were equally ineffective. An example of the latter were poorly publicized open houses at key schools just before summer's end.[7]

Judge Garrity brought in the federal Community Relations Service to assist with desegregation preparations, but frenetic conditions among EPC staff greatly reduced the service's capacity to aid. It is also likely that some EPC planners did not believe desegregation would proceed under such circumstances.[8]

Some city governmental agencies had discussed implementation of racial balancing before Judge Garrity's ruling, and, once it became reasonably clear that the judge would find against the school committee, more planning was done. In keeping with Mayor White's emphasis on decentralized programs, however, the main thrust was to involve neighborhoods through their "little city halls." Deputy Mayor Robert Kiley and other officials put together twelve neighborhood-safety teams comprising district police commanders and fire captains, members of the Youth Activities Commission, and, in about seven areas, headmasters or other school officials. The ostensible purpose of these teams was to meet with residents and convince them to comply with the law.[9]

Mayor White also visited neighborhoods urging calm and compliance with the federal-court ruling. Yet the mayor sometimes let slip his ambivalence toward Phase 1, as in a televised speech on 9 September in which he distinguished between "acceptance" of a law and "compliance" with it. He also said parents were free to keep their children at home, but urged against doing so because of the educational disadvantages to follow.[10]

Most city police were even less enthusiastic about upholding a busing order, and their union president was outspokenly opposed. Thus it was no accident that Judge Garrity tried to instruct the police in their duty to enforce his orders through a memorandum given to counsel for the Boston Police Patrolman's Association (BPPA). Police Commissioner Robert di Grazia was determined to maintain the peace, but he and other high police officials were convinced the best way to do so was to offer the least provocation possible by stationing only a few officers near schools. The elite Tactical Patrol Force (TPF) of 125 officers would be used in case of emergency. The "low key" police plan extended to supervision of operations, as no central command post was established for desegregation, and the superintendent had to manage events from his car or his office when trouble did occur.[11]

The police would soon have plenty to contend with, for resistance to busing had organized in almost every white neighborhood by midsummer under the Restore Our Alienated Rights (ROAR) banner. ROAR staged marches, rallies, and other events, such as a motorcade of over a thousand cars in South Boston.

A ROAR rally downtown at Government Center attracted Senator Kennedy, by now identified as a proponent of busing. When Kennedy tried to speak, some turned their backs while others cursed and jostled him. A shaken senator fled into the nearby John F. Kennedy federal building with some of the crowd in pursuit.[12] It was an omen of what would follow when school began three days hence.

Phase 1 Encounters Violent Resistance
in Defended Neighborhoods

Sixty-two percent of the anticipated citywide student total reported for classes on 12 September, and Phase 1 proceeded relatively smoothly in most districts. But national attention was drawn instead to South Boston, where defiant slogans and racial insults decorated walls, windows, sidewalks, and intersections by the score. Youths stoned a school bus when it took a wrong turn, injuring eight black students and one adult inside. Throngs of residents jeered and shrieked as buses arrived at neighborhood schools. Only 112 whites out of a projected 2,074 reported to the two high schools of the Roxbury-South Boston district.

City officials realized the low-visibility police strategy had been a mistake, and Mayor White ordered police in South Boston to escort the buses, keep the streets clear, and prevent gatherings of three or more near schools. He also imposed a curfew on South Boston.

The crowds outside South Boston High were even larger on the following day, and three departing buses were stoned. When school began again on 16 September, a small riot erupted near the high school with police making twenty-one arrests. A black youth was beaten up when several hundred white rampaged though the Andrew Square subway station. Police dispersed two-hundred residents at the M Street playground, and all bars and liquor stores in South Boston were closed.

Some form of demonstration or violent outburst accompanied almost every school day during the rest of 1974. TPF and other police were often hard pressed to keep mobs away from the buses, and a national television audience grew accustomed to images of mounted police, snarling dogs, and angry crowds, as all networks devoted most of their coverage of Boston school desegregation to events in South Boston.

Two days after the assault on André Jean-Louis (described in chapter 1), Mayor White and the plaintiffs made separate requests of Judge Garrity for federal marshals. White wanted 125 to give symbolic as well as actual reinforcement to police at South Boston High, whereas the plaintiffs did not trust local police to protect black children from mob fury. Judge Garrity held that local resources had to be exhausted before federal assistance could be given. Mayor White turned to Governor Sargent and obtained 400 state and Metropolitan District Commission (MDC) police. Federal Bureau of Investigation (FBI) agents started questioning and shadowing antibusing activitists.[13]

President Ford added to the situation by criticizing Judge Garrity's decision as "not the best solution to quality education in Boston."[14] Made casually in reply to a reporter's query, Ford's remark was hailed by ROAR and condemned by a furious Mayor White. On 12 October, after strong pressure from Senator Edward Brooke and others, Ford made a radio speech appealing to Bostonians to reject "hatred and the shrill voices of the violent few"[15] He did not revise his view of the Garrity decision, however.

When violence in South Boston still persisted, an alarmed Sargent mobilized 450 national guardsmen, placing most in a federal facility just inside South Boston. Mayor White refused to deploy them, however, citing their inexperience in riot control.

In mid-December, Judge Garrity reaffirmed previous orders making local officials responsible for protecting students in desegregated schools. Earlier he had ended Mayor White's claim that the school committee rather than the mayor was responsible for student safety by making White a codefendant in the case.[16] Now the judge expanded an already considerable hold on the police by requiring daily reports on the South Boston situation and by stipulating procedures to keep protestors away from schools and students. He banned gatherings of three or more within 100 yards of any South Boston school, and set 50 yards as the forbidden zone elsewhere. He ordered police to prevent demonstrations along bus routes during delivery and pickup hours. And he directed the school committee to write a discipline code in which "racial slurs" were prohibited.[17]

Phase 2 and School Committee Recalcitrance

Judge Garrity moved ahead with preparation of a more comprehensive Phase 2 program despite events in South Boston and other defended neighborhoods. Following Denver's example, he added racial/ethnic parent and student councils to the implementing population. Ideas from these groups were to be channeled to the court via the Citywide Parent Advisory Council (CPAC).[18] He also lifted suspensions of federal school aid to Boston.

During the summer, Judge Garrity had directed the school committee to devise a new desegregation plan by 16 December, and he repeated this order on 31 October.[19] Reacting to these orders, the EPC prepared a plan to bus 31,248 students out of a projected 1975-1976 total of 71,957. Magnet and special schools featuring multilingual and vocational instruction were also proposed by the EPC. The uniform grade structure established for Phase 1 was to be extended to the examination and vocational schools; problems of handicapped students were given unprecedented attention; and an implementation timetable was proposed.

The EPC plan also proposed reduction in the number of district high schools, from ten to six, with some existing schools paired to serve new combined districts. However, the EPC recommended dissolution of the Roxbury-South Boston arrangement. Instead Roxbury and Dorchester high schools were to be paired while South Boston's district would replace parts of Roxbury with North Dorchester and the South End.[20]

John Kerrigan, Paul Ellison, and John McDonough rejected this plan in a 16 December school-committee meeting. The EPC plan was given to Garrity anyway by the school committee's attorney, who then withdrew from the case. When the school committee majority refused to endorse the EPC plan, Judge Garrity held them in civil contempt and set 8 January as the final date for submission of an acceptable plan. Weekly fines were to commence thereafter.[21]

After losing their appeal to overturn their contempt citations, McDonough, Kerrigan, and Ellison produced a new plan on 7 January. It differed from the EPC version mainly in a "program preference" feature that permitted parents to decide whether to keep their children in racially balanced district schools or transfer them to magnet schools. Children whose parents indicated no preferences could then be bused to district schools to promote desegregation.[22] Already unhappy with the judge's finding of civil rather than criminal contempt against the defendants, the plaintiffs insisted this new proposal would simply perpetuate segregation and should not be accepted as sufficient to remove the citations. However, Judge Garrity held the plan to be evidence of good-faith compliance, lifted the citations, and gave the school committee three weeks to amend its version.[23]

Masters and Experts

The school committee majority's reluctant offering was hardly the sole blueprint submitted for Phase 2. Judge Garrity had received fourteen other plans of varying scope from the state board, the Boston Home and School Association, and parent and bilingual groups.[24] He also had the EPC plan.

Following common practice in desegregation cases, Judge Garrity appointed four "masters" to review all proposals and prepare a Phase 2 plan. The first master, Francis Keppel, had been dean of the Harvard School of Education and U.S. Commissioner of Education. He had helped implement southern desegregation in the 1960s. John McCormack, Jr., belonged to a dynasty second only to the Kennedys in Massachusetts politics. In 1962 he had given Edward Kennedy a bruising contest for the Democratic U.S. Senate nomination.[25] A South Boston native and South Boston High graduate, McCormack was a prominent attorney with a long record of political office, civic involvement, and liberal views when appointed. Jacob Spiegel was a former member of the Supreme Judicial Court, having retired after thirty-three years on the bench, when appointed by Judge Garrity. The only black master, Charles Willie, was a Harvard urban-studies and education professor.

Judge Garrity named Robert Dentler and Marvin Scott as experts to aid the masters in evaluating desegregation proposals. Both men were on the faculty and deans in the education school at Boston University when selected. Dentler was especially experienced as a desegregation consultant.[26]

The school committee objected to several of these choices because of previous memberships in, or financial support for, the NAACP. According to the school committee, such ties made unbiased assessment of issues impossible. Judge Garrity in part took the rather legalistic line that the NAACP was not party to the case, but also simply denied the presence of any bias. Of course, his replies did not prevent antibusing groups from exploiting the affiliation in their denials of legitimacy to subsequent desegregation programs.

Almost immediately, the masters heard testimony on the sixteen plans. Each was found faulty in some important respect during eleven days of hearings, and it was decided to draw up a composite plan incorporating features from most plans considered. A new version resulted from several weeks of closed sessions, and was given Judge Garrity at the end of March. After a 10 April session on the plan in the judge's courtroom, and subsequent submission of written objections by the parties, the masters produced a second version. To obtain needed information for this draft, Judge Garrity ordered school-department release of data on Hispanic and METCO students, examination procedures, and school facilities. Judge Garrity released the final version on 10 May, and followed on 5 June with supplementary legal findings in support of the plan.

The Phase 2 Plan

Unlike Phase 1, devised by state planners and adopted as an expedient, Phase 2 very much was Judge Garrity's own program. He swept school committee objections aside with the comment that "years of obstruction" had brought Boston to such remedies. In reply to complaints from black parents that East Boston schools were unduly exempted from desegregation, he found justification for the difference in "equitable considerations of geography, education, and the burden of transportation."[27]

Of the seven issues addressed by the new plan, three must be covered in some detail here: (1) community school districts, (2) the citywide school district, and (3) citizen participation.

Community School Districts

Phase 2 divided Boston into eight community school districts, each with the same grade structure (K-5, 6-8, 9-12) and administrative relationship to the school department (a district assistant superintendent who reported to the superintendent downtown). Each district would provide bilingual education in some schools and programs for handicapped students in all. Pupil assignments to schools would be decided by geocode, and would be somewhat affected by closing thirty-two schools, including ten already scheduled for abandonment by the school committee.

Each district would have one or, at most, two high schools. Students turned away from district high schools filled to capacity would be given places in citywide schools. Formerly area high schools were designated to share the same district. The most controversial of these arrangements was the pairing of Roxbury and Charlestown high schools in the new Madison Park district. As the South End was also made part of Madison Park, a reduced South Boston district was extended southward into North Dorchester. The plan made English High into a citywide facility. Capacities at all high schools were adjusted to reflect declining student population.[28]

The Citywide School District

The citywide, or ninth, school district consisted of all examination and vocational high schools, thirteen primary and junior high magnet schools, and an English language center. Judge Garrity set a 35 percent quota of blacks and Hispanics for examination school entering classes, and required that tutoring be made available to these students. However, tracking was permitted. Working with area businesses and cultural institutions, the planners had matched all citywide and some district schools with firms, universities, and other institutions in a support arrangement. In South Boston, for example, the Gillete Safety Razor Company established a special program with the high school.

Citizen Participation

Once again Judge Garrity increased his implementation population by encouraging citizen involvement. In part, this was done to make the court less dependent on the school department and defendants for essential information. In any case, Judge Garrity left no doubt that the citizens who were to become involved were to be supporters of his efforts.

At the top of an expanded structure of popular participation was the Citywide Coordinating Committee (CCC), whose functions were to monitor and aid desegregation while providing public information. Judge Garrity in a separate order on 30 May 1975 appointed the forty-two CCC members, all chosen to reflect ethnic, racial, and occupational variety, but uniformity with respect to endorsement of his program. CPAC and the racial/ethnic councils were incorporated into the structure as well, and sent representatives to the CCC. Nine Community District Advisory Councils (CDACs), one for each school district, were also created. They were instructed to submit yearly reports on school racial enrollments, faculty and staff racial composition, standardized test results by race, student suspensions by race, facilities use, transportation, institutional pairings, and various other matters.[29]

Other Details of Phase 2

The remaining Phase 2 plan did not greatly alter existing vocational education programs, and the school committee was given until early September to suggest improvement. Phase 2 also spelled out student transfer policy, permitting changes only when they reduced racial imbalance or placed pupils in bilingual and special education programs. The plan entailed busing twenty one thousand students, but details were left to the school department. Judge Garrity gave the EPC a July deadline to accomplish this task. (In July the school department abolished the EPC and replaced it with the Office of Implementation.) Finally, the plan was inconclusive about financial costs of desegregation, now a serious strain on the city.[30]

Phase 2 and the Receivership Controversy

After a tense summer punctuated by several episodes of racial violence, school began on 8 September on an ominous note, as police staged a massive show of might in Charlestown and South Boston. High schools in these neighborhoods remained nearly empty, as hundreds of helmeted police on foot, horseback, and motorcycles lined and patrolled streets while helicopters hovered overhead. A small riot erupted in Charlestown, and an estimated ten thousand demonstrated for or against desegregation across the city. Later in September a teacher strike compounded problems, but was ended after eight days of negotiations. Judge Garrity did not intervene in the strike, but kept close watch on the progress of negotiations.

Racial fighting and class disruptions plagued high schools in Hyde Park, Charlestown, and South Boston throughout the fall. South Boston High had the worst record in this respect, and, in November, Judge Garrity summoned students, teachers, administrators, and various others for five days of hearings on the South Boston situation. Although black students were unable to substantiate allegations of racist behavior against several white faculty, black and white witnesses generally agreed in the picture of near-anarchy and collective paranoia sketched by their testimony. Judge Garrity twice visited the school accompanied by his masters and a brace of marshals to gain firsthand impressions.

On 9 December a week after his second visit, the judge placed South Boston High in federal receivership and removed the headmaster.[31] A stunned Dr. Reid first learned the news from reporters.[32] In explaining this step, Judge Garrity cited evidence of racial conflict and hostile surroundings, but emphasized most the "pervasive lassitude and emptiness" he observed during his visits.[33] As receiver he first named Joseph McDonough, brother of the school committeeman and an assistant superintendent in the school system. Later the new superintendent, Marion Fahey, was appointed receiver.

Probably more than any other Garrity action, receivership infuriated South Bostonians and handed antibusing leaders a powerful symbol to exploit in a bicentennial year. Printed placards proclaiming "Remember Black Tuesday" blossomed throughout the neighborhood, and another boycott of classes immediately went into effect. Three days later, *The New*

York Times noted attendance by only eighteen whites, all members of the basketball and track teams who had to come in order to play sports.[34] Unknown persons firebombed the NAACP headquarters the night of 9 December, and antibusing demonstrators observed a "day of mourning" on 12 December by creating enormous rush-hour traffic jams on city expressways.

An end to the boycott brought no corresponding end of racial tensions in South Boston High. Now the the city joined with plaintiffs in recommending closure, and, through issuance of numerous orders, Judge Garrity exercised direct authority over school decisions even passing on such matters as the purchase of basketballs and a case of a half-inch wide ankle wrapping tape for physical education classes.[35]

At the same time, Judge Garrity oversaw recruitment of a new South Boston High headmaster, insisting that the new principal was to be committed to "alternative education" and to come from another school system. Eventually the search narrowed to Jerome Winegar, a junior-high assistant principal in St. Paul, Minnesota with the prescribed curricular bent and school desegregation experience. Although not widely known in educational circles at the time, Winegar nonetheless came highly recommended by Mario Fantini, a recognized urban education expert and consultant to Garrity's court.[36] The school committee initially balked because of Winegar's educational approach and NAACP membership, not to mention the circumstances of his selection, but soon accepted legal advice and bowed to a Garrity decree extending a contract through the 1978-1979 year. Several assistants to Winegar were similarly installed, adding to local resentment. No sooner did Winegar arrive than printed yellow signs reading "GO HOME JEROME" were attached to scores of telephone polls throughout the neighborhood.

Phases 2B and 3

No slackening of judicial power was evident in 1976-1977 modifications of Phase 2, but the modest changes made suggested Judge Garrity saw Phase 2 as the foundation upon which subsequent desegregation programs were to be built.

One problem not yet resolved to the judge's satisfaction was recruitment of black teachers. As part of starting Phase 2, Garrity had ordered the school department to hire black faculty on a one-for-one basis until 20 percent of the total teaching staff were black.[37] He repeated this order in February 1976, and established a complex screening system to involve participants in his councils. Evidently the judge intended to take the hiring process out of the exclusive domain of the school committee and department, as well as see that more black administrators and teachers were recruited.[38]

The masters essentially played no part in formulating Phase 2B. Most planning was done instead by two experts, who now enjoyed daily access to the judge and were able to obtain better information from the school department. When Judge Garrity received a suggestion from the councils or other groups, he passed these along to experts.[39]

Phase 2B was issued on 3 May 1976. As implied by its name, it was not a major transformation of the Phase 2 program. For the most part, it consisted of details on school repairs, provisioning, and closings. Isolated East Boston, an overwhelmingly Italian-Catholic defended neighborhood, was still largely exempted from desegregation. The new Office of Impementation had to make comparatively few changes in meeting the court's deadline for student assignment, but Judge Garrity nonetheless vested his experts with authority to review all transfers when possible violations of desegregation policy were uncovered. Later in the summer the judge streamlined the CCC, replacing all members except the chairman, Robert Wood, and reducing its size to seven whites, five blacks, an oriental and a Hispanic.

The court released Phase 3 for 1977-1978 in spring 1977. Again the result of work by Dentler and Scott, the new plan was another extension of the basic structure set down in Phase 2. Two important changes were made.

First, the plan called for inclusion of kindergarten children in desegregation, with some children to be bused. The Office of Implementation was charged with preparation of the details, which were forthcoming in August. Busing to assure racially diverse enrollments was part of the program approved by the judge on 12 August.[40]

Second, Judge Garrity moved to shore up the much-criticized Office of Implementation and bring it under his protection. Both this office and its predecessor, the EPC, had been caught in a bureaucratic no man's land between the court's experts and plaintiffs in one trench and the school committee in the other. In 1975-1976 the judge had temporarily suspended school-committee control of the EPC. Now he ordered creation of a Department of Implementation to be funded by the school committee; its functions, budgeting, and work schedules, however, were prescribed by him in a 13 May decree.[41]

Phase 3 required additional and less noteworthy adjustments, such as a slightly revised transfer policy, a new Madison Park district high school, closing four schools and building two others, and further revision of estimated school capacities. The plan also gave a timetable for implementation.

Although collective resistance to busing was visibly waning, Judge Garrity remained entangled in school operations. Partly it was so because of bureaucratic battles inside the Boston School Department. Some of the problem arose out of the confusion caused by the division of labor resulting from creation of the new Department of Implementation. Student transfer policy was one such contested domain, a problem much compounded when the experts discovered thousands of improper assignments under previous plans. Additional complexity followed Superintendent Fahey's replacement of Charles Leftwich with John Coakley as the new departmental head, and by her attempt to establish twenty-odd new positions in the department. Judge Garrity ordered Leftwich retained until the improper assignments had been corrected.[42]

Leftwich and the court experts then attempted to revise assignments, and provoked outcries from affected parents and students. After hearing from his councils, who endorsed making changes, and parents, who pleaded such changes would wreak havoc, the judge decided in favor of stability and allowed most assignments to stand. Although about three thousand changes were rescinded, Garrity's decision came too late to adjust transportation plans, and some students were not given rides the first day of school. Racial incidents were few, however.[43]

Judicial Disengagement, 1977-1978

Judge Garrity began to draw back from involvement in nearly every facet of implementation in the fall of 1977. His limited disengagement was facilitated by changes in the mood of certain local officials.

By this time, for example, even bitter opponents were realizing Garrity would not be overturned by the higher federal courts. Not only were his orders consistently upheld on appeal, but the lesson of futile legal challenges had been driven home in spring of 1976 by a tawdry political episode.

Then locked in a desperate struggle with Ronald Reagan for the Republican nomination, President Ford sought conservative support in the Kentucky primary by hinting that his attorney general was looking for an urban compulsory-busing program to challenge in court. Press speculation and Ford's known distaste for Judge Garrity's policies inflated local anti-busing hopes that Boston would be chosen. These hopes were just as quickly dashed when Ford dropped the idea once Attorney General Edward Levi balked. In Boston a most ironic shift of positions occured in little more than a week. When Ford's hint first was dropped, black leaders promised such a step would ignite the ghetto, while Mrs. Hicks and other prominent busing foes insisted the law must be obeyed. These positions were precisely reversed when Ford was persuaded by Levi not to pursue the idea.[44] Anti-busing frustrations were also vented when the Supreme Court refused to review the Boston case the following week.[45]

These events doubtless influenced the school committee's more decorous handling of Judge Garrity and his satellites in 1977. Hardly thrilled with federal control, the school committee still chose negotiation and cooperation more often than bluster and delay. Détente was further helped by the defeat of incumbent Elvira "Pixie" Palladino in the November 1977 school-committee runoff. She had been one of the group's most outspoken opponents of Judge Garrity and busing. Her replacement by John O'Bryant, the first black elected to the school committee in memory, further moderated matters. The voters also turned back Richard Laws of Hyde Park, an articulate antibusing leader.

Related to these defeats was the collapse of ROAR as a citywide coalition and the consequences of its bifurcation for organized antibusing opposition. This subject is discussed in the next chapter, and is mentioned only to round out the reasons making Judge Garrity's withdrawal possible.

Evidence of a less-conflictual period could be seen in the school department's cooperation with the judge in making student assignments for the 1978-1979 academic year. With the court's permission these assignments were released in early 1978. This was the first time since Judge Garrity's 1974 ruling that students had been notified considerably in advance of the schools they would attend.[46]

Unquestionably the most important symbol of this new period was ending South Boston High's receivership. Intense negotiations preceded this move, with removal following school-committee acceptance of a nondiscrimination guarantee covering school operations, tenure for Winegar and top staff, funding of Winegar programs, faculty desegregation in accordance with court guidelines, employment of security personnel, and assorted physical-plant improvements. Judge Garrity ended receivership on 20 September 1978 and ordered the Department of Implementation to monitor conditions and periodically report to him.[47]

A short-lived sign of harmony was the school committee's unanimous choice of Robert Wood to replace Superintendent Fahey in 1978. Wood's selection was remarkable partly because of his record of support for Judge Garrity's policy, including service on the CCC. Once he became superintendent, however, Wood occasionally complained about the degree of judicial control over school matters. That was a minor issue compared to the 1979 return of Pixie Palladino to the school committee. On 21 August 1980 the committee fired Wood in a three-to-one vote on grounds of "inadequate leadership" and "general dissatisfaction."[48] The consequences of this action and a newly constituted school committee for school desegregation are not fully apparent at the time this is written.

Even before the Wood episode it was clear that greater cooperation had not dissolved all areas of dispute between the parties. One such issue was disciplinary action against black students. In 1975 and 1976 the two sides clashed over higher rates of black suspensions. The school department subsequently cautioned faculty against suspending minority students without just cause, but the proportion of suspensions given to black students markedly increased, as is shown in table 7-1. Of course, the percentage of all those enrolled who were black also increased simultaneously with white decline.

Minority faculty proved to be another enduring controversy. In June 1978 the plaintiffs took the school department to task for not recruiting more black faculty, and pointed up a recent drop in the actual number of nonwhite teachers. Phase 1 had ended with 592 black teachers in the system, and, by the end of Phase 2B, the number had increased to 630. In June 1978, however, it was 600. In response, school officials must have demonstrated that the black proportion of all faculty had remained between 11 percent and 12 percent during the entire desegregation period, for the number of white teachers had also dropped. Of course, 12 percent was still short of the court's 20 percent quota, and here the school department argued the difficulty of finding qualified applicants. Although Judge Garrity did not rule on the point, the school department set up an affirmative-action unit to expedite black recruitment efforts. No doubt, the parties found greater cheer in statistics on school administrators, the black proportion of which had increased from 8 percent in 1976 to 17 percent in 1978.[49]

Dynamic Aspects of Judicial Implementation

This concludes the account of judicial implementation begun in chapter 6. One cannot examine events in Boston without discovering Judge Garrity's critical role. After the legal ruling that Boston schools were segregated, Garrity engaged in continual development and transformation of equitable remedies to end the segregation. His example suggests a model in which the relationship between definition of equitable remedies and implementation is reciprocal and adaptive, with remedial steps informed by feedback from

Table 7-1
Student Suspensions, by Race, Boston Public Schools, 1973-1978

Race of Suspended Students	1973-1974	Phase 1 1974-1975	Phase 2 1975-1976	Phase 2B 1976-1977	Phase 3 1977-1978
White	49.6%	37.9%	40.1%	39.5%	29.7%
Black	45.8	58.1	55.9	55.7	63.0
Other	4.6	4.0	4.0	4.8	7.3
Totals	100.0%	100.0%	100.0%	100.0%	100.0%
Ns	4,838	10,152	6,324	5,799	4,891

Source: Undated statistics provided by the Citywide Coordinating Council.
Note: In Phase 2, South Boston High accounted for 1,471 of all the suspensions, 44 percent of which were given to black students.

experiences with implementation. Hence a judge's response to implementation shocks basically consists of revising or affirming what he thinks equity demands or can tolerate. A less-doctrinaire jurist might have decreed less change, perhaps exempting the venerable Latin School and a few other examination schools. A less-resolute judge might have been less prepared to slash Gordian knots by issuing scores of orders. A less-meticulous legalist likely would not have so carefully grounded every order in precedent.

A few examples from the Phase 1 period illustrate the diversity of problems encountered by the judge and the extent of his day-to-day involvement in implementation:

25 June 1975: Arthur Gartland, CCC chairman, complains that John McDonough, school-committee chairman, will not return phone calls or otherwise facilitate a meeting of the two groups. Judge Garrity orders McDonough's cooperation, and sets 1 July as a deadline for the meeting. He also sets a new date for racial/ethnic parent council elections.

27 June: The first CCC and school-committee meeting ordered by the court is set for 30 June. Judge Garrity ponders hiring computer experts to expedite Phase 2 student assignments.

11 July: Until the school department reports to him, Judge Garrity refuses to allow teacher-assignment changes. He orders a report to be produced by 15 July, and stipulates a focus on teacher vacancies, resignations, and retirements. The judge also directs the department to supply the numbers and school locations of all minority faculty for 1974-1975.

29 July: Robert de Grazia, city police commissioner, is to submit a Phase 2 safety plan to the judge, who will also examine overtime pay for teachers and administrators, minority teacher and administrative recruitment, and busing plans for Phase 2 in hearings on 30 July. The judge receives a school-committee request via the CCC for an appeals and transfer policy to respond to student complaints about assignments. The school committee refuses to formulate a policy unless so ordered by the court.

4 August: The school committee proposes delaying classes until teachers and administrators have received six weeks of special desegregation training. Judge Garrity announces he will set the starting date for Phase 2.

6 August: Judge Garrity permits school-department contracting for school repairs without following customary competitive-bidding procedures.

20 August: Having marked 8 September 1975 as the first day of Phase 2, the judge orders special transportation be provided teachers assigned to schools in "potentially dangerous" areas. He also considers a request to place the school committee in receivership until all schools have been integrated.

25 August: Still considering receivership, Judge Garrity rejects a school-committee proposal to charter buses for transporting white students to predominantly black areas, while blacks evidently are to rely on public transportation or their own means of getting to schools in predominantly white areas.[50]

In this manner, Judge Garrity penetrated such traditionally local domains as education, police, and property taxes. He made extensive use of judical authority in overcoming resistance or reluctance, thus restraining Mayor White, reforming the school bureaucracy, taming the school committee, and amassing a sizable implementing population of dependable supporters. Compliance was exacted, but were policy goals accomplished? Chapter 9 examines selected consequences of judicial policy. At this point, however, our interest shifts to South Boston's response to "forced busing."

Notes

1. See the comparison of Judge Garrity to Judge Stanley Weigel in San Francisco's school desegregation case in David L. Kirp's "Race, Politics, and the Courts: School Desegregation in San Francisco," *Harvard Education Review* 46 (November 1976):572-611. See also Robert T. Nakumara and Frank Smallwood, *The Politics of Policy Implementation* (New York: St. Martin's Press, 1980), pp. 99-100.

2. Equity powers developed out of preventive measures to halt further injustices to individuals and were transformed into positive and longer-term methods of settling issues for collective benefit. See Abram Chayes, "The Role of The Judge In Public Law Litigation," *Harvard Law Review* 89 (April 1976):1281-1316; and Owen M. Fiss, *The Civil Rights Injunction* (Bloomington, Ind.: Indiana University Press, 1978).

3. See J. Woodford Howard, "Adjudication Considered As A Process of Confict Resolution," *Journal of Public Law* 18 (Spring 1969):339-370; and, Donald L. Horowitz, *The Courts and Social Policy* (Washington, D.C.: Brookings, 1977) pp. 35-36.

4. Interview by Buell, 29 June 1977.

5. *Morgan* v. *Kerrigan,* 505 F.2d 580 (1st Cir. 1974). For other accounts of Judge Garrity's early orders, see Charles W. Case, "History

of The Desegregation Plan In Boston," in *The Future of Big City Schools,* Daniel U. Levine and Robert Havinghurst, eds. (Berkeley, Calif.: McCutchan, 1977), pp. 153-176; Ralph R. Smith, "Boston: Two Centuries And Twenty-Four Months," in *The Limits of Justice,* Howard I. Kalodner and James J. Fishman, eds. (Cambridge, Mass.: Ballinger, 1978); and, *Desegregating The Boston Public Schools* U.S. Commission on Civil Rights (Washington, D.C.: U.S. Government Printing Office, 1975).

6. *Morgan* v. *Kerrigan,* No. 72-911-G (D. Mass. 31 July 1974), order on hiring. Hereafter references to *Morgan* v. *Kerrigan* and *Morgan* v. *McDonough* will supply only citation numbers and dates.

7. See "Open Houses Precede Start of School," *Boston Globe,* 9 September 1974, p. 1; "School Integration: 10 More Days To Go," *Boston Globe,* 2 September 1974, p. 1; "Split Desegregation Authority Could Mean Confusion," *Boston Evening Globe,* 21 August 1974, p. 4; "Hub Planners Put Finishing Touch On School Assignment," *Boston Evening Globe,* 12 August 1974, p. 3; see also the testimony by John Coakley and Ann Foley in *Hearing Held in Boston, Massachusetts June 16-20, 1975,* U.S. Commission on Civil Rights (1975), pp. 71-89.

8. See Case, "History," pp. 156-157.

9. See Kiley's testimony in *Hearing Held in Boston,* pp. 32-53.

10. An excerpt of White's speech is found in *Desegregating The Boston Public Schools,* pp. 29-30; see also Christine Rossell, "The Mayor's Role in School Desegregation Implementation," *Urban Education* 12 (October 1979): 247-270.

11. See the appraisal of police planning in *Desegregating The Boston Public Schools,* pp. 94-148. For a sympathetic account of police performance, see John Kifner, "The Men In The Middle," *The New York Times Magazine,* 12 September 1976, p. 36. See declaratory memorandum concerning peaceful desegregation by Judge Garrity, 8 September 1974.

12. "Sen. Kennedy Jeered and Punched At Rally," *Boston Globe,* 10 September 1974, p. 1.

13. Several antibusing activists interviewed by Buell maintained they had been both interviewed and followed by FBI agents. On Garrity's refusal of White's marshal request, see "400 State, MDC Police Ordered Into Boston," *Boston Globe,* 10 October 1974, p. 1.

14. See "The President's News Conference of October 9, 1974," in *Public Papers of the President: Gerald Ford, 1974* (Washington, D.C.: U.S. Government Printing Office, 1975), p. 127.

15. "Remarks on Boston School Desegregation Violence, October 12, 1974," *Public Papers: Gerald Ford,* p. 143.

16. Order joining Kevin H. White as party defendant, 30 September 1974.

17. Order on motion for relief concerning security, 17 December 1974.

18. Memorandum and order establishing racial/ethnic councils, 4 October 1974. The CPAC consisted of fourteen members chosen by district and race.

19. Order to Boston School Committee, 31 October 1974.

20. Student Desegregation Plan, 16 December 1974.

21. Memorandum and order as to sanctions on civil contempt and citation of civil contempt, 27 December and 30 December 1974.

22. Student Desegregation Plan of Boston School Committee, 27 January 1975; the lost appeal was *Morgan* v. *Kerrigan,* 509 F 2d. 618 (1975). (1975).

23. Memorandum and conditional order as to three defendants' civil contempt, 8 January 1975; interview by Brisbin 16 June 1977.

24. See "Court Gets 16 Proposals On Integration," *Boston Globe,* 21 January, 1975, p. 1.

25. See Murray B. Levin, *Kennedy Campaigning* (Boston: Beacon Press, 1966).

26. See "Two BU Deans To Help Draft High School Plan," *Boston Globe,* 1 February 1975; interview by Brisbin, 28 June 1977.

27. Memorandum of decision and remedial orders, 5 June 1975, pp. 55-57.

28. Student Desegregation Plan, 10 May 1975, pp. 1-42.

29. Ibid., pp. 86-100. Cf. Robert A. Dentler, "Improving Public Education in Boston," *The Advocate* 7 (Fall 1975):3-8.

30. Student Desegregation Plan, 10 May 1975, pp. 69-85.

31. Order concerning South Boston High School, 9 December 1975.

32. Interview by Buell, 29 June 1977.

33. Supplementary findings and conclusions on plaintiffs' motion concerning South Boston High School, pp. 4, 6-24; reprinted as *Morgan* v. *Kerrigan,* 409 Supp. 1141 (D. Mass. 1975).

34. John Kifner, "Whites Boycott South Boston High, *The New York Times,* 12 December 1975, p. 28.

35. First order as to facilities at South Boston High School, 24 December 1975.

36. Interview by Buell and Brisbin, 30 June 1977.

37. *Morgan* v. *Kerrigan,* 388 F. Supp. 581, 582-585 (D. Mass. 1975).

38. Order for desegregation of administrative staff, 24 February 1975.

39. Interviews by Brisbin 28 June 1977 and 6 January 1978.

40. Memorandum and orders as to kindergarten desegregation, 12 August, 1977.

41. Memorandum and order on Boston School Committee motion for modification filed 11 May 1977 and 13 May 1977.

42. See "Illegal Pupil Assignments to End, Garrity Aide Says," *Boston Evening Globe,* 22 July 1977, p. 1; "Garrity Firm On Student Assignment," *Boston Globe,* 23 July 1977.

43. "2300 Boston Students Lack First-Day Rides," *Boston Globe,* 5 September 1977, p. 1; "First Day of School Peaceful But Chaotic," *Boston Globe,* 8 September 1977, p. 1.

44. "Levi Report Stirs Dispute," *Boston Herald-Advertiser,* 16 May 1976, p. 1; "Atkins Decries Suggested Plan," *Boston Globe,* 16 May 1976; "Busing Opponents Blast Levi Logic," *Boston Herald-American,* 4 June 1976.

45. See John Kifner, "Boston Busing Foes Assail Court's Refusal To Review Case And Hint Violence May Result," *The New York Times,* 15 June 1976, p. 23.

46. Memorandum and preliminary orders as to student assignment plan, 31 January 1978.

47. Consent decree, Goodwin, Procter & Hoar. Case materials included in CCC files are now located in the Special Collections Division of the Boston College Library.

48. See Michael Knight, "Boston School Opening Clouded By Dismissal of Chief," *The New York Times,* 27 August 1980, p. A-14.

49. Final report of the Citywide Coordinating Council to the United States District Court, August 1978, Appendix C.

50. Selected from Wendy Bauman, "Boston Busing: A Chronology, 1849-1975." *Boston Globe* microfilm.

Implementation and Resistance—Defending the Neighborhood

Protest and Community Involvement

Earlier we distinguished between the defended neighborhood and neighborhood protest, and pointed out that the latter draws upon and exaggerates certain features of the former. Protest may sharpen common understanding of community plight, add to an already acute territorial orientation, refurbish good community ideals, and confer legitimacy upon literal neighborhood defense.

Since the defended neighborhood is a community to which inhabitants exhibit uncommon loyalties, formulations about protest in such a place must address earlier research showing little relationship between political behavior and community attachment. For example, a 1962 study of four medium-sized Wisconsin cities discovered no correlation between political activity and identification with community. The study in question, however, did not investigate neighborhood commitments and limited political activity to electoral involvement.[1]

"Breakdown" theory in the sociological literature of collective behavior poses a more formidable challenge. According to the "discontent" model, social strain heightens discontent to the point that some segments of an affected population protest. Since discontent is a critical intermediate step, it is important to observe who becomes discontented enough to protest. According to the model, the poorly integrated and socially excluded are generally more discontented than well-integrated members of the community who also belong to secondary associations and communications networks of substantial size. Since strain raises the general level of discontent, the threshold of discontent necessary to protest involvement would be found more often among those already more discontented than the comparatively satisfied and quiescent. It follows, in other words, that protest issues primarily from the most discontented.[2]

"Solidarity" theorists have reached quite different conclusions about who protests and why. In their research, protest involvement correlates strongly with participation in more-normal community activities and belief in community values. Therefore, people are moved to protest out of commitment to their community, not isolation from it. Without such an emotional compass, the solidarity theorists argue, a protest would lack coherence and purpose.

125

The defended-neighborhood model is wholly compatible with parts of both discontent and solidarity theory. Even though the former contains a view of protest participation contrary to the defended-neighborhood model, its focus on disturbance or strain, leading to discontent, is, of course, analogous to externally imposed crisis—or even subtler forms of the common plight leading to greater cohesion and determination by residents to preserve the neighborhood way of life. By the same token, the solidarity theoretic explanation of protestor motivations and characteristics is equally compatible with our model, for it suggests an effort to maintain the good community. Joining a protest for this reason presupposes some prior stake in neighbrohood life.

Bert Useem found evidence supportive of both theories in a recent study of antibusing protest participants and sympathizers in three white Boston enclaves, one of which was South Boston.[3] The respondents who scored high on his community attachment and secondary group membership measures were more likely than lower scorers to endorse or take part in the antibusing movement. Useem concluded that strong neighborhood ties were important, perhaps necessary, to participation. At the same time, he discovered a correlation between protest support or involvement and feelings of relative deprivation in comparison to blacks and other reference groups. Since relative deprivation often is taken as evidence of discontent, Useem found a place for discontent theory as well. His conclusion that solidarity theory can comfortably accommodate relative deprivation is both plausible and consistent with earlier formulations of the deprivation concept: "Not only are isolated individuals without the resources to engage in protest, as the solidarity theorists would argue, but isolated individuals are less likely to experience relative deprivation sufficient to motivate protest."[4]

Although Useem made no reference to the defended-neighborhood model, the importance of neighborhood variables in his analysis is straightforward. For example, he asked respondents in the three neighborhoods, at least two of which are defended types, to place themselves on a five-point continuum in which "1" designated "very strong ties" to their community while "5" indicated "almost no ties." The overall mean was 2.5; it was lower, of course, for those who took part in, or endorsed, the protest against busing. Useem also arrayed respondents along a six-point continuum of identification with reference groups; "1" designated "a great deal in common" with a particular group, while "6" stood for "very little in common." The lowest overall mean was 2.09, obtained for "people in your neighborhood." Again, of course, protestors and movement sympathizers evidenced even stronger identification with neighbors.[5]

Encouraging as these findings may be for the defended-neighborhood model, first-hand observation of South Boston's protest cautions against stretching the solidarity canvass too far. On the one hand, almost every acti-

vist interviewed for this study conformed to the solidarity model of protestor characteristics: they expressed strong emotional loyalty to the
neighborhood, exhibited personal histories of prior community involvement, and were otherwise integrated into local society. But most belonging
to the South Boston Marshals, a para military vigilante organization, exhibited characteristics closer to the discontent model. An undetermined but
likely significant number were unemployed or underemployed; some had
prior arrest and conviction records, and at least a few were named in
outstanding warrants.[6] A contemptuous South Bostonian who did not support the movement lent anecdotal support to our observations by referring
to the marshals as "jail fodder," lower-class "products of the barroom and
the street," and "thugs" who turned instinctively to violence:

> They're animals who don't care if they're beating the shit out of their
> father, their mother, their son, or their wife. In that sense, they're very
> democratic. They'd just as soon bust each other as a cop or a black. . . .
> They need something like this to make them legitimate.[7]

Without pushing such impressions too far, we may conclude that the
South Boston movement exhibited enough diversity in the characteristics
and motivations of its members to point up the need for yet another
theoretical construct. Neither discontent nor solidarity theory can account
for such diversity, and neither can explain the movement's bifurcation. A
useful addendum is found in William Gamson's "challenging group"
framework for the study of social protests.[8]

The Antibusing Protest as a Challenging Group

In order to qualify as a challenging group, a protest movement must condemn existing conditions or policies, exhibit a formal organizational structure, acquire a name, maintain a membership, follow rituals in its gatherings, and periodically demonstrate a capacity to act. Rather than lash out
blindly, the movement must identify specific antagonists to be destroyed or
displaced. It must mobilize at least part of a primary constituency, and
designate a secondary population of likely beneficiaries in the event of success. It can accommodate a variety of supporters.

A "challenge" ends when the group ceases to exist, when *de facto* activity stops despite continuing pro forma existence, or when antagonists
fully accept the challenging group as the legitimate voice of its constituency.
"Acceptance," however, is a highly complex process that can occur in four
ways.

First, a measure of acceptance may be adduced from permitting the
group to represent its constituency in an official forum, for example, in

testimony to the U.S. Commission on Civil Rights. Acceptance may also be inferred from periodic negotiations between the group and any antagonist. A third way of conferring acceptance is to include the challenging group in formal documents or organization charts. Finally, including challenging-group members in an antagonist's organization without requiring them to surrender their protest roles constitute yet another form of acceptance.

Obviously, acceptance hardly requires capitulation by the antagonist. Each of Gamson's acceptance forms may be little more than symbolic politics. Formal presentations, negotiations, designations, or even employment need not extend any concrete benefits to the challenging group, but each implies some degree of recognition of the group's representation of its constituency. As Gamson points out, acceptance is only "a response to the challenging group itself rather than to its issues or a program."[9] Indeed, an antagonist may embrace the group in one or more of these ways in order to co-opt its leadership.

Acceptance is complicated by the presence of multiple antagonists. The more antagonists, other things being equal, the more difficult it will be for the challenging group to win genuine recognition as the legitimate representative of its constituency. Hence Gamson provides for "minimal acceptance," in which only one or some of a group's antagonists bestow recognition in one or more of the ways noted above.

In classifying tactics employed by fifty-three challenging groups between 1800 and 1945, Gamson found violence significantly correlated with acceptance. Not all protest leaders need embrace violence consciously in order for it to be effective, as the following passage makes apparent:

> Violence should be viewed as an instrumental act, aimed at furthering the purposes of the group that uses it. . . . This is especially likely . . . when the normal condemnation which attends to its use is muted or neutralized in the surrounding community. . . . It occurs when hostility toward the victim renders it a relatively safe and costless strategy. The users of violence sense that they will be exonerated because they will be seen as more the midwives than the initiators of punishment. The victims are implicitly told, "See how your sins have provoked the wrath of the fanatics and . . . brought this punishment upon yourselves."[10]

Other tactics employed by challenging groups were boycotts, marches, ad hominem indictments, and personal intimidation.

The "combat readiness" of a movement depends critically on leadership ability to maintain the protest organization, particularly in creating and sustaining "a single center of power." In this connection, averting factionalism is a crucial task, for factionalism has been the bane of challenging groups.[11]

Having sketched these theoretical fragments, it remains to combine them with the defended-neighborhood model in a useful mosaic for analysis of the South Boston antibusing protest. We first take up the protest rationales expressed by antibusing respondents.

Voices of Protest

Elite interviews underscored the centrality of neighborhood defense in South Boston's protest against busing. What follows is a selective but representative presentation of this and related themes.

Asked why South Boston's resistance to busing had been so powerful and enduring, a spokesman for the South Boston Information Center answered with a description of community life exemplifying both the defended-neighborhood and solidarity models:

> I would say definitely it is the makeup of the people of South Boston. This has always been a very close-knit community. Generations live here and grow up with one another. My father lived here, I'm living here, and I expect my children will live here. We don't want to live anywhere else, and, besides, why should we? We already live in the most beautiful section of the city.[12]

What possible connection was there between busing and the choice to live in South Boston? A Catholic priest in South Boston's St. Augustine's Parish who had observed the movement made the link when he pointed out:

> . . . . It's nearly impossible to come here without crossing over a bridge, and people prefer it that way. . . . You can live here a long time and still be considered an outsider. . . . We have our share of fear and bigotry here, but I think you must dig deeper to understand [the protest], get down to the sense of community. After all, the need to belong is one of our most powerful needs. Most people in South Boston belong to the community, and they are sure busing, affirmative action, and other changes they can't understand will destroy it.[13]

The same theme was struck by an activist much involved in the National Association for Neighborhood Schools (NANS):

> Busing is not the only issue at stake in what's happening in this town. . . . In some ways you could even say it's a smokescreen because it blinds us to some of the more important problems. It comes down to things like where and how people wish to live and bring up their families. The government is trying to force everybody . . . to live . . . one approved lifestyle; it's trying to take away our way of living, the neighborhood concept that we have,

our moral code for raising our children. Some people, believe it or not, still believe in old-fashioned ideas like giving thanks to God for what He gives you in this life, or working for a living instead of being taken care of by affirmative action or special treatment. The government can't understand how families can be happy here, how they can be content to live here for generations, how they might even think Southie is the best place in the world to live. . . . Well, maybe all that's happened [over busing] will help them get the picture. What we have in this community is very special. They bit off more than they could chew when they took on South Boston.[14]

Of course, preservation of community was hardly the sole theme stressed by our respondents. Most combined neighborhood defense with one or more additional arguments, such as unlawful violation of rights and racial preference through affirmative action. Thus some tied school desegregation to welfare, employment quotas, and lower scholastic standards. Those who did generally felt the federal government had abandoned common sense and basic fairness out of an obsession to appease blacks. Strong indications of relative deprivation surfaced in such commentaries. A Hyde Park ROAR leader best exemplified this perspective:

. . . . To tell me that I have to hire somebody . . . just because the guy is black. . . . That's wrong, absolutely wrong. And, then, I just get so aggravated when I think about these things, I have to work. . . . I am a supervisor. I sit in the unemployment office, and I see people walk by me and get a check, and I've got a sign there with [announcements for] jobs. They don't want the job. They do not want the job because they are getting unemployment, they are getting medical care, and they're getting food stamps. They've got it made! They are getting a rent subsidy. These people demonstrate in front of the Statehouse for color television sets. They want to go for sheets and towels in Jordans up on the top floor. My wife has to wait for the white sale and go to the basement. I work for a living. I have to have my teeth fixed. I have to wait until I have the money to pay the dentist. I don't have a magic card to go and hand them and let the commonwealth pay for it. You know? It's crazy. It's absolutely crazy and upside—the whole world is upside down! Everything that I've ever worked for, or believed in, all my life in this country—I believed it was a republic, a democratic republic. It's a ripoff![15]

A closely related theme voiced by a few activists and sympathetic observers was the arbitrariness of race as a basis for policy. For example, a West Roxbury activist who had researched racial imbalance and the state's short-term plan recalled her main reason for publicly opposing the latter at a 1972 meeting:

I said, "You cannot . . . classify people as W's and NW's and O's because what you're doing is [taking away] their identity. . . . These children will have no identity. They will go by numbers . . . and . . . if we are going to do that,'' and I was philosophizing here, ''we're taking a black person and saying . . . the only difference in the world is [between] NW and W. And . . . we're going to classify all the other people under O. . . . What's an 'other?' Are you an 'other?' I'm an 'other.''' That's what I told them. ''I was not born here, for instance, so that makes me an 'other.'''[16]

Much the same point was expressed by an exercised South Boston High teacher who blamed busing for ruining the school's educational environment and who felt working-class, barely assimilated ethnics were having to pay for slavery: ''Their ancestors weren't even here when there was slavery; they were serfs in some old country.''[17]

It was no great conceptual leap to castigation of stereotypical ''limousine liberals'' and ''Wellesley whites'' who prescribed busing for the city while sending their own children to expensive private schools or living in suburban districts beyond Judge Garrity's reach. This argument was made with considerable gusto by a city councilman, who explained that busing was a conspiracy by liberal elites to deny ordinary citizens the freedom to choose neighborhood schools for their children. He predicted more violence until busing was extended to the suburbs, at which time court-ordered desegregation would be doomed: ''Let it happen to them [affluent suburbanites] and it'll turn around soon enough.''[18] The Hyde Park ROAR leader quoted earlier was equally passionate in his opinion of elected officials:

> I see people like Kennedy, a United States senator, prestigious, all for black people . . . on the surface. I had lunch with him, and his chauffeur was telling ethnic jokes and making me sick to my stomach. But that's in private. The same man, who is a two-faced hypocrite, tells Senator Biden from Delaware, ''Do something to stop busing, I can't. It would hurt my national image.'' That's how two-faced they are. And yet they sit up there, holier than thou . . . telling the whole country how to live. And why don't they live by example? How many of them send their children to the Washington public school system?[19]

A South Boston protest leader summarized the same argument by declaring, ''it's the old game of 'do what I say, not what I do.'''[20]

The passages quoted in this section offer at least anecdotal evidence to support the defended-neighborhood, solidarity, and discontent models. All antibusing respondents had been active in school and other community affairs prior to busing, and their frequent references to neighbors and neighborhood further validate both the defended-neighborhood thesis and the solidarity model of protester characteristics. But the same passages suggest an important role for discontent theory too, for it is obvious that antibusing activists in Boston viewed contemporary social priorities as distorted and irrational. Indications of relative deprivation, political estrangement, and simple dismay stood out in almost every interview. Such perceptions no doubt greatly reinforced their conception of the defended neighborhood as a haven against such an outside world.

In this context, the candid admission by most antibusing respondents to racial prejudice fits. Rather than conceding that racial bigotry made them oppose busing, they reversed the causal order to claim that the busing controversy and what it had taught them about the outside world had made them more prejudiced. As one South Boston protester put it, "Oh sure, the government's just about made a racist out of me."[21] Yet it was equally clear that some had entered the busing fray with an ample reservoir of hatred for blacks. For example, a South Boston Marshal repeatedly promised at an antibusing rally he would "call a spade a spade no matter who goddamned don't like it."[22]

Conducted about the same time as our elite interviews, the Useem survey affords an opportunity to compare popular opinion in South Boston and two other enclaves with the perspectives discussed above. First, the opposition to busing expressed by our respondents was generally representative of neighborhood opinion; 89 percent of the Useem sample condemned the 1974 Garrity decision, and 87 percent felt it violated their constitutional rights. Second, antibusing activists interviewed for this study were not alone in resenting federal affirmative-action efforts; 83 percent of Useem's respondents agreed that federal policy reverse discriminated against whites. Third, activist ire against the suburban double standard evidently was widely shared; 84 percent of the Useem sample agreed that compulsory busing was unjust, partly because most of its proponents lived outside Boston and thus were unaffected. Another 76 percent felt "unsympathetic" elites had taken over the city schools.[23]

Useem's survey is, of course, very relevant to the present analysis because it provides an idea of actual neighborhood involvement in the antibusing movement. Table 8-1 reports the extent of resident endorsement of, and actual participation in, several aspects of the protest.

Two trends appear in these data. First, verbal support greatly exceeded reported participation in all comparisons. Two-thirds of the combined sample favored antibusing marches, for example, but less than a third actually marched. Second, South Boston evidenced substantially higher support and participation levels than less intense Hyde Park or West Roxbury. Nearly half of the South Boston subsample claimed to have marched in protest against busing, and almost a third said they had joined an antibusing group. More than a third had expressed their discontent in letters to public officials.[24] Such findings give credence to earlier conclusions derived from observation and elite interviews.

Table 8-1
Antibusing Involvement in Three Boston Neighborhoods, 1977

	West Roxbury (%)	Hyde Park (%)	South Boston (%)	Combined Sample (%)
Favored protest marches	49	68	81	66
Participated in protest marches	15	24	49	30
Favored protest organizations	51	62	83	65
Joined protest organizations	8	19	31	19
Favored private academy	62	66	86	71
Donated money or helped otherwise to establish a private academy	8	12	22	14
Wrote antibusing letter to public officials	20	28	35	28
Ns	159	148	161	468

Source: Special tabulation provided by Bert Useem, 24 October 1980.

Note: Respondents "strongly" and "mildly" favoring marches, organizations, and private academies were combined for this tabulation.

Structure of the Antibusing Protest

Having examined the chief reasons given by antibusing elites for their protest, we now apply the Gamson framework to the Boston movement. The first particulars are the movement's organizational structure, ritual, and identification. According to Gamson, a protest must exhibit at least three structural levels, one of which is a formal rank and file. All of these features were evident in the ROAR coalition of the 1970s.

At the grassroots level, rank and file participated in ROAR primarily by joining quasi-autonomous chapters in at least seven city neighborhoods and perhaps two or three suburbs.[25] The near complete independence of chapters in South Boston, Charlestown, East Boston and other enclaves, of course, was rooted in the historic isolation and parochialism of these defended neighborhoods. The eventual ROAR split demonstrated that even the most passionate single-issue politics could not fully bridge such cleavages or overcome the traditional pulls and tugs of Boston political culture.

While it lasted, the citywide coalition was governed by an eighteen-member executive board largely comprised of neighborhood representatives.

South Boston's Rita Graul, long-time political ally and personal secretary of Mrs. Hicks, served as board president and, in effect, as the voice of her old friend and benefactor. Other strong Hicks supporters on the board were South Boston's Virginia Sheehy and Hyde Park's Richard Laws, ROAR treasurer.

As "national" chairwoman of ROAR, Mrs. Hicks occupied the top organizational rung. Alone in this status, she formally did not sit on ROAR's "E-board," a technicality later carried to absurdity by her supporters in a lame attempt to minimize her domination of the organization's policies. After all, Mrs. Hicks had virtually created ROAR out of the small Save Boston Committee in July 1974. Two characteristics of the Save Boston Committee, a research group dedicated to repealing the Racial Imbalance Act, were thus imprinted on ROAR: First, the organization consisted mostly of women activists, and, second, these women were intensely loyal to Mrs. Hicks. Thus ROAR could not be divorced from the political interests of Louise Day Hicks.[26]

Until spring 1976, when factional strife led the executive board to require formal enrollment, neighborhood ROAR chapter meetings were open to interested residents of the respective communities where gatherings were held. In South Boston, at least, the intimacy of the defended neighborhood prevailed when chapter officers routinely instructed members to inspect persons to their immediate left and right and report any strangers to the marshals. Anyone so identified had to prove residence in South Boston to avoid being ejected.[27] In 1976 members were issued identification cards in return for a $1 fee. In this way ROAR—what was left of it—obtained a formal membership list and a means of excluding various categories of undesirables.

Ritual was important to South Boston chapter meetings, each of which began with the pledge of allegiance and the singing of "Southie Is My Home Town" and "ROAR's Way."[28] A ROAR flag, probably intended to resemble the Irish tricolor, was displayed at all antibusing gatherings, until factional strife made it impolitic in some neighborhoods.

More so than in other neighborhoods, the South Boston movement proliferated structurally beyond ROAR to produce an information center, a legal defense fund, a monthly (later weekly) newspaper, a private school, a vigilante organization, and a small terrorist underground. Other neighborhoods had information centers, but only Charlestown spawned a vigilante organization comparable to the South Boston Marshals. In South Boston, of course, organizational leadership and membership overlapped extensively. Thus the head of the defense fund, James Kelly, also became head of the information center and held important posts in the neighborhood ROAR chapter as well. Mrs. Sheehy was an officer in both the information center and the neighborhood chapter as well as an executive-board member of citywide ROAR. Evidently, the least overlap existed between the South Boston Marshals and all other organizations except the clandestine South Boston Defense League, whose membership probably came almost totally from the marshals.

Antagonists and Constituencies

As would be expected, the different elements of the antibusing movement evidenced substantial agreement in identifying most of their antagonists. On every list were Judge Garrity, the *Globe*, both U.S. senators from Massachusetts, various affluent white liberals, and such leftist organizations as the Committee Against Racism (CAR), the Progressive Labor Party (PLP), and the National Student Coalition Against Racism (NSCAR). As will become clear shortly, the movement was less in agreement about Mayor Kevin White.

The paramount constituency for most South Boston protest elites was their own neighborhood. In some cases, this was true to the point that almost any other population was regarded as beyond the pale. Although activists from other neighborhoods attended South Boston rallies, even a common cause could not overcome traditional neighborhood parochialism. There is every reason to believe a similar localism prevailed in the other defended neighborhoods. When East Boston ROAR leader Pixie Palladino complained publicly about being snubbed at a Charlestown antibusing rally, the response by the head of the Charlestown Marshals was most revealing: "This march was sponsored by Charlestown people and it was held within Charlestown territory. What right does a person from East Boston have to demand anything from us? If Mrs. Palladino has an 'axe to grind,' I suggest she does it in East Boston at rallies she herself sponsors."[29]

A few leaders, such as Mrs. Hicks and Richard Laws, had a broader perspective, but, in the main, the "national" designation for ROAR was hardly appropriate. Even when they trekked to Washington and demonstrated with other antibusing groups for a constitutional amendment to end court-ordered busing, most of the ROAR delegation seemed unable to view the busing issue in a context more general than their neighborhood.

The Uses and Justifications of Violence

Gamson's analysis of how movements are served by violence proved highly relevant to the Boston case. Extraordinary violence was associated with the busing controversy in one way or another, and most of it was perhaps committed by individuals and groups acting on behalf of the antibusing movement. Gamson's insight usefully supplements the literal defense part of the defended-neighborhood model and helps us comprehend the ways in which violence against blacks, white leftists, and other enemies of the movement was condoned.

For example, black people entering South Boston after 1965 often were attacked without provocation. The list of black victims included fishermen, D Street project residents, motorists, people waiting for trains at one of the South Boston subway stations, bus drivers, and passengers. Indeed, strangers of any race ran some risk if they sought to enjoy South Boston's beaches when tensions were high. Although protest spokesmen generally expressed regret about such incidents, invariably they went on to absolve local assailants of personal responsibility for their actions. The rationale generally began by enumerating previous instances of black mayhem against whites and almost always ended by transferring responsibility to Judge Garrity for having created an environment in which such violence had become commonplace.

Such reasoning dominated a South Boston ROAR meeting soon after the 1976 assault on Theodore Landsmark at City Hall (described in chapter 1). Incensed by extensive press coverage of the affair, ROAR members raged against the news media for not reviewing the case of a white nurse set afire by black youths in Roxbury, the stoning to death of an elderly white man fishing near Columbia Point, and other incidents of racial violence in which whites were the victims. An especially exercised resident recounted a recent school fight in which a white boy's nose had been broken. Noting the lack of press coverage of this injury and pointing up Landsmark's much reported broken nose, he angrily asked, "Ain't his nose as good as the other?" Someone promptly declared that nobody's nose would have been broken had Garrity kept his own nose out of Boston's affairs. Garrity, another member of the audience proclaimed, really was responsible for Landsmark's drubbing.[30] All antibusing activists interviewed after the Landsmark affair took the same position.

Extensive press coverage of black violence against whites seldom penetrated the anger of most antibusing respondents. When such reporting was acknowledged, it was almost invariably dismissed as projecting a double standard under which blacks were always victims of white racism and whites were always bigoted hoodlums. One respondent made the point with great conviction:

My wife was called a white honkey whore, a white slut. She was told they were going to take over her daughters and her home. These are these poor little deprived Negro children that weren't getting a quality education that were screaming these things out the window. But all you ever see is people in South Boston screaming, you don't see what the blacks do. You don't see the people that go into Columbia Point housing project. They made a wrong turn, and they got hit with pieces of sidewalk and everything else . . . It's always white people that are doing these things. It's always those awful bigots from South Boston.[31]

Another context in which violence won unanimous aproval was defending the neighborhood against invasions in force. A case in point was the 3 May 1975 "march against racism" which the PLP, CAR, and other leftist groups intended to hold in South Boston. As the main column moved out of North Dorchester, it was preceded by a "strike team" outfitted in combat boots and studded leather straps; some wore helmets or carried canes and bats. An accompanying sound truck blared, "Hitler, Hicks, Same Old Tricks" and "Death to the Fascists." Police later blamed the strike team for starting the actual fighting. In any event, perhaps a thousand South Boston men and boys fell upon the march as it entered the neighborhood. Rocks, bats, hockey sticks and other lethal weapons were used without restraint in the ensuing melee. The march was stopped.[32]

Two months later, several black salesmen from out of town unknowingly stopped to enjoy Carson Beach in South Boston and instantly came under attack. Governor Michael Dukakis proclaimed the beach open to all, and vowed police would enforce public access if necessary. Any lingering misgivings on the part of South Boston residents about local youths attacking blacks likely evaporated when black leaders vowed to test the governor's promise on 10 August with hundreds of demonstrators. Now the issue became an invasion of South Boston territory, at least in the eyes of residents, and scores of police were required to separate the two sides on the announced day. Perhaps forty were hurt in the exchanges of rocks and bottles. Carson Beach was the site of a similar confrontation two years later.

Violence against the despised TPF also found general acceptance in South Boston and Charlestown, where the elite police unit was accused of wanton brutality.[33] A "men only" march against busing on 15 February 1976 brought this issue to a head in South Boston.

According to their parade permit, two columns of antibusing marchers were supposed to leave the Andrew Square and Broadway MBTA stations at 1:00 p.m., converge at Perkins Square, and proceed together to nearby Dorchester Heights for a rally above South Boston High. Tensions were already high when the two groups moved out on schedule, and they heightened further when some marchers in the Broadway contingent produced clubs and hockey sticks, while others scrounged for rocks and bottles along the route. Reacting to similar preparations and considerable drinking in the Andrew Square group, nine police tried to divert it from the rendezvous at Perkins Square. Instead the Andrew Square marchers swept the police aside, but not before several protesters had been clubbed to the pavement. A roar of triumph resounded when the two columns met. At this point, the marchers and several hundred onlookers surged up G Street directly to South Boston High, thus violating a Garrity order and local police restrictions. At this point they were met by perhaps sixty police, including TPF in riot gear, mounted and canine units. Inexplicably, none of the several high-ranking police officers spoke so much as a word to redirect the gathering crowd or demand its dispersal. Instead, a silent police line temporarily dammed what was swiftly becoming a raging tide of cursing, chanting marchers, frustrated to the point of turning on strangers in their midst. Rocks soon arched overhead into police lines and, when someone tossed an enormous firecracker at police horses, the TPF charged. Scores of police and civilians were injured in the next hour's seesaw battle for control of G Street, finally decided by police reinforcements. Reportedly, the South Boston Marshals gave out clubs and other weapons nearby, introduced tear gas to the riot by using it on police, and monitored all police radio calls.[34]

The battle for G Street had hardly ended before the police and South Boston antibusing leaders began to fight for symbolic control of how the riot was to be interpreted. Police Commissioner di Grazia presided over a press conference where all manner of cudgels confiscated from rioters were displayed, and promised to put 500 police in South Boston if necessary to suppress its "hoodlums." Antibusing leaders immediately began referring to the event as the "fathers march," and held their own press conference to recount instances of police brutality during the riot. They correctly accused the police of having violated a valid parade permit, but overlooked that many of the injured had come armed and spoiling for a fight. The saga of innocents savagely beaten without provocation by police stormtroopers soon became an important movement myth.

Another tacitly approved application of violence was the selective expulsion of residents who objected to the protest and wished to comply with federal policy. Drawn to one another by common disapproval of South Boston's response to Phase 1, a handful of parents who met frequently at a local Catholic center decided in 1975 to form a countervailing organization, the South Boston Task Force for Positive Action. One member explained the group's purposes in a newspaper interview:

> I've lived in Southie all my life, and it hurts me that people around the world know us only as violent people. That's got to be changed. The South Boston Task Force for Positive Action wants the area free of stoning of people, stoning of school buses, free of tire slashing and violent demonstrations in front of schools and buses. We want no more . . . insults or racial slurs. And we want the slurs and racial epithets removed from buildings and streets.[35]

The task force attracted immediate media notice, and those members identified by newspaper stories soon found themselves victims of property destruction, hate mail, obscene phone calls, and other harassment. At least one member's car was firebombed, and several were driven out of the neighborhood. A woman later forced to leave recalled neighbors' reactions to her position:

> I had terrible reactions . . . when I spoke out for black people. . . . "Don't you realize the niggers will take over?" they jeered. "Don't you know that those black kids have been in jail, that they're from the youth service board and they're coming to take over our schools? We'll never send our kids to school." That's the way they talked . . . and they were wild because I had a different viewpoint. They no longer talked to me. They slashed my tires. The pressure was terrible. Then I got mad. "I have a choice," I told them, "I can send my kids or not send my kids to school." I don't interfere with how they raise their children, so why should they interfere with me? But please don't retaliate. Don't hurt my children.[36]

By January 1976 the task force no longer existed.

There was also a tendency in some quarters to justify violence simply on the grounds that it was done by local people. Speaking to this point, an important member of the South Boston Information Center staff averred: " . . . . We have never offered excuses for our actions. We may be guilty, but we'll still fight you. We might go out in back here and fight, and I might tear your eyes out. It's wrong, maybe, but we'll stand by our actions."[37]

The most extreme stand on violence was taken by the underground terrorists belonging to the South Boston Defense League. Police and FBI focused chiefly on this group in a 1975 investigation of rumored plans to blow up all South Boston bridges. Evidently, members of the defense league carried out the 14 June 1975 baseball bat attack on CAR pickets in North Dorchester. On 19 May 1977 the defense league claimed credit for the firebombing of a communist bookshop in North Dorchester the previous evening. In a tape released to a Boston radio station the Defense League set out its policy:

> . . . . Not only will we not tolerate these [leftist] groups in South Boston, but we will seek them out wherever they go as a defensive measure. . . . We do not want these left-wing scum to infect our community with their social sickness. . . . We will use violence to protect our community. South Boston is tough, independent, and white, and will stay that way forever. God help any outsider who tries to change it.[38]

An interesting footnote to such violence is that some antibusing elites condoned even the defense league, but would have no part of the Ku Klux Klan or Nazis, both of which attempted to join the neighborhood protest. When the Nazis tried to set up a storefront in South Boston, antibusing activists picketed the building and otherwise persuaded its tenants to depart in March 1975. Outsiders, with their separate perspectives, simply were not wanted.

The extent to which violence over busing became commonplace in South Boston cannot be fully understood until one turns to the almost daily strife inside South Boston High during the first two phases of desegregation. Inspection of the school's attendance records of the period revealed wild fluctuations from one day to the next as fighting, walkouts, mass refusals to attend classes, early dismissals, and so on, made a shambles out of the educational process. Police installed metal detectors in October 1974 to keep knives, brass knuckles, hatpins and the like out of the school, but combatants of both races soon made innovative use of padlocks, hairpicks, pencils, and shop tools. State police patrolled the hallways and faculty teams conducted corridor sweeps while classes were in session. Black and white students apprehended for troublemaking were placed in separate holding rooms.

December 1974 was one of the worst of many turbulent periods for South Boston High. Six days suffice to illustrate the point:

4 December: Two students hurt in racial fight in the metal shop; one arrested for assault with a deadly weapon.

5 December: Fifty to sixty black and white girls involved in fighting throughout the main building; thirty black girls sent home early while one hundred twenty-five whites walkout.

6 December: Police escort three hundred white students from the school after a meeting with the headmaster; extra police are summoned to disperse the group, which reformed outside the school; outraged parents start protesting this action.

9 December: Several students injured in fights; the South Boston Home and School Association asks that classes be suspended.

10 December: Additional police inside and nearby the school as parents picket outside to show ire over the 6 December incident; several students suspended after fighting in the cafeteria; two black girls arrested for beating a white girl with padlocks.

11 December: Perhaps the worst day in the school's history; at 10:00 A.M., a white student is gravely wounded by a knife-wielding black student and removed by ambulance; classes are canceled and all whites sent home; word spreads rapidly through the neighborhood, and a hostile crowd forms outside before buses arrive to pick up black students; Mrs. Hicks appears and appeals to the ever growing crowd to allow the buses through to collect black students, but neither her pleas nor 125 riot police were able to move the crowd; using the school buses as decoys to divert crowd attention, police evacuate the black students in other vehicles; the school does not reopen until 8 January 1975.[39]

Why so much violence for so long in South Boston High? Most antibusing respondents began answering the question by denying racial problems were unique to their school. According to information center spokesmen, almost every middle and high school in the city experienced serious racial tensions, and violence was far more commonplace than generally recognized. White students at Madison Park High, for example, supposedly paid extortion money to blacks in order to use the restrooms, and a recent stabbing of a white at Boston Technical reportedly had brought previous violence there to light. If South Boston seemed different in kind, according to antibusing respondents, it was because of a greater degree of violence and an official cover-up of the true incidence of it in other schools.[40]

Most respondents went on from this point to argue that black students generally were disruptive products of an "alien" culture. Although some attempted to separate race and class in making the claim, very few avoided lapsing into sweeping characterizations of the black population. From the respondents' point of view, the vast majority of black students were predators, socialized into an underclass culture in which sloth, chronic dependency, immorality, violence, and crime were normative. Egged on by black nationalists and given judicial fiat to menace the "racists" of South Boston, they came to school primed for violence and full of shrill demands that the neighborhood students swallow local pride, confess error, and bend to the new order. Violence thus was inevitable, according to respondents, for local youth already embittered over the disruption of their education, and filled with pride of neighborhood, were unwilling to react meekly to such provocations.

In summary, violence was central to the antibusing protest in numerous ways. So much had occurred by the time this research began that most respondents refused to engage in abstract distinctions between the justifiable and the unjustifiable. Events had undermined the capacity to look upon outrages, such as a tire-iron beating of an elderly black man in the Boston Common, as wrong per se. Instead, the incident was judged minor in comparison to what a hundred blacks did to a white mechanic in Roxbury. Moreover, blaming Garrity for creating the climate causing such violence permitted neighborhood defenders to evade individual responsibility for their own violence.

Other Protest Methods

The antibusing movement also practiced aggressive "civil disobedience" tactics. In addition to pray-in's, sit-in's, and other nonviolent resistance, they also confronted antagonists in situations where a high potential for violence was created.

A fairly common ROAR tactic was intimidation of other groups by invading their public meetings. Antibusing activists arrived in force and simply drowned out anyone else with their chants and screams. In this way protesters against busing forced an early end to an Equal Rights Amendment rally at Faneuil Hall on 9 April 1975. On 12 February 1976 ROAR supporters of George Wallace in the Massachusetts Democratic presidential primary hounded Senator Henry Jackson from a Charlestown stage. Later in the same day, several busloads of activists drove from the South Boston Information Center to English High, where they disrupted a CCC meeting called to discuss Phase 2B. Allowing no one else to speak, they took over the microphone and chanted or sang until CCC Chairman Arthur Gartland adjourned the session. Although Boston police observed the affair, they took no action other than to escort the buses back to South Boston. At the next CCC meeting, however, fifty or more police were on hand and no disruption occurred.

ROAR liked to drive its point home in literal fashion by massing at the residences or offices of individual antagonists. Thus about three thousand assembled at the home of Governor Dukakis on 1 December 1974. A huge motorcade with seven hundred participants drove to the Wellesley home of the 1974 United Way chairman on 13 April 1975 to express displeasure over allocation of funds to probusing groups. On 8 June 1975 another thousand trekked to South Natick to intimidate *Globe* publisher John Taylor. A month later, perhaps fifty ROAR activists seized Mayor White's hospitality suite in the Sheraton-Boston hotel to dramatize their cause to the U.S. Conference of Mayors, hosted by White. Shortly after Judge Garrity placed South Boston High in receivership, antibusing demonstraters took over four senatorial and congressional offices in the John F. Kennedy federal building. The sit-in's ended after telephone conversations with representatives O'Neill and Moakley and both senators. About twenty-five ROAR members camped in the office of Massachusetts Attorney General Francis Bellotti on 27 May 1976 until he agreed to meet with them to explain a recent brief supporting Boston busing.[41]

Easily the most objectionable politician to the antibusing movement was Senator Kennedy, and some ROAR members undertook a campaign to make his every visit to Boston miserable. Thus on 6 April 1976 Kennedy was physically harassed by about three-hundred protesters in Quincy and forced to flee aboard a subway train after someone disabled his limousine. As the chief organizer of this campaign, Pixie Palladino of East Boston denied responsibility for the damage to Kennedy's car, and promised more harassment:

> We told Senator Kennedy many months ago, until he changes his position on busing, we'd be everywhere he would be. He refuses to acknowledge what we're all about. He's voting his conscience instead of the will of the people. . . . He said let the chips fall where they may and the chips are coming down like a snowstorm.[42]

In subsequent Boston visits Kennedy had to contend with ROAR pickets and hecklers, but managed to avoid physical contact with his tormentors.

Another protest tactic, as noted by Gamson, is to discredit individual antagonists by exposing unsavory aspects of their personal background. Several respondents in South Boston claimed to know of investigations into the personal lives of elected officials and reporters, but little appeared to come of such efforts.

Apparently, economic boycotts against selected antagonists were no more successful. The *Globe* supposedly was the target of such a campaign in 1975 and 1976, and perhaps subscriptions and classifieds were reduced in South Boston, but the paper sold well at neighborhood newsstands and obviously was read by protest leaders.[43] One respondent claimed residents had punished the Catholic hierarchy's probusing posture by withholding significant sums from the annual Cardinal's Stewardship Fund, but the archdiocese maintained no knowledge of any such gesture and reported overall increases in the fund for the years in question.[44]

Of course, the movement expressed its grievances through marches and rallies, at least one of which drew about thirty-thousand people to downtown Boston. After ROAR's fatal split however, such demonstrations were staged in a few defended neighborhoods and the number of participants steadily declined over time. Antibusing activists received a sympathetic hearing on one or two local radio talk shows. A few did extensive research into school-desegregation case law, busing programs in other cities, and conditions in the Boston schools.

Acceptance and Factionalism

It makes sense to group acceptance and factionalism because acceptance greatly exacerbated the factionalism that split the citywide antibusing coalition asunder. ROAR gained acceptance in at least three ways stipulated by Gamson. First, Mrs. Hicks and a few others gained recognition as authoritative representatives of the movement by testifying before the U.S. Commission on Civil Rights and the state legislature. Frequent press interviews reinforced their status. Mayor White gave the movement another form of acceptance by periodically negotiating with Mrs. Hicks and other protest leaders. And the mayor's distribution of city jobs to protesters through Mrs. Hicks amounted to yet another form of acceptance: inclusion of challenging group members in an antagonistic organization without apparent loss of their roles in the movement.

When the formal ROAR schism of 1976 is examined, Louise Day Hicks again emerged as the central figure. ROAR had been founded on the premise that busing took precedence over politics-as-usual. Hence the organization's by-laws proscribed endorsement of candidates for public office without executive board approval, and members of the executive board were not supposed to themselves become candidates. The point of these restrictions was to steer ROAR clear of the treacherous currents of local politics so that it could function as a unified force. In 1975 ROAR demonstrated what its unity could mean by taking a decisive role in defeating Mayor White's Question 7, a referendum by which he sought to gain control of the school committee.

Sobered by this defeat and worried about his own reelection that year, White reportedly started to cultivate his old adversary. Just returned to public office after losing her congressional seat, Mrs. Hicks evidently found more gain than loss in reciprocating. As head of the city council's Ways and Means Committee, she was well-positioned to assist or hinder city hall budgets.[45]

No doubt the new White-Hicks relationship was crucial to the subsequent splintering of ROAR into two factions. The pattern first became evident when ROAR began to debate its position in the 1975 mayoral campaign, and it reappeared the following year in a dispute over endorsement of presidential candidates and acceptance of federal busing funds.

Reportedly, Mayor White and Mrs. Hicks agreed that ROAR would not endorse any mayoral candidate in 1975. While White had no chance of winning such an endorsement, denying it to his opponent in the runoff was said to be critical to his strategy. Weakened by busing, allegations of corruption in his administration, and general voter disaffection, White did not want ROAR's full might again used against him. In any case, the Hicks majority on ROAR's executive board refused to endorse any candidate in the preliminary election, including South Boston's Ray Flynn whose antibusing stand was unequivocal. When the contest narrowed to White and State Senator Joseph Timilty, the Hicks faction against kept ROAR neutral despite general rank-and-file contempt for "Mayor Black." White eked out a victory.

The cleavage formed in 1975 was deepened in the following year's Massachusetts Democratic presidential primary. Most ROAR members enthusiastically endorsed George Wallace, but Mrs. Hicks embraced Senator Henry Jackson, Mayor White's candidate. She even journeyed to Washington, D.C., to testify in favor of a Jackson measure to fund special programs and jobs in school systems ordered to undergo busing. Although

Mrs. Hicks carefully distinguished between her views and ROAR positions, her appearance set off a sharp debate in ROAR. Most ROAR leaders were outspoken in favor of Wallace, who was given an enthusiastic welcome in South Boston.

In reality the rift went much deeper than mere disagreement over candidates and extended to fundamentally divergent conceptions of what the antibusing protest was all about. To some ROAR members, White was no less the enemy than Garrity or the *Globe*, and accepting extra federal money under Jackson's bill, if ever passed, was tantamount to accepting busing. Not until matters reached crisis proportions would enough Americans support the constitutional amendment required to stop busing, the argument continued, and bringing Boston to the brink of fiscal collapse was one way of speeding the crisis. Helping White obtain more desegregation money would only forestall the crisis and subsequent public awakening.

Evidently, Mrs. Hicks entertained a different view, one educated in the byzantine byways of Boston politics, in which yesterday's foe is tomorrow's potential ally and no cause depends upon heaven for its rewards. Hers was a more discriminating perspective on the movement's antagonists, one that did not place White in the same class with Judge Garrity. If the mayor was hardly all the movement had hoped for, he had greatly disappointed blacks, liberals and other busing supporters too. Destroying Boston's credit would not stop busing, but the Jackson bill would provide tangible resources for city hall and its friends.

These issues came to a head on 29 February 1976 when ROAR's executive board expelled Mrs. Palladino by a twelve-to-six vote, ostensibly for holding a school-committee office while serving on the board. By even larger margins, the board banished several other members for actions "counterproductive to the anti-forced busing movement," and cut ties with the rebellious Hyde Park Information Center, whose members were notified not to attend future ROAR meetings.[46] Soon afterward, Mrs. Palladino and her supporters formed United ROAR, while the Hicks-dominated organization became ROAR, Inc.

Once this conflict became public, the two factions exchanged recriminations through the press. The Palladino side won the media battle by revealing numerous ties between city hall and the Hicks faction. Doubtless it assisted Joe Conason of *The Real Paper*, who exposed a large number of Hicks supporters to be city employees, especially in the school department.[47] One of the most interesting disclosures was the South Boston High transitional aide job given in 1975 to Warren Zaniboni, the hulking chief of the South Boston Marshals. "There is a certain inconsistency in his taking the job," Conason wrote, "its description is helping teachers and administrators with peaceful implementation of school desegregation."[48] Zaniboni had obtained a better-paying position with Parks and Recreation by the time this report was published. Virginia Sheehy of the ROAR executive board and South Boston Information Center was incorrectly identified as a clerk-typist for the school department; her real title was "information specialist."[49] Another board member supervised evening meetings in school buildings, and his son worked as a school supply attendant. Several vociferous foes of busing who wrote for South Boston weeklies were also named as school employees, although at least one had been hired before desegregation. Likely the same was true for others in the story, but a certain irony lingered over these revelations nonetheless. Trust the Palladino faction to drive it home: "Here we are breaking our butts to fight forced busing, and her [Hicks'] people are all holding jobs and making money off it."[50]

Conclusion

Ironically, by gaining acceptance from city hall, Mrs. Hicks unwittingly hastened the collapse of her citywide organization. White could not have asked for a better return on his investment of a few, mostly low-paid and temporary jobs.

Even if the ROAR presidium had remained united against White, however, the local political culture eventually would have taken its toll. ROAR embraced too many "mortal friends" in the persons of Mrs. Hicks, John Kerrigan, Albert "Dapper" O'Neil, and others whose ambitions often conflicted. Moreover it was constructed atop the sociological equivalent of the San Andreas fault, the fiercely autonomous enclaves whose parochialism undermined any common cause. Although single-issue politics might breathe new vigor into each defended neighborhood, an enduring coalition of such communities was quite another matter.

This chapter reiterated the point that the defended neighborhood and protest are not the same thing; a protest is but a brief moment in the longer life of a defended neighborhood. This distinction pointed up the need of additional perspectives to understand the South Boston response to busing.

Such perspectives are found in solidarity and discontent models and in the Gamson framework. Of course, solidarity theory reinforced the defended-neighborhood image of protesters as well-integrated and deeply concerned members of their community, but it lacked an explicit linkage to events outside sufficiently threatening to generate organized protest. Discontent theory furnished the connection and provided a further corrective with its emphasis on the marginal character of at least some protesters. Indeed, both views inform analysis of the South Boston backlash, which drew upon a wide spectrum of residents, from long-active parents to petty hoodlums and inebriates often unable to stand at protest functions. Gamson's framework provided insights into the uses and justifications of violence. Gamson might well have emphasized more the corrosive effects of long-term violence, and the fading capacity to discriminate between self-defense and indefensible brutality. Finally, Gamson informed our understanding of the costs and benefits of protest acceptance, including the greater risk of factionalism.

Despite all of the resistance described above, the federal desegregation program moved inexorably from one phase to another. In the process of forcing this change, antibusing activists charged, Judge Garrity and his allies destroyed the Boston public schools. The next chapter examines the particulars of their indictment.

Notes

1. See Robert R. Alford and Harry M. Scoble, "Sources of Local Political Involvement," *American Political Science Review* 62 (December 1968):1192-1206.

2. This discussion of discontent and solidarity theory primarily relies upon Bert Useem's account in "Solidarity Model, Breakdown Model, And The Boston Anti-Busing Movement," *American Sociological Review* 45 (June 1980):357-369.

3. Ibid. The other neighborhoods were Hyde Park and West Roxbury.

4. Ibid., p. 368.

5. See items 37 and 106 in Bert Useem, "The Boston Anti-Busing Movement and Social Movement Theory" (Ph.D. diss., Brandeis University, 1980), pp. 156 and 167.

6. See David O'Brian, "On Patrol: Night-Riding With The Marshals," *Boston Phoenix*, 18 May 1967, p. 6.

7. Interview by Buell, 19 July 1976.

8. William A. Gamson, *The Strategy of Social Protest* (Homewood, Ill.: Dorsey, 1975).

9. Ibid., p. 33.

10. Ibid., p. 81.

11. Ibid., p. 101.

12. Interview by Buell, 14 June 1977.

13. Interview by Buell, 29 June 1977.

14. Interview by Buell, 16 June 1977.

15. Interview by Buell, 11 July 1977.

16. Interview by Buell, 15 July 1977.

17. Interview by Buell, 17 June 1977.

18. Interview by Buell, 14 July 1977.

19. Interview by Buell, 11 July 1977.

20. Interview by Buell, 14 June 1977.

21. Interview by Buell, 16 June 1977.

22. Buell's notes of South Boston ROAR rally, 29 February 1976.

23. Computed from the frequency distributions given for items 4, 14, 28, 36 and 107 in the appendix to Useem, "The Boston Anti-Busing Movement," pp. 148-167.

24. Bert Useem's generosity in making these neighborhood breakdowns in a special tabulation is most appreciated. Useem's sample frame included only white residents between twenty-five and fifty-three years of age who were U.S. citizens. See Useem, "Solidarity Model, Breakdown Model," p. 30 for more information on sample design.

25. The neighborhoods were West Roxbury, Roslindale, Jamaica Plain, Hyde Park, East Boston, Charlestown, and South Boston.

26. Interview by Buell, 15 July 1977. See also Kathleen Kilgore, "Militant Mothers: The Politicization of ROAR Women," *The Real Paper*, 13 November 1976, p. 4.

27. Always picked out as a stranger at ROAR meetings, Buell had to prove he resided in South Boston at every meeting attended.

28. The song had no less than four verses and is sung to the tune of "I Did It My Way." See the *South Boston Tribune*, 10 June 1976, p. 10 for the lyrics.

29. Quoted in "Tug of ROAR," *Boston Phoenix*, 25 May 1976, p. 8.

30. Buell's notes of ROAR meeting on 6 April 1976 at South Boston's Cathedral Hall.

31. Interview by Buell, 11 July 1977.

32. See "Clashes Mar May Day March in S. Boston," *Boston Globe*, 4 May 1975, p. 1; "Anti-Busing Violence in South Boston and Dorchester: ROAR And The Vigilantes," *The Real Paper*, 9 July 1975, p. 4.

33. Two violent episodes brought into the open the antipathy between TPF officers and antibusing protesters. After TPF officers were assaulted outside an Andrew Square taproom 4 October 1975, a larger number of TPF returned the following day and wrecked the place, beating up numerous marshals and other protesters. One year later, three South Boston men charged TPF officers had attacked them without provocation. Movement spokespersons in South Boston and Charlestown demanded the TPF's removal from their neighborhoods on several occasions.

34. This account is based on Buell's observation of the riot and the following sources: "Police, Busing Foes Battle in South Boston," *Boston Globe*, 16 February 1976, p. 1; "Busing Protest Explodes Into Riot," *Boston Herald-American*, 16 February 1976, p. 1; "Police, Marchers Blame Each Other For Southie Clash," *Boston Globe*, 17 February 1976, p. 1; and, "Anarchy, Not Busing, Blamed for Riots," *Boston Herald-American*, 18 February 1976, p. 3.

35. Quoted in "South Boston: The Voices of Reason," *Boston Sunday Herald-Advertiser*, 24 August 1975, p. 1.

36. Ibid.

37. Interview by Buell, 14 June 1977.

38. Quoted in Joe Conason, "Southie Group Threatens Left With Violence," *The Real Paper*, 9 April 1977, p. 3; see also "Southie Goons Strike Again," *The Real Paper*, 4 June 1977, p. 3.

39. Selected from Wendy Bauman, "Boston Busing: A Chronology, 1849-1975," *Boston Globe* microfilm. National television network news extensively reported the stabbing incident. See the following videotapes at the Vanderbilt University Television News Archive: ABC Evening News, 11 December 1974, 5:07:10 p.m. to 5:08:50 p.m.; CBS Evening News, 5:39:30 p.m. to 5:45:30 p.m. (includes a special segment on South Boston's "isolated Irish"); and, NBC Nightly News, 5:43:50 p.m. to 5:45:50 p.m. All times CST.

40. In various publications the U.S. Commission on Civil Rights has contended that only a few Boston schools experienced serious racial disorder during the first two years of busing, but this claim rests on police *arrest* statistics, surely a gross understatement of true violence. See *Desegregating the Boston Public Schools* (1975), p. 95; and, *Fulfilling the Letter and Spirit of the Law* (1976), p. 17. Claims by antibusers that school administrators elsewhere in the city deliberately understated violence in their facilities to protect their positions cannot be verified, hence the dispute is not amenable to empirical resolution.

41. *Boston Globe* microfilm chronology; see also "Busing Foes Invade Congressmen's Offices," *Boston Herald-American*, 17 December 1975; and, "Protesters Crowd Bellotti's Office Over His High Court Brief On Busing," *Boston Globe*, 28 May 1976, p. 5.

42. Quoted in "Anti-Bus Group Acts To Ruin Kennedy Politically," *Boston Herald-American*, 8 April 1976, p. 5.

43. A South Boston doctor and prominent antibusing activist interviewed by Buell 29 June 1976 characterized the *Boston Globe* as "left of Stalin," and swore he never read it. Months later Buell observed him at a downtown athletic club engrossed in the *Boston Globe* sports section.

44. Unfortunately it was not possible to obtain parish data on Stewardship Fund collections.

45. This account draws primarily on "Tug of ROAR"; "ROAR, Hicks Differ On U.S. Busing Funds Bill," *Boston Evening Globe*, 10 March 1976, p. 4; "Palladino Sets Steps For Her To Quit ROAR Board," *Boston Evening Globe*, 11 March 1976, p. 12; Joe Conason, "The ROAR Split Over Money And Wallace," *The Real Paper*, 17 March 1976, p. 3; and, also by Conason, "On The Other ROAR," *The Real Paper*, 14 April 1976, p. 4.

46. "Results of February 29, 1976 ROAR Executive Board Meeting," (ditto), distributed 3 March 1976 at ROAR meeting in South Boston's Cathedral Hall.

47. See "I Got My Job Through ROAR And Louise Day Hicks," *The Real Paper*, 9 June 1976, p. 16.

48. Ibid.

49. Joe Conason, "ROAR's Job Deniability," *The Real Paper*, 16 June 1976, p. 3.

50. Quoted in "I Got My Job Through ROAR And Louise Days Hicks," p. 17.

9

The Disputed Impact
of Boston Busing

Antibusing Claims

Almost every antibusing activist interviewed for this study maintained that busing had devastated Boston in at least four ways: first, "forced busing" had caused prodigious white flight from the public schools; second, enough schools had resegregated since Phase 1 to make racial imbalance worse than ever before; third, educational quality in the public schools had been ruined in the process, thus proving there was "nothing at the end of the bus ride" for blacks or whites; and, fourth, the costs of implementing Judge Garrity's programs were directly responsible for the city's 1976 fiscal crisis and a staggering property tax increase.

This chapter investigates each assertion to the extent allowed by limited information, insufficient passage of time for assessment, and time and space constraints. While some contentions cannot be fully confirmed or rejected at this time, each at least can be discussed.

White Flight

Few subjects have generated as much professional rancor in the social sciences as the disputed impact of school desegregation on already declining white enrollments.[1] Although leading antagonists in the debate now agree on some busing effects, other important issues remain in dispute.[2] Ideally, it should be possible to disentangle the various causes of steadily dropping white public-school enrollments. Yet most white-flight studies to date have relied upon aggregate analysis rather than surveys with students and parents, hence the importance of such factors as dissatisfaction with city school quality, rising violence in the schools, racial prejudice, and so on, are rarely addressed directly.[3] Unfortunately, the present discussion is similarly limited, for it rests upon simple enrollment data.

Numerous white-flight studies have found school desegregation-related white enrollment dropoff to be most severe in big city districts where black students are a third or more of total enrollments. Reynolds Farley and Clarence Wurdock reported that significant desegregation efforts in such districts generally produced a white loss rate in the implementation year twice the normal attrition in previous years.[4] Christine Rossell saw a "temporarily disintegrative effect'' in doubled and even tripled white attrition during the first several years of school desegregation.[5] By the fourth year, however, white decline had almost ceased; in some districts the white proportion of total enrollments even increased slightly. But this was not so in "city districts at or above 35 percent black with two-way reassignment plans," where the white proportion fell in the fourth year of implementation, albeit at a slower rate.[6] Another study attributed 24 percent of white student decline in nonsouthern central-city districts between 1968 and 1976 to school desegregation. Possible reasons for this loss were public repudiation of unpopular judicial policy, powerful neighborhood school attachments, and difficulties associated with big-city school desegregation.[7]

Turning to Boston, table 9-1 compares white student dropoff associated with busing to previous white decline. The table reports yearly white enrollments from 1964-1965 through 1980-1981 gives annual white percentages of total enrollments, and indicates both the numerical and proportional falloff in white enrollments over the previous year.[8]

Of course, court-ordered busing was associated with steep decline in white enrollments during the first two phases of Judge Garrity's program. Clearly a large, if undetermined, number of white parents took their children out of

Table 9-1
White Enrollment Decline in Boston Public Schools, 1964-1980

Academic Year	White Enrollments	White Percentages	Numerical Change from Previous Year	Percentage Change from Previous Year
1964-1965	69,919	75.6	− 784	− 1.1
1965-1966	69,136	74.3	− 783	− 1.1
1966-1967	68,050	73.9	− 1,086	− 1.6
1967-1968	67,028	72.5	− 1,022	− 1.5
1968-1969	64,500	68.5	− 2,528	− 3.8
1969-1970	62,657	66.0	− 1,843	− 2.9
1970-1971	62,014	64.1	− 643	− 1.0
1971-1972	59,390	61.5	− 2,624	− 4.2
1972-1973	56,893	59.5	− 2,497	− 4.2
1973-1974	53,593	57.2	− 3,300	− 5.8
1974-1975[a]	44,937	52.4	− 8,656	− 16.2
1975-1976[b]	41,407	48.7	− 3,530	− 7.9
1976-1977	34,561	46.8	− 6,846	− 16.5
1977-1978	31,014	41.7	− 3,547	− 10.3
1978-1979	28,094	39.4	− 2,290	− 9.4
1979-1980	25,527	37.3	− 2,567	− 9.1
1980-1981	24,067	35.4	− 1,460	− 5.7

Sources: Data for 1964-1965 (an estimate), 1965-1966, and 1966-1967 were taken from Christine Rossell, "Boston's Desegregation and White Flight," *Integrated Education,* 15 (January-February 1977), table 1, p. 36; all other data provided in a special tabulation by the Department of Implementation, Boston Public Schools.
[a]Phase 1.
[b]Phase 2.

the public schools because of busing and related issues. On the other hand, as the table also shows, white enrollments had fallen steadily throughout the previous decade. As the fifth column illustrates, however, comparable numerical losses register as greater and greater *proportional* reductions when computed on a steadily declining numerical base. Hence the 2,624 drop in white enrollment for 1971-1972 amounted to only a 4.2 percent loss, while the 2,290 whites lost between 1978 and 1979 came out to be a 9.4 percent drop.

Almost no survey data were available at this writing to provide a clearer picture of motivations underlying such reductions. One bit of census information suggests that school concerns mattered little in decisions by Bostonians to move to the suburbs.[9] A recent study of the Boston school-desegregation controversy found no meaningful link between busing opposition and moving to suburbia.[10] However, suggestive, such findings hardly exhaust all the possibilities. "White flight" need not be expressed in suburban migration. Many families with school children in South Boston and other defended neighborhoods simply could not afford to move out of the city. Hence dropout statistics and transfer to private schools are more likely better indicators of their behavior.

In overwhelmingly Catholic Boston a private school typically is a Catholic school. In 1974 Cardinal Medeiros authorized an archdiocese proclamation closing Catholic schools to whites seeking to escape busing.[11] Yet reports persist that archdiocese schools were a haven for whites leaving the Boston public schools after Phase 1.[12] Did the Catholic schools take a significant number of whites fleeing desegregation?

A complete answer cannot be provided without additional information about transfer students. Available data suggest that few, if any, Catholic schools were havens for Boston whites. Analysis of all archdiocese school enrollments for 1970 through 1978 disclosed a 29 percent drop in white suburban parochial-school enrollments and a 28 percent drop in white city parochial-school enrollments over this period. The trend hardly suggests significant absorption of whites from Boston's public schools.

Yet closer examination of schools by location and grade level uncovers an interesting discrepancy between suburban Catholic high schools and all other suburban and city Catholic schools. In the three years preceding Phase 1, Catholic suburban high schools exhibited a 10.9 percent decline in white enrollments. Boston's initial year of busing saw a 1.6 percent *increase* in white students, however, and the rate of white decline over the next four years was merely 2.8 percent. In contrast, Catholic high schools in the city continued to drop in white enrollments at about the same pace as before; in the four years following Phase 1 their overall white loss was 12.9 percent. Catholic elementary and middle schools in the suburbs had declining white enrollments comparable to sister institutions in the city after busing started.[13] If some suburban Catholic high schools bent the rules and admitted Boston whites, as was claimed by antibusing activists, the actual numbers of students involved suggest an insignificant impact.

In sum, antibusing spokepersons were partly right in maintaining that busing had drained the Boston public schools of white students. Although it is impossible to derive individual motives directly from enrollment data, by anyone's reckoning the figures for 1974 and 1975 reflect significant white flight. Afterward, however, the actual number of "lost" whites soon aproximated annual reductions noted in the late 1960s and early 1970s. Whether the students withdrawing in busing years differed significantly from those withdrawn earlier is impossible to say. Just how much of the drop after 1974-1975 can be attributed to busing remains at issue, but it is unlikely that earlier reasons for falling white enrollments, such as lower birthrates, ceased to have an effect when busing started.[14]

Racially Imbalanced Schools

Investigation of the second antibusing claim, that busing has made racial imblance worse than ever before, is greatly complicated by shifting definitions of imbalance. The old 50 percent or more nonwhite standard of the Racial Imbalance Act was made obsolete by Phase 2, which divided the Boston public schools into nine districts and established black, white, and "other" racial goals for each district.

These goals and the degree schools could deviate from them varied substantially by district. To make matters even more complex, school administrators and the court's experts changed goals and permitted deviations each year.

In 1976, for example, the court set ideal white enrollment in any district 7 school at 31 percent, but allowed actual enrollments to vary by ±8 percent. Hence, no district 7 school was supposed to have a student body more than 39 percent or less than 23 percent white. In 1977 the white goal was reduced to 29 percent and the range to ±7 percent. The 1976 East Boston (district 8) black goal was only 4 percent, with only ±1 percent permitted by way of deviation. These figures contrasted starkly with the 53 percent black goal and ±13 percent range assigned district 5 schools the same year. In effect, an East Boston school with 6 percent black enrollment exceeded the maximum for black students, but a 66 percent black Dorchester school did not. The ideal combination of American Indians, Asian-Americans, and Hispanics for 1976 varied from 29 percent in district 7 to 2 percent in district 4.[15]

According to judical policy, then, a school could become racially imbalanced on account of enrolling too few or too many whites, too few or too many blacks, too few or too many students of other races. Schools in South Boston illustrate some of the possible combinations.

For example, in 1976 the O'Reilly (K-5) had 34 percent more whites, 23 percent fewer blacks, and 11 percent fewer others than allowed by the district 6 racial goals. Four of the other six South Boston elementary schools were similarly imbalanced. Four years later, the O'Reilly still was over the white maximum by 34 percent, still fell 23 percent below the least-acceptable black figure, and still lagged 11 percent behind the lowest acceptable other goal, even though goals and ranges had been slightly changed. Two of the four primary schools thrice imbalanced in 1976 remained so in 1980, but two others had corrected one type of 1976 imbalance. The Tuckerman (P-5), still excessively white and insufficiently black, had obtained enough pupils of other races, and the Tynan (P-5) had enrolled enough blacks, even though it remained overly white and without enough American Indians, Asians, and Hispanics.

Table 9-2 is the product of a laborious comparison of every Boston public school's racial composition from 1975 through 1980 with the court's annually adjusted district goals over the same period. The table takes account of changing ranges of allowable deviation as well and, in effect, presents Judge Garrity's view of racial imbalance in Boston schools. Despite the dramatic drop in white enrollments reported in table 9-1, according to judical policy, the number of schools with too *many* whites actually increased in recent years. By the same token, the number of schools with too *few* black and other students increased as well. Hence judical policy easily adjusted to circumstances in which whites have become a steadily diminishing minority in the public schools.

Table 9-2
Racial Imbalance in Boston Public Schools according to District Court Guidelines, 1975-1980

Schools with:	1975	1976	1977	1978	1979	1980
Too many whites	20	24	29	23	35	35
Too few whites	47	49	41	47	43	44
Too many blacks	43	43	27	43	27	21
Too few blacks	24	29	28	25	25	37
Too many others	41	36	42	44	33	34
Too few others	52	49	57	48	55	57
Total number of schools in system	162	154	156	156	154	152

Source: Computed from court racial guidelines and yearly enrollments provided in special tabulations by the Department of Implementation, Boston School Department, October and November 1980.

Note: Since a school often exhibited more than one form of racial imbalance, and was counted more than once accordingly, the imbalance cell entries do not sum to the total number of schools in the system for any given year.

Of course, busing foes receive such conclusions with scorn and regard them as additional proof that Boston school desegregation is only an arbitrary numbers game by which massive white losses are translated into Orwellian excesses. Certainly the contemporary judical definition of racial imbalance ill-comports with the old 50 percent or more nonwhite standard of 1965.[16]

Another perspective is obtained by comparing all schools over time, according to a single standard. This is done in table 9-3, where some of the changes wrought by Judge Garrity stand out boldly. An especially sharp break with the old order is apparent in the reduction of schools with less than 1 percent black enrollment and, similarly, in the reduction of 75 percent or more black schools after 1974.

Yet the table also points up a contervailing pattern giving some credence to antibusing claims of steadily growing imbalance. The number of 55 to 64 percent black schools crept upward in the late 1970s and a less consistent trend for 65 to 74 percent black schools also warranted concern. If racial imbalance is defined as 50 percent or more black, a seemingly reasonable figure since black students were never fully half of total enrollments in any year observed, one may even conclude, by inspecting the proportion of 50 percent or more black schools, that racial imbalance was worse after 1977 than before busing began.

Of course, as Mrs. Hicks argued in the 1960s, a desegregated school system can still have imbalanced schools. The real issue is what is done

Table 9-3
Boston Public Schools, by Black Enrollments, 1970-1980

Schools with:	1970	1972	1974	1975	1976	1977	1978	1979	1980
<1% black	41	32	29	1	3	2	2	4	4
1-14% black	65	64	35	11	13	13	12	9	8
15-34% black	23	27	38	47	31	36	28	30	37
35-49% black	14	19	26	67	60	60	63	59	50
50-54% black	3	5	10	11	13	11	12	11	11
55-64% black	6	3	23	16	16	18	18	19	20
65-74% black	9	8	1	8	13	17	16	11	14
75% + black	43	44	27	1	5	1	5	11	8
Total schools 50% + black	61	60	61	36	47	47	51	52	53
Total schools	204	202	189	162	154	156	156	154	152
Percentage of all schools with 50% + black enrollments	30	30	32	22	30	30	33	34	35

Sources: 1970, 1972, and 1976 data published in HEW/OCR reports of enrollments by race and ethnicity for elementary and secondary school districts; data for other years provided by the Department of Implementation, Boston School Department, in special tabulations.

with students of different races within such a system. Table 9-4 reports two conventional measures of the desegregation accomplished through Judge Garrity's orders. The Taeuber scores show the significantly greater proportions of students enrolled in schools with racial compositions approximating overall racial proportions in the entire student population, whereas Coleman standardized indexes capture an enormous increase in the probability of the average black pupil having white classmates after 1974. Although the two indexes correlated reasonably well, they tapped somewhat different aspects of desegregation. Hence the Coleman index uncovered no consistent reduction in the probability of interracial student contact in the late 1970s, while the Taeuber index tapped the creeping imbalance discussed above.[17]

In sum, the simple claim that Judge Garrity only made racial imbalance worse than ever before is wrong. Despite the increase in 50 percent or more black schools documented above, his edicts virtually eliminated the less-than-1 percent and 75 percent or more black enrollments so common before busing. Moreover, despite dwindling white enrollments, his programs have drastically reduced racial isolation in the Boston schools—for the time being. Ever-changing demographics and at least some continuing white flight already have diminished these gains, and the 1980s promise a hard test of how much imbalance can be maintained by a desegregated school system.

Declining Educational Quality

No issue is more difficult to resolve than the hotly contested impact of judical desegregation policy on "educational quality" in the Boston schools. Nowhere are the limitations of available data and insufficient expiration of time more restrictive.

Any analysis is immediately sobered by divergent conceptions of educational quality. Educators and working-class parents typically differ on what is basic and worthwhile in schooling, but this familiar dispute took on

Table 9-4

Boston School Desegregation as Measured by the Taeuber and Coleman Standardized Indexes, 1970-1980

	1970	1972	1974	1975	1976	1977	1978	1979	1980
Taeuber (%)	25	26	48	73	74	72	71	70	70
Coleman	.377	.364	.650	.887	.847	.871	.852	.859	.881

Source: Computed from 1970, 1972, and 1976 HEW/OCR racial-ethnic enrollment data and from special tabulations for other years provided by the Department of Implementation, Boston School Department, October and November 1980.

added dimensions when Judge Garrity began making curricular and person-nel policy in the process of ordering desegregation. Hence, busing in Boston has come to mean much more than involuntary pupil reassignment; it also means new forms of citizen participation in school affairs and various educational innovations promoted by the judge. Supporters see great im-provement in such changes while opponents of busing regard them as ruinous to educational quality.

Popular writing on the Boston schools before busing described a system long stagnating under the weight of patronage politics, pedagogical rigidity, ethnic parochialism, strangulation finances, and encapsulated recruitment practices. Only the elite examination schools won any praise in such ac-counts, and growing racial isolation, along with deteriorating schools, figured prominently in a generally gloomy description.[18]

Martin Katzman acknowledged such problems in his cross-sectional analysis of 1964-1965 Boston school data, but nonetheless contradicted cer-tain other commentaries of the period, especially the 1965 Kiernan Commit-tee report.[19] Katzman regressed measures of school resources against selected indicators of student performance, controlling on race and social class. He found surprisingly little correlation between race and class, and uncovered little advantage for student performance owing to newer buildings, small class size, or more-educated teachers. Nor did he find the harmful educational effects attributed to racial imbalance by the Kiernan Committee. Without denying that segregation could inflict psychological harm on black students, he nonetheless concluded:

> In Boston, the average student in a Caucasian school does not perform bet-ter than the average student in a Negro school when social class and school resources are equal. Similarly the average student in an integrated school does not perform differently from the average student in mostly Caucasian or mostly Negro schools. In other words, there do not seem to be clear gains to both black and white by integration per se when social class and school resource(s) . . . are held constant, at least for the aspects of the per-formance measured here.[20]

Whatever import such conclusions may hold for a better understanding of the racial-imbalance controversy of the 1960s, readers will have to weigh the limitations of a cross-sectional analysis against the loosely supported claims of the Kiernan Committee. At this writing there does not exist a published longitudinal study, with before- and after-measures and adequate controls, of the educational effects of Boston school desegregation. Yet the absence of such data seems to matter very little in the continuing debate over Boston school desegregation and consequences for educational quali-ty. Whatever information becomes available is quickly pressed into service by one interested party or another, and it is common for foes and proponents of busing alike to take comfort in different interpretations of the same statistics.

No statistics are more exploited than student reading and mathematics-achievement test scores. Hence a 1976 *Globe* report of reading gains during the first year of Boston busing got everyone's attention.[21] But careful reading of the story disclosed that much ado had been made of very little information. The "gains" were well within normal fluctuations, the data had been "pooled" rather than broken down by race, and not enough information was supplied about high-school students to reach any conclusion. Of course, busing critics pounced on such shortcomings and dismissed the report as yet another example of biased *Globe* coverage.

Another flap over test scores occurred when the Boston School Department applied for emergency federal education aid in 1977. In emphasizing the need for more funds, school officials cited declining achievement levels and rising discipline problems in desegregated schools. Robert Dentler, the court-appointed expert, sharply criticized the report's methodology and conclusions.[22] A *Globe* feature repeated these criticisms, and Superintendent Fahey responded to this publicity by trying to defend the report and desegregation at the same time.[23] Naturally, busing foes capitalized on the controversy by citing the school department's findings as proof of their argument against busing while conveniently ignoring Dentler's valid methodological critique.[24]

Unfortunately, it was not possible to obtain before- and after-Phase 1 achievement scores, but table 9-5 at least allows a comparison of black and white performance on 1976, 1977, and 1978 reading tests. Mean scores for each group were converted into grade equivalents and stanines ("standard nines" used to divide a distribution into ninths with the fifth stanine as the mean point) for the first eight grades, and stanines only for high-school grades. The data are for all schools in the system.

Each comparison reveals essentially the same pattern. The group averages for black and white first graders were only two months or so apart in grade equivalency terms and, even though both groups gained steadily over time, the white group progressed more rapidly. The white eighth-grade average was two years above the black eighth-grade average, and in two of the three years observed, the white eleventh-grade mean was two stanines above the black eleventh-grade mean.

Similar patterns surfaced in fourth-, sixth-, and ninth-grade mathematics achievement test data for 1976 and 1977. In both years the fourth-grade black mean was at the fourth stanine and translated into a 3.5 grade equivalency; the white mean was ahead by one stanine and one year in grade equivalency terms. By the ninth grade, the white average was two stanines higher and more than two years ahead in grade equivalency.[25]

Table 9-5

Black and White Reading Achievement Scores, by Grade, 1976-1978

	Grade										
	01	02	03	04	05	06	07	08	09	10	11

1976 black
  mean grade
  equivalent
	1.8	2.5	3.1	3.7	4.4	4.9	5.6	6.0	—[a]	—	—

Stanine	5	5	4	4	4	4	4	3	3	4	3

1976 white
  mean grade
  equivalent
	2.0	3.1	3.8	4.9	5.7	6.4	7.6	8.4	—	—	—

Stanine	6	6	6	6	5	5	5	5	5	5	5

1977 black
  mean grade
  equivalent
	1.8	2.6	3.1	3.8	4.5	5.0	5.8	6.4	—	—	—

Stanine	5	5	4	4	4	3	4	4	4	3	4

1977 white
  mean grade
  equivalent
	2.0	3.1	3.8	4.8	5.6	6.6	7.4	8.4	—	—	—

Stanine	6	6	6	5	5	5	5	5	5	5	5

1978 black
  mean grade
  equivalent
	1.8	2.6	3.2	3.7	4.6	5.0	5.6	6.4	—	—	—

Stanine	5	5	5	5	4	3	4	4	4	4	3

1978 white
  mean grade
  equivalent
	2.0	3.2	3.8	4.6	5.6	6.2	7.6	8.2	—	—	—

Stanine	6	6	6	5	5	5	5	5	5	5	5

Source: Annual Reports of the Boston Public Schools, 1976, 1977, and 1978, Marion J. Fahey, superintendent.

[a]Grade equivalents generally are not reported for high school years; scores are total reading results from the Metropolitan Reading Examination.

According to Boston school administrators, in 1977 there were thirty-nine elementary, middle, and high schools where the mean black math score fell two or more stanines below the white mean. South Boston High and two South Boston elementary schools were on this list. In fifty other schools the black mean was one stanine lower, and the Bigelow (1-5) in South Boston was in this category. Black and white stanines were equal in nine other schools, including South Boston's Gavin Middle School.[26]

Such findings are depressingly familiar to urban school officials. The fact that Boston's ninth-grade black math test mean fell into the third stanine and translated into sixth-grade equivalency should distress a diverse audience. In Boston, however, this type of information cannot be interpreted independently of the busing controversy, even though the data pertain to groups and say nothing about the effects of busing. To busing proponents such statistics merely identify a continuing problem only enlightened policy can ameliorate. In so short a time, they avow, it is grossly unfair to expect the shackles forged by segregated schooling to be broken. Desegregated education is the surest way to end such inequalities, they conclude, and busing is but the "stick" that "lifts the rock" to expose such injustices. For busing foes the same data confirm the inability of desegregation to eradicate the pernicious results of lower-class and ghetto subcultures. If racial-achievement gaps are to be taken seriously, they insist, the pace of white instruction must be slowed so lagging black pupils can be accommodated; educational quality inevitably suffers in the process. Hence busing forces whites to become educational "guinea pigs" while black achievement is improved not one whit. Of course, such arguments show strikingly the preoccupation of busing proponents with helping minority children and an equally singular concern of busing foes to help white children. Despite tacit agreement that most black students are somehow culturally deprived, this fundamental divergence leads to conflicting prescriptions and perspectives unlikely to be changed by more and better information.

A simpler indicator of educational quality is the high-school dropout rate, a mirror image of "continuation" rates used by Katzman to measure a school's "holding power."[27] Did busing correlate with higher dropout rates? Table 9-6 shows that the answer depends on the school.

Table 9-6
Dropout Rates in Selected Boston High Schools, 1964-1979
(percent)

Year	South Boston	Charlestown	Hyde Park	East Boston	English	J.E. Burke	Citywide
	Schools in Defended Neighborhoods				Long Desegregated Schools		
1964	5.9	6.9	4.0	8.3	2.8	5.5	5.1
1965	6.0	5.1	3.6	12.9	2.6	5.2	5.6
1966	16.4	7.0	5.5	10.9	7.3	5.6	7.0
1967	10.4	7.6	2.0	11.0	10.0	5.2	6.8
1968	8.9	5.7	3.7	8.1	5.4	7.0	5.8
1969	9.7	5.9	4.2	8.1	7.6	3.9	7.1
1970	9.9	6.8	4.1	6.2	5.7	1.9	5.3
1971	12.3	7.7	3.1	6.2	6.6	1.7	6.1
1972	12.3	5.9	3.3	5.4	4.1	1.1	6.3
1973	9.4	4.9	3.1	4.1	2.7	0.6	4.4
1974	4.5	4.1	0.9	4.2	3.9	1.5	2.9
1975	11.9	11.6	2.1	11.7	9.7	2.1	6.4
1976	19.3	14.6	4.1	9.6	9.0	2.3	6.7
1977	14.4	10.8	4.0	9.4	10.8	1.2	8.5
1978	20.9	17.3	2.5	15.6	2.3	9.5	10.2
1979	16.5	7.4	3.9	12.5	9.7	8.1	10.5

Source: Guidance Department tabulations, Boston School Department.

For example, the South Boston High dropout rate averaged 17 percent over 1975-1979, actually exceeding a fifth of all students in 1978-1979. Such statistics, coupled with chronic absenteeism, comported poorly with press accounts of the school's "turnaround," and unquestionably reflected both racial tension and student alienation. But two earlier periods of high dropout rates at South Boston High hardly could be blamed on busing.

Until 1979, when its rate returned to near normal, Charlestown High seemed a straightforward case of increased dropout owing to busing, but equally unruly Hyde Park High reported only slightly worse dropout with busing than in 1965-1967. Long-desegregated Burke and English had higher rates in the late 1970s, but in neither case was the connection to busing clear.

Another yardstick of educational quality might be the percent of high-school graduates going directly to college. Did busing coincide with appreciable change in the proportion of college-bound seniors? The *Globe* implied this was true of South Boston High when it credited the school's judically installed administration with sending a record number of graduates to college in 1979.[28]

The claim is inaccurate, whether based on absolute numbers or class proportions. For 1970-1974 the average South Boston High graduating class numbered 406; for 1976-1980 the average was 150. Of the 2,034 graduated during the former period, 17 percent directly enrolled in four-year colleges and another 5 percent in two-year colleges. Of the 749 graduated in 1976-1980, 16 percent went to four-year colleges and 7 percent to junior colleges. In 1979, the best of the new administration's first five years, 31 of 157 seniors entered four-year colleges and 8 more went to junior colleges. But South Boston had sent bigger proportions of larger classes to colleges in 1969, 1972, and 1974.[29]

Similar data for other Boston high schools revealed a mixed pattern. In the defended neighborhoods of Hyde Park and East Boston, college-bound proportions remained about the same as before. Charlestown High's much-reduced senior classes in 1976-1980 had slightly higher college-bound proportions. Comparison of all city high-school graduates in the two periods uncovered a 2 percent increase in the proportion of seniors entering four-year colleges and another 2 percent increase in the junior college proportion in 1976-1980.[30]

Another important indicator is teacher perception of educational quality. How did Boston teachers view desegregation's impact on their schools? A 1977 survey found that faculty perceptions varied most consistently by years of classroom experience. The most-seasoned teachers were more often negative.[31] For example, 45 percent of those with eleven years or more experience agreed that "most of our problems would be solved if the courts would just leave the schools alone." Only 19 percent of those with four-to-ten years in the profession felt this way, as did 17 percent with three or fewer years background.[32] When asked about student performance since judicial intervention, almost half the senior faculty saw decline while only 13 percent reported improvement. Teachers with four-to-ten years in the classroom were more evenly divided.[33] Thirty-nine percent of the most experienced teachers said their work had grown "less rewarding" with busing, while 43 percent saw no meaningful change. Among teachers with four-to-ten years experience, one-fifth said the job had become less rewarding, another fifth replied it had gotten more rewarding, and the remainder saw no change. Most of the least-experienced teachers expressed no opinion.[34] As would be expected, the senior teachers were most convinced their jobs had gotten harder and their schools more dangerous with busing.[35] But large majorities of each group rejected statements that "no real education is going on in the school system" and "students are so upset as a result of the court order that they cannot concentrate on their studies."[36] Teaching experience correlated inversely with participation in magnet education programs and pairings with universities, business, and cultural institutions established by Phase 2.[37] In sum, the 1977 survey yielded mixed, but scarcely surprising, results. Disruption of the old order proved understandably most traumatic for teachers longest in the system, but newer teachers, many of whom would not have been hired under the old order, generally were upbeat about desegregation's present and future impact on schools and students.

Educational quality in Boston cannot be discussed without considering use of the magnet or special school designed to draw students of all races from all parts of the city. In 1977 Superintendent Fahey referred to district 9, comprising twenty-two magnet schools, as the "heart and soul" of Judge Garrity's program, and predicted the Boston magnet school would become a model for the nation.[38] Indeed, by almost all accounts, the magnet schools are the success story of Boston busing, and it is to them that the press are inevitably drawn when reporting desegregation progress.

Most magnet schools began to surpass the other district schools from the start of Phase 2. Fifteen of the initial twenty magnet schools designated by the court managed to enroll 90 percent or more of their projected 1975 student totals, a feat matched by fewer than a third of the schools in districts 1-7, and less than two-thirds of the nearly all-white district 8 schools.[39] This did not change in subsequent years.

What accounts for the stronger pull of Boston's magnet schools? Although the average number of students bused was greater for magnet than other schools, the option of choosing them over schools in home districts apparently was important enough to offset traditional apprehensions about distance, strange neighborhoods, and safety. Moreover, several magnet schools enjoyed excellent academic reputations long before busing, and numerous others came to be known as "good schools" because of emphasis on the "basics." All were given "learning themes" by the court in 1975 to enhance their scholastic images and foster diversity, but distinctiveness seems to have rested on perceptions of general quality rather than specific themes. Magnet school teachers were younger and regarded as more aggressive than teachers in other schools. In the aggregate, magnet schools compared favorably to other schools in such areas as the average student/teacher ratio, per pupil expenditures, building age and upkeep, and attendance. Most were located in sections generally viewed as safe and were seldom disrupted by serious racial conflict. No small factor proved to be the district 9 racial guidelines (designed to replicate system-wide proportions), which prevented any magnet school from becoming overwhelmingly black.[40]

To see one magnet school, however, hardly was to see them all. For example, the faculty and administration of the King Middle School were astonished by their designation as a language-arts magnet in 1975, and had to labor heroically thereafter to attract enough whites to their ghetto location.[41]

As for magnet high schools, analysis of college entry and dropout statistics after Phase 2 suggests three fairly distinct categories. The elite examination schools of the old system constitute an exceptionally high college entry and exceedingly low dropout group: Latin (93 percent college entry and 0.1 percent dropout), Latin Academy (92 percent college entry and 0.2 percent dropout), and Boston Technical (47 percent college and 2 percent dropout). Copley Square High (47 percent college and 6 percent dropout) might be placed in this category as well. A second relatively high college entry but relatively high dropout class included English (39 percent college and 13 percent dropout) and Madison Park (25 percent college and 13 percent dropout). Finally, a low college and high dropout grouping consisted of Boston High (8 percent college and 18 percent dropout) and Boston Trade (9 percent college and 8 percent dropout).[42] Looked at individually, then, magnet schools had some of the same advantages or problems used to label other schools as successful or failing.

The final item in this survey of the relationship between busing and educational quality is "magnet educational programs," or special courses with twin objectives of curricular innovation and racial integration. Not to be confused with magnet schools per se, such offerings were available to district schools upon application. In order to get funded, a course proposal had to specify cognitive, affective, and interracial learning goals. Some cognitive objectives mentioned in one account were pottery, political advocacy, ecology skills, story telling, and art appreciation. Affective concerns included "growth," "increased self-awareness," and "self-understanding." Interracial learning goals included the exposure of stereotypes and the development of mutual respect. Participating students earned full academic credit from their home institutions, and were not required to make up lost time in regular coursework.[43]

Although some welcomed such courses as innovative, especially in a system notorious for curricular rigidity, others regarded rap sessions and museum trips as poor substitutes for work in science, literature, history, reading, and other "basics." Even some teachers supportive of busing expressed reservations:

> . . . . So long as magnetic options operate after school or in free periods or on Saturdays, school staff . . . are usually glad to allow students to participate. But when they are asked to substitute . . . an integrated outdoor environmental program for part of the science curriculum, or a week exploring the city as a unit of social studies . . . or twenty sessions at an art center as part of the reading curriculum, all during school hours, many teachers will object strenuously, despite their express pro-integration values. The same holds true of many parents.[44]

Hence a recent pronouncement that "desegregation is not an educational treatment" has a hollow ring in Boston, where busing became the vehicle for judical transformation of an entire school system, including its curriculum.[45]

To sum up, evaluation of busing's educational impact in Boston at this point must be limited. Yet we can confidently reject sweeping claims that busing "ruined" the public schools. Rot was evident long before federal intervention, especially in dilapidated ghetto schools. Moreover, unless busing foes had a very brief crisis in mind, at least some alleged educational ill-effects of busing should have surfaced in steadily falling white achievement levels after Phase 1. As noted above, no such collapse occurred in the late 1970s.[46] Further, some aspects of judicial intervention were undeniably beneficial to education, such as building renovations, greater minority parental involvement in school affairs, more open and merit-determined teacher recruitment practices, and at least some school pairings. Many magnet schools offered exciting programs, although the best ones had long enjoyed reputations for academic excellence.

But there was a debit side as well. Violence and confusion repelled middle-class Bostonians and doubtless hastened the flight to private and suburban schools. Many remaining good students were siphoned off by magnet schools, thus worsening the plight of schools in their home districts. In turn, such schools increasingly became grim respositories for the city's disadvantaged youth. In a handful of schools, such as half-empty South Boston High, racial tensions still soured the learning environment and boosted dropout rates. Dubious "alternative education" courses may have contributed further to dropout by convincing working-class students and parents that more schooling was pointless. Conditions in such schools lent credibility to characterizations of Boston desegregation as a "forced conclave of the poor."[47]

Busing and Boston's Fiscal Woes

On 16 September 1976 Mayor Kevin White announced a $56.20 property tax increase, the biggest in Boston history. This raised the rate per $1,000 assessed valuation to $252.90—probably the steepest for a major American city. Forewarned, the public reacted less vociferously than probably otherwise would have been true, but talk of tax revolt and accelerated middle-class suburban exodus was heard nonetheless. Taking the political offensive, White did not dwell on busing in accounting for the increase, but did lash out against "uncontrolled" school spending as a major cause.[48] Several city councilors and other antibusing elites were less hesitant to pinpoint busing as a major factor. The increase coincided with an adverse municipal-bond market, a big deficit, and inflation. To what extent did busing contribute to the 1976 fiscal "crisis"?

Numerous newspaper investigations reached the same general conclusion: Busing certainly added to Boston's burden, but the main reasons for the city's financial illness in 1976 predated desegregation and eventually would have forced a day of reckoning in any case. All acounts further agree that reliance on the property tax for 65 to 70 percent of total city revenues was, and is, the crux of the problem. Many complications issued from this dependency.

Not the least of such difficulties was a steadily dwindling tax base, with increasing middle-class and business migration to the suburbs. Hence in 1976 the city could tax only 23 percent of its metropolitan "marketing area," as compared to 68 percent for New York, 62 percent for Houston, 40 percent for Los Angeles, and 36 percent for Cleveland. Inflation also cut in the tax base by reducing real income. Using 1972 dollars to compare, Boston's 1972 tax base was valued at $1.7 billion; it dropped half a billion dollars over the next five years. Seeking to slow suburban exodus, city hall sacrificed immediate cash by granting tax abatements. Such abatements increased by 102 percent between 1972 and 1975, resulting in a $38.5 million shortfall for the city in 1976. Revenues were further constrained by tax exemptions. According to Mayor White, between 55 and 58 percent of Boston was tax exempt, including some of the most valuable downtown parcels.[49]

While Boston's tax base declined, its public sector expanded, especially during White's first term. Between 1967 and 1972 the city workforce grew by 3,072 employees, or 14.5 percent, excluding another thousand absorbed by the commonwealth in 1968 when it assumed Boston's welfare programs. The most dramatic growth occurred in the mayor's office and those agencies most directly under his control; the number of such employees shot up from 94 in 1967 to 608 in 1972.[50] Accompanying all this hiring were new collective-bargaining arrangements and formation of municipal unions committed to raising government salaries to competitive levels. City salaries were increased an average of 8 percent each year of White's first two terms.[51]

Although city hall attracted some federal money and persuaded the state to assume certain obligations, its growth still impacted heavily on the property tax. The rate climbed from $118 in 1967 to $197 in 1972. In 1971 the city budget director predicted a $300 rate unless the brakes were applied; he was joined in 1974 by the city treasurer in recommending another rate increase. But Mayor White was unwilling to begin his 1975 reelection bid with a tax increase, and city hall instead eliminated some jobs while transferring more than a thousand others to a federal Comprehensive Employment Training Act (CETA) payroll. He also used the interest on banked federal revenue-sharing funds and state aid to tide the city over until 1976. Hence, few observers of city hall doubted another tax hike was imminent, the only real question being how much.[52]

That issue was much complicated by Boston's typically byzantine school finances. Although run by an independently elected school committee, schools depended on the same property-tax revenues as other city agencies. A statuory formula fixed school proportions, and supplementals required council and mayoral approval. Armed with a veto over school budgets, the mayor nonetheless had to bargain with school committees and accept the politcal consequences of a higher tax rate. In 1974 White sought to have the city charter amended by referendum so he could appoint the school committee and take over its budget, but was soundly defeated. Thus control over school finances remained split when Judge Garrity ordered busing.

Like other city agencies, the school department grew markedly during White's first term, from 6,782 employees in 1967, to 8,159 in 1972, despite a corresponding enrollment decline. Like the mayor, school-committee members rewarded supporters with well-paid administrative posts and less remunerative, if largely custodial, sinecures. Hence the Boston schools had an excessive ratio of employees to students when busing began.[53]

Money to pay for desegregation was a major concern from the outset, but federal and state funds, available once again because of compliance with desegregation orders, helped defray Phase 1 costs. Nonetheless, city police expenditures on Phase 1 alone topped $7.5 million, and continuing disorder over busing promised to drive such costs even higher.[54]

The real revelation was a school budget request of $177 million for fiscal 1976, which was 35 percent more than the previous year's budget. Although desegregation costs accounted for only some of this increase, White discovered he had to bargain with Judge Garrity, as well as the school committee and Boston Teachers Union (BTU), in order to reduce the 1976 figure by $30 million. The school department eventually ran up a $19 million deficit anyway.

Now faced with a massive deficit of $33 million overall, the mayor had no choice but to advocate a $16.40 tax increase and cutbacks in almost every city agency. A plan to save $19 million by laying off 615 city workers was soon abandoned after union strike threats, and the best White could get was an agreement whereby city employees gave up their customary pay raise. The city council killed his $16.40 property tax increase, which several councilors blamed wholly on busing.

White fared about the same in negotiations with the school committee and the school department. Here, an interesting but hardly novel (for Boston) factionated conflict configuration emerged in which, often as not, a school-committee majority backed White, whereas the school department's deficit spending won Judge Garrity's critical approval. Already deeply involved in monitoring school finances, Judge Garrity directed the school department to suggest cost reductions. The school committee proposed firing 220 provisional teachers and 204 teaching aides, thus leaving administration untouched. In April 1976 Garrity consented to firing the aides, but not the teachers, whom he deemed necessary to desegregation. An irate White spoke of closing schools early for lack of funds, and promptly was summoned to Garrity's courtroom for a two-hour discussion of federalism, city finances, and his obligations to carry out judicial orders. After this hearing, Garrity ordered White to divert $8.6 million in "surplus" funds from other departments to schools, and served notice of his intent to review school finances periodically. A more extensive order on 10 May directed the mayor to keep the schools open until 22 June, the normal end of the 1975-1976 term. Finally, the judge ordered meetings between White and the other principals responsible for school finances.[55]

Thus stymied in his efforts to cut back, Mayor White's options were further reduced when New York's fiscal crisis impacted on the municipal bond market. Boston's bond rating fell and its debt service costs soared as a result. Other woes forcing the mayor's hand were steadily rising pension costs, the expense of operating Suffolk County government (borne entirely by Boston), state rejection of a special payroll tax on all who worked in the city, and maintenance of the Massachusetts Bay Transportation Authority (MBTA).[56]

Hence the $56.20 property-tax increase that was finally agreed to by the city council and reluctantly announced by White in September.

Showing that school desegregation per se was merely one source of Boston's 1976 fiscal emergency and tax increase is easier than establishing exactly how much desegregation cost the city each year. This is so partly because Boston got millions in desegregation-related aid from the state and federal governments. The use of state troopers in South Boston and other trouble spots reduced local police overtime, a major burden, and at least spread the cost to other Massachusetts taxpayers.[57] Excessive and possibly fraudulent bus-company charges further inflated the city's desegregation bill.[58]

Only a partial picture of desegregation costs can be obtained from school department annual reports. Some desegregation items are clear enough in each report, for example $4,225,868 for "racial balance transportation" in 1976-1977 and another $3,855,760 in 1977-1978. Court-appointed experts were paid $60,000 each of these years. But other desegregation costs probably were hidden in items such as "special education" and "program support." The 1976-1977 report was more revealing than others because it stipulated a gross "desegregation" item in a detailed projection of 1977-1978 school outlays. According to this estimate, desegregation would cost $10,708,500 (or 7 percent of total costs); based on optimistic enrollment projections, this came to $143 per student.[59]

Conflict between city hall and a judicially backstopped school department hardly ceased with alleviation of Boston's 1976 fiscal crunch. Responding to White's accusations of uncontrolled school spending, Superintendent Fahey charged both the mayor and the school committee with being more concerned about patronage than the school children of Boston. All Mayor White wanted, she continued, was to take over the schools. To illustrate her department's sacrifice, Mrs. Fahey announced the transfer of twenty-three administrators from her office to various schools.[60] Sounds of the same battle were heard in January 1981; only now the passage of the so-called Proposition 2½ promised to slash property-tax revenues to the point of closing numerous schools. Operating with a $210 million budget, the school department's actual spending was at $250 million. As before, Judge Garrity was deeply involved. Lashing out at both Mayor White and at counsel for the black plaintiffs in Boston's school desegregation suit, Garrity praised the school department, whose good faith he now took for granted.[61] In February 1981, however, plans were announced to close twenty-seven Boston schools.[62] And, by April, it was not clear whether any schools would reopen after spring break. Another, and possibly more severe, fiscal crisis lay ahead for Boston and its public schools.

Conclusion

In South Boston and other defended neighborhoods, few doubted that "forced busing" was a castrophe. Some respondents likened its impact on their personal lives and communities to that of a war or natural calamity. Spokespersons for the antibusing movement, however, could hardly limit their indictment to neighborhood effects. Hence the four claims reviewed in this chapter.

At least three of the four claims contained some substance, but none put desegregation in the broader context necessary to full analysis of the problem. Busing had indeed hastened white flight, but middle-class whites had been leaving the public schools long before Judge Garrity's intervention. The low repute of so many Boston schools no doubt explained much of this predesegregation loss. Even though busing's immediate impact on white enrollments could be discerned in the growing number of schools that were at least half black, other factors, such as birthrate differentials, eventually would have rendered whites a minority in the Boston school system, continuous monitoring of racial enrollments notwithstanding. Numerous officials, including Mrs. Hicks, foresaw this development in the mid-1960s. Although busing costs certainly exacerbated Boston's fiscal problems, and school deficits continue to be a major problem, economic efficiency has not been a cardinal virtue of Boston government for a very long time. An archaic tax system and patronage politics were more to blame than busing for Boston's 1976 fiscal crisis. If court-ordered busing did not harm white academic achievement, it is by no means clear that its educational programs improved the lot of district 1-8 schools.

What could be done to make court-ordered busing more legitimate, less conflictual, and perhaps more educationally viable to cities with defended enclaves similar to Boston's? The final chapter addresses this question.

Notes

1. For example, see Michael Knight, "Scholars in New Rift Over 'White Flight,'" *The New York Times,* 11 June 1978, p. 27. Some of the leading disputes are summarized in Diane Ravitch, "The 'White Flight' Controversy," *Public Interest* 51 (Spring 1978): 135-149; Christine H. Rossell, "A Response to "The 'White Flight' Controversy," *Public Interest* 53 (Fall 1978): 109-111; and Ravitch's reply, *Public Interest* 53 (Fall 1978): 111-115. See also Christine H. Rossell, "School Desegregation and White Flight," *Political Science Quarterly* 90 (Winter 1975-1976): 675-695; Thomas F. Pettigrew and Robert L. Green, "School Desegregation in Large Cities: A Critique of the Coleman 'White Flight' Thesis," *Harvard Educational Review* 46 (February 1976): 1-53; Coleman's reply, *Harvard Educational Review* 46 (May 1976): 217-224; and, finally, the Pettigrew and Green rebuttal, *Harvard Educational Review* 46 (May 1976): 225-233.

2. For a good summary of the literature see Karl E. Taeuber and Franklin D. Wilson, "An Analysis of the Impact of School Desegregation Policies on White Public and Nonpublic School Enrollment," draft report, 26 November 1979, Institute for Research on Poverty, University of Wisconsin-Madison.

3. Research by Michael Giles and associates does employ interview data; cf. Everett F. Cataldo, Michael W. Giles, and Douglas S. Gatlin, *School Desegregation Policy* (Lexington, Mass.: Lexington Books, D.C. Heath and Company, 1978); and Michael W. Giles and Douglas S. Gatlin, "Mass-Level Compliance With Public Policy: The Case of School Desegregation," *Journal of Politics* 42 (August 1980): 722-746.

4. Reynolds Farley and Clarence Wurdock, "Can Government Policies Integrate Public Schools?" Population Studies Center, University of Michigan (March 1977), pp. 16-17.

5. Christine H. Rossell, "The Effect of School Integration On Community Integration," *Journal of Education* 160 (May 1978), p. 47.

6. Ibid., p. 59.

7. Taeuber and Wilson, "An Analysis," pp. 24-25.

8. Readers should be aware that other authors have reported somewhat different white enrollments for the academic years noted in table 9-1. Most of this discrepancy is probably attributable to choice of reporting periods (the Boston School Department issues enrollment figures in October and March of each academic year). State figures sometimes differ from those provided by local authorities, and it is not uncommon to find minor disagreement between data supplied by the Department of Implementation and other departments in the Boston school bureaucracy. Periodic reports by the Office of Civil Rights (Department of Health, Education, and Welfare) in the 1970s also differed slightly from locally gathered statistics. But none of the above would seem to explain substantial differences in reported white enrollment for 1975-1976. Table 9-1 used a state figure of 41,407 for November 1975; the statistic was subsequently endorsed by the Department of Implementation of the Boston School Department. But Diane Ravitch's estimate for the same year was only 36,243 whites; see table 5 of "The 'White Flight' Controversy," *The Public Interest* 51 (Spring 1978): 135-149. Christine Rossell's figure for 2 February 1976 was 36,522; see "Boston's Desegregation and White Flight," *Integrated Education* 15 (January-February 1977): 36-39. Of course, a difference of several thousand students importantly affects computation of loss rates for subsequent years. Hence estimates of white flight during this tumultuous period must be regarded with appropriate caution.

9. 1974-1975 Annual Housing Survey cited by Taeuber and Wilson, "An Analysis," p. 8.

10. See D. Garth Taylor and Arthur L. Stinchcombe, *The Boston School Desegregation Controversy,* unpublished manuscript, pp. 55-56.

11. A five-point statement of Church policy appeared in "Board of Education Publishes Guidelines On School Imbalance," *The Pilot,* 1 March 1974, p. 1.

12. For example, see John Kifner, "White Pupils' Rolls Drop A Third in Boston Busing," *The New York Times,* 15 December 1975, p. 1.

13. Computed from special tabulations kindly provided by the Department of Education, Archdiocese of Boston.

14. Declining birthrates unquestionably had an effect. See *Boston School Enrollment Projections 1977-1981, 1986* (Boston: Harbridge House, 1977).

15. See appendix A for district racial guidelines.

16. Although the black proportion of all enrollments grew from 33 percent in 1972 to 46 percent in 1980, the actual number of black students decreased from 31,728 to 31,082. In contrast, Hispanic students increased by 80 percent, from 5,138 in 1972 to 9,274 in 1980; and their proportion of total enrollments jumped from 5 to 14 percent in the same period.

17. See Michael R. Fitzgerald and William Lyons, "Measuring Urban School Desegregation: A Cautionary Note," *Political Methodology* 5 (August 1978): 511-530, for a good discussion of these measures. The Coleman standardized index is particularly useful for situations where whites are a minority of total enrollments, but this index may have inflated the 1970 and 1972 probabilities noted in table 9-5. Some may prefer the simpler Coleman index, which yielded .241 for 1970 and .217 for 1972, as nonblack minority enrollments were below 10 percent both years.

18. See especially Jonathan Kozol, *Death at an Early Age* (Boston: Houghton-Mifflin, 1967) and Peter Schrag, *Village School Downtown* (Boston: Beacon Press, 1967).

19. Martin T. Katzman, *The Political Economy of Urban Schools* (Cambridge, Mass.; Harvard University Press, 1971).

20. Ibid., p. 62.

21. See "Pupils' Reading Ability Better Since Busing Began," *Boston Globe,* 26 May 1976, p. 4.

22. Dentler's criticisms first appeared in his memorandum to Judge Garrity, parts of which surfaced in "School Report for U.S. Aid Called Biased," *Boston Globe,* 30 January 1977; see also "Report Cites Negative Effects of Desegregation," *Boston Globe,* 16 January 1977, p. 1.

23. See Muriel Cohen, "Boston Schools: Deterioration and Future," *Boston Globe,* 19 January 1977, p. 7; and, Peter Mancusi, "Fahey Defends Education Since Busing," *Boston Globe,* 17 January 1977, p. 1.

24. See statements by Raymond Flynn, Virginia Sheehy, and "Pixie" Palladino quoted by Mancusi, Ibid.

25. As reported in a school-department memorandum from Thomas R. Deveney to John Coakley, "Math Achievement Data for School Years 1976-77 and 1977-78," 28 May 1978.

26. Ibid., table A.

27. Katzman, *Political Economy,* pp. 46-47.

28. Muriel Cohen, "Turnaround at Southie," *Boston Globe,* 25 June 1979, p. 1.

29. See annual Boston School Department reports on the distribution of graduating high-school classes, prepared by the Guidance Department and Office of Pupil Services under direction of John Diggins.

30. Ibid.

31. Citywide Coordinating Council, "An Analysis of Teachers' Attitudes Toward the Public Schools in the City of Boston," CSR No. 891 (April 1977), pp. 15-17, 24-25, and 76.

32. Ibid., computed from data on pp. 58-59.

33. Ibid., computed from data on p. 31.

34. Ibid., computed from data on p. 42.

35. Ibid., pp. 38 and 54.

36. Ibid., p. 48.

37. Ibid., p. 45.

38. Quoted in Charles B. McMillan, "Magnet Education in Boston," *Phi Delta Kappan* 59 (November 1977), p. 159.

39. "Education and Enrollments [in] Boston During Phase II," (Boston, Mass.: Massachusetts Research Center, nd.), p. 54.

40. Ibid., pp. 54-56. See also Christine H. Rossell, "Magnet Schools as a Desegregation Tool," *Urban Education* 14 (October 1979): 303-320.

41. See Kim Marshall, "The Making of a Magnet School: A Personal Account of the Journey from Chaos to Quality," *Journal of Education* 160 (May 1978): 19-35.

42. Computed from data compiled by the Guidance Department and Office of Pupil Services, Boston School Department. The college entry percentages were computed from the total number of graduates entering four-year colleges in 1975-1976, 1976-1977, 1978-1979, and 1979-1980 for each of the magnet high schools listed. The high-school dropout percentage is the average percentage of the four years noted above for each school. Since the citywide dropout average for the same period was 8.4 percent, Boston Trade might better be classified as a low college entry and average-dropout school.

43. George B. Thomas and Charles B. McMillan, "Magnetism and Integration in Massachusetts," *Theory Into Practice* 17 (April 1978): 140-143.

44. McMillan, "Magnet Education in Boston," p. 162.

45. Robert L. Crain and Rita E. Mahard, "Desegregation and Black Achievement: A Review of the Research," *Law and Contemporary Problems* 42 (Summer 1978), p. 30.

46. Any showing of harmful effect on white test scores would have been most surprising, for, as Crain and Mahard point out, "every writer on the subject has agreed that the test performance of white students is unaffected by school desegregation." Ibid., p. 18.

47. J. Harvie Wilkinson, III, *From Brown to Bakke: The Supreme Court and School Integration, 1954-1978* (New York: Oxford University Press, 1979), p. 214. Numerous others have made the same point, for example, Robert Coles.

48. David Rogers, "Hub Gets Bad News: Tax Rate Up $56.20," *Boston Globe*. 17 September 1976, p. 1.

49. White's "minimum" 55 percent estimate was offered in a 21 November 1977 interview with *Barron's,* "No Last Hurrah: Reports of Boston's Demise Are Grossly Exaggerated," p. 3. The 58 percent figure was quoted in "Boston's Fiscal Mess—Where it Started, Where it's Headed," *Boston Globe,* 5 December 1976, p. A-1. As noted in the latter source, however, the bigger estimate included streets and parks owned by the city.

50. As reported by Warren T. Brookes, "City Could Cut Payroll $64M Without Slashing Services," *Boston Herald-American,* 19 October 1976.

51. "Boston's Fiscal Mess," p. A-4.

52. Ibid. See also Warren T. Brookes, "How Can the City Find $90 Million Dollars? [sic]" *Boston Herald-American,* 18 October 1976, p. 13.

53. See Warren T. Brookes, "Boston Running Most Expensive Schools in U.S.," *Boston Herald-American,* 20 October 1976.

54. By the end of Phase 2B (1976-1977), total police expenditures were $16,533,829. See "Operation Safety Cost 74-77," undated release by the Boston Police Department.

55. *Morgan* v. *McDonough,* 72-911G (10 May 1976).

56. "Boston's Fiscal Mess," p. A-4. See also "Dukakis Tells White 'No' on New Taxes," *Boston Globe,* 19 November 1976, p. 1.; and, "Inflation Could 'Eat Up' $64M Savings of Cost of City Services," *Boston Herald-American,* 22 October 1976, p. 15.

57. In order to share overtime earnings, state troopers were "rotated" to Boston, some driving the length of the state to do desegregation duty. See "Taxpayers Work Overtime, Too," *Boston Herald-Advertiser,* 18 February 1976, 5-4.

58. "White Hit on Bus 'Waste,'" *Boston Herald-American,* 19 April 1976, p. 1; "Boston School Bus Audits Find $250,000 Discrepancy," *Boston Globe,* 29 September 1976, p. 1; and "Jury Investigates Busing Contracts," *Boston Globe,* 23 February 1977, p. 11.

59. "Annual Report of Total System for the 1976-77 School Year," [Boston, Mass.: Boston School Department, 15 July 1977 (processed)], Exhibit IV, p. 7.

60. "Fahey Lashes Back at White, Demands End of Patronage," *Boston Globe,* 18 September 1976, p. 1.

61. "Garrity Raps White on Budget," *Boston Globe,* 14 January 1981, p. 1.

62. "Boston Closes 27 Schools," *Oregonian,* 26 February 1981.

10 Desegregating Defended-Neighborhood Schools

Defiance and Compliance in Boston

"Forced busing" soon led to school desegregation in defended neighborhoods, but at enormous cost. Few today would say that the same schools truly have been integrated.[1] Although much less turmoil accompanied desegregation of other Boston schools, Judge Garrity's intervention in local affairs appalled many Bostonians and probably millions of other Americans. Placing these results in perspective is partly the task of this final chapter. Another task is to offer policy recommendations for desegregating the schools in defended neighborhoods of other cities.

To establish a perspective for reviewing the findings of previous chapters, let us return to the questions listed in chapter 3. It will be recalled that these questions were listed under three general sets of variables: substance of judicial policy, implementor and enforcer factors, and characteristics of the compliance environment.

Substance of Judicial Policy

As noted in chapter 2, the Supreme Court's Denver decision in 1973 gave Judge Garrity ample authority to order system-wide correctives when unlawful segregation was found in some, but not all, public schools. Official segregative intent could not be concealed in considerable evidence of dogged school-committee opposition to any racial balancing, rigged feeder patterns, odd grade differences, dubious districting, and curious bus routing brought out during the 1973 trial in Boston. Using the Denver ruling and earlier legal precedents, Judge Garrity devised remedies to reduce racial isolation and associated educational problems. His measures must be characterized as redistributive, especially if we examine what was extracted from local government and the white target population. Of course, his policy also had enormous impact on the nonwhite consumer population.

Perhaps the most redistributive part of judicial policy was the wholesale reorganization of schools begun with Phase 2. Chapter 7 described that transformation and other instances of judicial policymaking for schools. Chapter 9 furnished additional details of this type, including the judge's penchant for innovative education. Another instance of redistributive policymaking was judicial intervention in city finances and the resulting coercion that forced reallocation of city revenues. However rightly, many Bostonians blamed Judge Garrity for the stiff property-tax increase of 1976. Redistributive aspects also were present in denial of parental and student choice of schools, at least with respect to whites. Table 10-1 provides indirect illustration of how school children were affected by reporting both compulsory and voluntary busing statistics for three recent academic years.[2] Although black and other students were bused more than whites, the proportion of each group bused increased each year. In 1978-1979, over half of all Boston students were bused.

Adverse reactions to judicial power were hardly limited to antibusing activists. For example, several *Herald-American* editorial cartoons caricatured Judge Garrity as a dictator. One such drawing depicted a roadside billboard outside Boston bearing the following message:

Welcome to Bicentennial Mass. 1976

Governor: W. Arthur Garrity

Supt. of Schools: W. Arthur Garrity

Mayor: W. Arthur Garrity

Pres. of City Council: W. Arthur Garrity

Budget Director: W. Arthur Garrity

You Name It: W. Arthur Garrity.[3]

Table 10-1
Boston Public-School Students Bused, by Race and Academic Year, 1977-1979

	Whites	Blacks	Others	Totals
1977-1978 enrollments[a]	31,014	31,478	11,488	73,980
Number bused[b]	12,315	15,768	4,648	32,731
Percentage bused	39.7	50.1	40.5	44.2
1978-1979 enrollments	28,094	31,091	12,077	71,262
Number bused	12,547	18,157	5,920	36,624
Percentage bused	44.7	54.4	49.0	51.4
1979-1980 enrollments	25,527	31,274	11,673	68,474
Number bused	11,680	17,783	6,163	35,626
Percentage bused	45.8	56.9	52.8	52.0

Source: Special tabulations provided by Department of Implementation, Boston Public Schools.
[a]Enrollment subtotals for October of each academic year
[b]Busing data computed at end of academic year.

Whatever the degree of overstatement, the judge was far too modest in describing the limits on his authority. After receiving numerous calls and letters concerning "every facet" of school operations, Judge Garrity referred to himself in the third person in a rather legalistic complaint expressed in open court: "Judge Garrity is not running the schools. He cannot run the schools unless the system is placed in receivership. And a receiver has been appointed for only one school."[4]

A crucial aspect of policy substance is the role of causal theory. Did Judge Garrity's desegregation policy enjoy a justification going beyond recitation of legal precedent? Did he connect specific remedies to particular educational and social problems arising from segregation or gross racial imbalance? Remarkably little by way of causal explanation is found in the judge's official pronouncements and hundreds of newspaper accounts of his actions. A rare hint of why his remedies were necessary was his 1975 reference to "inferior educational opportunities" resulting from school-committee discrimination.[5] On occasion, he expressed concern about educational quality and the general welfare of school children. For the most part, however, a detailed explanation of how judicial remedies related to particular problems was not provided. However evident the injustices of segregation and imbalance may have been to the judge and his supporters, they certainly were not obvious to busing foes, who continually wanted to know "what's at the end of the bus ride?"

If causal connections between constitutional wrongs and remedies remained mostly inarticulate in official pronouncements, standards for measuring compliance were made increasingly more precise after Phase 1. Chapter 9 described the annually adjusted racial guidelines issued under judicial authority. Early in the desegregation process, as noted in chapter 7, school administrators had to supply the court with detailed enrollment and employment information. Data processing further aided judicial monitoring of school balancing and racial composition of staff.

Chapter 7 described how Judge Garrity dealt with recalcitrant city officials. Use of civil contempt penalties against school committee-members was but one instance of judicial coercion leading to compliance. Compelling the school committee to accept Jerome Winegar as South Boston High headmaster was another. Hence the point was made: Judge Garrity would hold individuals accountable for carrying out his orders.

The final question of policy substance is the size and diversity of both target and consumer populations. As noted in chapter 9, whites were a minority in the public schools after 1975 and, by 1977, blacks alone outnumbered white students. Whatever the precise enumeration of racially motivated white flight, there can be no doubt of a future resegregation problem because of steadily shrinking white enrollments. A related problem will be lessening socioeconomic diversity of white pupils, as the white student minority comes more and more to consist of children of the poor and of the working class. Conversely, an already racially and culturally heterogeneous consumer population should become even more diversified with sustained nonwhite mobility and growth of the Hispanic population.

Implementor and Enforcer Variables

The racial-balance dispute of the 1960s won national recognition for Louise Day Hicks and hardened popular attitudes in Boston toward busing. A shift in the early 1970s to *de jure* segregation did not change white public rejection of busing or alter the public intransigence of Mrs. Hicks and other antibusing politicians. Not one important city official supported Judge Garrity's liability decision. Instead the spectrum of official reaction ranged from Mayor White's equivocations to the "never" sentiments of Mrs. Hicks. Fiery denunciations issued from the city council and school committee, one school committeeman even promising to appeal every word uttered by the judge. When Superintendent Fahey praised Judge Garrity in a 1976 newspaper interview, school-committee members sharply rebuked her at the next public meeting while ROAR activists in the audience demanded her dismissal.[6] Within two years of this event, however, open defiance of judicial policy had ceased in the councils of city government. Although the 1979 elections and the firing of Robert Wood suggested it was premature to count the school committee as a willing member of Judge Garrity's implementing population, it was fair to say that the school department had assumed such a role. At one point, the judge praised the department's cooperation in implementing desegregation and served notice of his good-faith acceptance of departmental efforts.[7]

Why was Judge Garrity able to overcome official obstacles to implementation in so brief a time? Although a full analysis of this aspect of the Boston busing controversy is beyond the scope of the present study, surely much of the answer must be found in the leverage given judicial policy by the development of equitable remedies. Unlike the policymakers described by Pressman and Wildavsky, Judge Garrity commanded unenthusiastic implementors through aggressive use of sanctions made available through equitable remedies. However much Mayor White might have preferred to stall or defer on grounds of insufficient funds, he was bound by court orders to carry out judicial policy. As described in chapter 7, Judge Garrity called upon the same source of authority to compel police enforcement and school-department compliance. Hence equitable remedies give a judge the power to cut through inertia, disagreement, dilatory administration, and jurisdictional squabbles sufficient to check implementation of other kinds of policy. In Boston, however, equitable remedies and punishment of noncompliance were enough to offset the political benefits of defiance in nearly all instances. Public officials who never conceded the legitimacy of judicial busing policy nonetheless were compelled to see to its implementation and enforcement. Creation of the Department of Implementation within the school bureaucracy made the process more mechanical and eventually permitted the judge to monitor progress from a distance.

Characteristics of the Compliance Environment

In a recent study of Los Angeles busing opposition, M. Stephen Weatherford points up the critical role of the context in which opposition forms. Merely aggregating individual replies to questionnaires, according to Weatherford, neglects "the presence of a highly charged atmosphere of personal interaction and involvement, which facilitates the spread of conflict beyond the original participants."[8] Inevitably, in aroused communities there is "movement away from the position the individual might have taken alone, and toward the position shared by the bulk of people in his social environment."[9]

The present study is predicated on the necessity of disaggregating the white target population into defended-neighborhood residents and others required to take part in court-ordered busing. Otherwise the basis for understanding Boston's turmoil is lacking for want of the proper analytic focus. Whites living outside defended neighborhoods objected to busing for the same reasons expressed everywhere: concerns about child safety and educational quality in ghetto schools. Many white Bostonians further resented judicial denial of their traditional "right" to enroll their children in the nearest neighborhood school.[10] Such concerns were joined with fears for the community ideal in defended neighborhoods. Here busing was regarded as fundamentally redistributive because it was but the beginning of forced change, of invasion and disruption of traditional relationships. The symbols of such change were no further away than the dreaded Columbia Point project, a stone's throw from Carson Beach. Moreover, Mrs. Hicks and other antibusing politicians had characterized school desegregation in precisely this way over the years.

Weatherford's point concerning the communal pull of individuals away from more moderate positions fits South Boston well. The dynamics of protest mobilization do not allow serious challenges to prevailing interpretations of the common plight. Never particularly tolerant of free thinking, the defended neighborhood in times of protest crushes dissent. Chapter 8 recounted examples of selective expulsion against renegades who dared argue for compliance with judicial policy.

Hence protest in defended neighborhoods looked very different than protest elsewhere. In most parts of Boston, resistance soon settled down to white flight and protest voting, but in South Boston and a few other places it was enduring and multifaceted. As noted in chapter 8, both discontent and solidarity theory contributed to understanding defended-neighborhood protest. This was because residents took part for various reasons. Protest was an opportunity for some hitherto disreputable elements to gain status. Of course, some were hoodlums whose mayhem against blacks and leftist whites nonetheless escaped vigorous condemnation by protest elites. The Gamson uses-of-violence thesis recounted in chaper 8 gave some insight into why this was so.

Weatherford observed Los Angeles antibusing groups to have a "strongly localistic tendency" that repeatedly inhibited citywide protest coalitions from forming.[11] Of course, the same phenomenon was described in chapter 8 with respect to neighborhood-based ROAR groups. Although a citywide coalition did briefly exist in Boston, its effectiveness as a challenging group soon succumbed to factionalism and co-optation.

Turning to other characteristics of the target population and compliance environment, we cannot neglect social class. Lillian Rubin stressed social-class antagonisms in her account of the busing struggle in Richmond, California during the late 1960s.[12] Noting that liberal proponents of busing were mostly upper-middle class while opponents were mainly working- and lower-middle class conservatives, Rubin concluded:

> The protagonists in this struggle occupy different places in the social structure. . . . That means they do different kinds of work, have different levels of education and different educational experiences, and hold different places in the power and status hierarchies of society. These differences lead to disparate orientations to political issues, to work, to the meaning and purpose of education, and to the family unit, which, in turn, condition their hopes, their fears, and their aspirations, and set the course of their collision once these issues become salient.[13]

These observations apply with comparable force to South Boston protesters, nearly all of whom were working- or lower-middle class. Social-class antagonisms intertwined with the defended-neighborhood syndrome in complex fashion, and perceptions of "limousine liberals" seeking to transform city neighborhoods informed notions of the common neighborhood plight. No doubt working-class values lay beneath the protesters' view of South Boston High's new curriculum; magnet education programs and field trips angered and dismayed antibusing activists already agitated over alleged decline in instructional quality and course substance. Like the conservative busing foes in Rubin's study, at least some defended-neighborhood protesters bitterly resented appropriation of their taxes to pay for "forced busing" and related programs.[14] Finally, as pointed out in chapter 5, class conflict themes had been an important part of Mrs. Hicks's appeal to Boston voters in the 1960s.

Yet another characteristic of the compliance environment noted in chapter 5 and worthy of reiteration here was the rapidly changing demographic picture. South Boston was becoming a white outpost surrounded by increasingly black neighborhoods. Although Roxbury and the South End had changed over some time earlier, most of North Dorchester in 1960 had been Irish. Absorption of North Dorchester into an ever expanding ghetto and the racial turnover in the Columbia Point project greatly added to perceptions of South Boston's common plight. And, like their counterparts in Richmond, California, South Boston busing foes compared their proximity to the ghetto with the distance enjoyed by suburban busing proponents.

The final aspect of the compliance environment to be considered is the success of antibusing protest. All research to date agrees that antibusing protest follows the critical desegregation decision and hence comes too late to prevent implementation. Typically, such protests dissipate within a year of the critical decision.[15] Of course, protest did not stop busing in Boston, but neither did it dissipate after a few months, as was true of other cities.

Although unble to halt busing, protest nonetheless can have powerful secondary effects on implementation. According to Christine Rossell, serious and sustained protest can lead to accelerated white flight, heightened racial tensions in desegregated schools, and, most importantly, crucial lags in a multi-phase process of behavioral and attitudinal habituation to school desegregation. In a recent review of community change in response to school desegregation, Rossell suggested that most districts ordered to bus are faced with a collective cognitive-dissonance problem. Initially, reduction of dissonance takes the form of negative reaction, for example, protest voting and white flight. Once white parents and their children recognize school desegregation to be irrevocable, however, behavioral change taking account of the new reality generally follows. Eventually this adjustment may foster more positive attitudes about desegregation, multiracial society, and individuals of different races. But protest and backlash can check this process and spawn deeper racial hatred so that every contact worsens relations. Hence protest of the sort exhibited by South Boston residents can disrupt desegregation, deepen prejudice, and delay positive adjustment perhaps for a generation.[16]

At this writing it is hard to say how much behavioral acceptance of school desegregation has taken place in South Boston. Outward appearances suggest a continuing and profound resentment of busing, stronger prejudice against blacks, and greater suspicion of outsiders. Perhaps recent violence in South Boston High was exaggerated by the news media, and, in any case, may not be representative of other schools in the neighborhood. Younger children may have already begun to accept classmates of different races and neighborhoods. If so, desegregation may eventually create the mutual understanding and related educational benefits hoped for by its proponents. As long as South Boston remains a truly defended neighborhood, however, such change will be slow in coming.

To conclude the review of findings organized under the headings of the chapter 3 framework, Judge Garrity's authority and readiness to coerce unwilling officials were probably the most important reasons that his desegregation policies were so thoroughly implemented. In equitable remedies federal lower-court judges are able to exercise a power resource unavailable to other political officials. If a judge is vigorous in seeing to the enforcement of his remedies, as was Garrity in Boston, his policy can be implemented in even the most difficult of compliance environments.

What about the consequences of implementation? Was implementation successful in achieving policy goals? Superficial measurement of changed school enrollments and probability of interracial student contact point to a successful desegregation policy in Boston. Rossell's conditions of positive behavioral and attitudinal change pose a harder test. Here the characteristics of the compliance environment are crucial, and it is no accident that organized opposition to busing in South Boston and a few other enclaves is only now ending.

Policy Recommendations

The final task of this chapter is recommending strategies for desegregating defended-neighborhood schools in other cities. What follows is intended to emphasize the desirable and feasible, to accomplish some degree of desegregation while sensitizing policy to characteristics of a special type of community.

Of course, the defended neighborhood is something of an anachronism in contemporary urban America, a relatively rare case of "community saved." Probably no school-busing plan can be devised that at once pleases and still desegregates a defended neighborhood. Even one-way busing of minority pupils to fill vacant seats likely will be seen by most residents as a threat to their community. An unpopular policy need not provoke the sort of fury vented by South Boston, however, and there should be ways of anticipating and reducing community outrage without sacrificing enforcement of constitutional rights.

Lower federal-court judges presently enjoy wide latitude in fashioning segregation remedies. No doubt this fact informed a recent comment that "no two desegregation plans are alike."[17] Indeed, Boston illustrates how much diversity can be encompassed within a single school-desegregation plan. The steadily shrinking white proportion of students was noted in chapter 9, yet no district 8 (East Boston) school was less than 75 percent white in 1980, and seven of ten remained 90 percent or more white. Even though the 1980 district 6 goal laid down by the court was 47 percent white, six of seven South Boston elementary schools were more than half white, and five were more than two-thirds white, well in excess of the maximum theoretically permitted by the court. Although community disapproval cannot dictate enforcement of the law, judicial policy can take account of special conditions. The figures cited just above suggest such conditions were so acknowledged, one way or another. Hence readers may wonder what all the uproar in South Boston and other defended neighborhoods was all about.

The probability of such turmoil was greatly increased in 1974, when Phase 1 planners decided to pair high schools in Roxbury and South Boston. Forewarned of South Boston's reputation, planners proceeded nonetheless with an arrangement bound to provoke fierce community resentment. Hence a critical symbolic conflict marked the beginning of federal busing policy. Justifications couched in terms of the short busing distances involved wholly overlooked the dread with which most South Boston residents regarded Roxbury. To them, Roxbury symbolized the very worst aspects of urban life; socially it might well have been on another planet.

In retrospect, it would appear that almost any other arrangement would have better served judicial policy, the educational process, and the emotional state of participating students. Even a temporary one-way busing plan whereby black students replaced Dorchester whites in South Boston High would have left indigenous youth intact in their neighborhood school and thereby deprived antibusing protest of one of its most effective arguments.[18] Local whites transferring to magnet schools, or fleeing the public system altogether, could have been replaced by additional black and other nonwhite pupils until a desirable balance had been reached. Or, reversing the order of desegregation and beginning with elementary schools and eventually incorporating high schools probably would have helped significantly the chances for positive behavioral adaptation. Even a temporary exemption of South Boston High from Phase 1, like the exemption given other schools, might have undercut protest and possibly demonstrated—by example elsewhere in the city—that desegregation was not so bad after all.

In any case, Phase 1 got off to a terrible beginning, largely because of a remarkably insensitive pairing scheme. And, of course, South Boston's fury in 1974 set the stage for violence in Charlestown when Phase 2 got underway. There is every reason to believe East Boston would have reacted similarly if it had been meaningfully included in Judge Garrity's busing orders. Hence the first policy recommendation: Desegregation planners should take neighborhood identities and sentiment seriously, especially when dealing with communities conforming to the defended-neighborhood model.

Second, implementors and planners must recognize that judicial policy is on trial. Even though the policy's legitimacy is denied by most defended-neighborhood residents, it is still essential to justify particular remedies. No parent compelled to participate in involuntary busing should be left without a clear idea of why the court deems such sacrifices necessary. In other words, the causal theory underlying judicial policy must be stated lucidly and extensively. Truncated proclamations that the law requires people to do something they vehemently oppose are not enough. Nor will brief references to minority disadvantages, as if no one else were socially and economically deprived, suffice. Reassurances about bus safety and short distances simply are not responsive to the apprehensions most white Americans have about compulsory busing. Indeed, what other redistributive policy is so sparsely justified? Without a better explanation of why busing is necessary, school desegregation is unlikely to be accorded legitimacy in urban white neighborhoods.

Third, and in keeping with the argument that busing policy is on trial, every effort must be made to demonstrate that busing does not lead to declining educational quality. It does not matter that educational quality in white ghetto schools may not have been high before busing. Since educational quality is so relative a concept, so much affected by social class perspectives, why not take the educational values and concerns of the neighborhood seriously? In most defended neighborhoods such an approach would emphasize traditional knowledge and skills rather than alternative programs. However well-intended or perhaps suited to the needs of some students, innovative approaches with their "noncognitive" concerns only convince working-class parents that educational ruin is at hand. Of all Boston schools to start such a curriculum, surely troubled South Boston High was the worst choice. Undoubtedly *no* program under receivership would have been given a fair hearing in South Boston, but probably one stressing academic excellence and the "basics" would have won grudging respect. In turn, such respect would seem fundamental to eventual positive adaptation by defended-neighborhood students and parents.

Finally, Weatherford suggests a fourth strategy possibly suited for defended neighborhoods: Break up community opposition by enlisting moderate parents and groups in planning and implementing desegregation.[19] In most cities the Parent Teacher Association (PTA) and similar groups likely would have an important role to play, but in South Boston the Home and School Association was taken over by antibusing activists (some of whom had no children in public schools). Probably the imbalance controversy of the 1960s undercut any such strategy in Boston's defended neighborhoods. In any case, the few South Boston residents who served on Judge Garrity's councils probably did not represent neighborhood sentiment, and chapter 8 described what happened to the short-lived South Boston Task Force For Positive Action. Perhaps if Phase 1 had treated South Boston differently, this attempt at co-optation might have been feasible despite hardened imbalance positions. In any event, it might work in cities where no comparable history of conflict over racial imbalance exists.

At this writing, the future of court-ordered busing is by no means assured. Demographic changes in American metropolitan areas continue to reduce the number of inner-city white students available for desegregation, and a Supreme Court endorsement of metropolitan busing programs for Northeastern and Middlewestern areas appears most unlikely. Busing foes have won an important victory in the 1981 termination of Los Angeles's state-ordered busing program. President Reagan has promised to support further congressional curbs on federal enforcement of busing. Federal judicial policy remains at odds with both the Congress and the White House; public opposition to busing has not lessened. All the more reason to take account of defended neighborhoods in fashioning future remedies for segregated urban schools.

Notes

1. See Howard Husak, "Boston: The Problem That Won't Go Away," *The New York Times Magazine,* 25 November 1979, pp. 30 34, 90 100.

2. These data must be viewed with important limitations in mind. First, it was not possible to differentiate students voluntarily bused to magnet schools from those bused to schools in districts 1-8. Second, school department annual reports do not jibe with figures provided by the Department of Implementation. For example, the annual report busing total for 1977-1978 was 6,882 less than the number provided in table 10-1. The Department of Implementation's data have been accepted as the more likely correct because of that department's role in Boston school desegregation.

3. *Boston Herald-American,* 8 June 1976, p. 17.

4. Quoted in Alan Eisner, "Garrity Denies He Is 'Running' City's Schools," *Boston Herald-American,* 26 March 1976, p. 9.

5. Memorandum of decisions and remedial orders, 5 June 1975, quoted in *Quality Education: Changing Definitions and Heightened Expectations,* Citywide Coordinating Council, 17 March 1977, p. 1.

6. See "Fahey Threatened With Ouster," *Boston Herald-American,* 3 February 1976, p. 1.

7. "Garrity Raps White on Budget," *Boston Globe,* 14 January 1981, p. 1.

8. M. Stephen Weatherford, "The Politics of School Busing: Contextual Effects and Community Polarization," *Journal of Politics* 42 (August 1980), p. 748.

9. Ibid., p. 758.

10. Whatever the legal basis for this argument, a long-standing tradition of parental choice existed in Boston. See Stanley Schultz, *The Culture Factory* (New York: Oxford University Press, 1973), pp. 103-131.

11. Weatherford, "Politics of School Busing," pp. 762-763.

12. Lillian B. Rubin, *Busing and Backlash* (Berkeley: University of California Press, 1972).

13. Ibid., pp. 51-52.

14. Ibid., p. 58.

15. A good summary of this research is found in Christine Rossell, "School Desegregation and Community Social Change," *Law and Contemporary Problems,* 42 (Summer 1978): 133-183.

16. Ibid., pp. 134-148.

17. Robert L. Crain and Rita E. Mahard, "Desegregation and Black Achievement: A Review of The Research," *Law and Contemporary Problems,* 42 (Summer 1978), p. 30.

18. The argument was that South Boston did not object to letting black students take empty seats in neighborhood schools, only to the involuntary reassignment of local youths to ghetto schools or, indeed, any schools outside their neighborhood. The racial-imbalance controversy discussed in chapter 5 suggests the claim was partly false.

19. Weatherford, "Politics of School Busing," p. 764.

Appendix:
Federal District Court Racial Goals and Allowed Variations for the Nine Boston School Districts, 1975-1980

Table A-1
Federal District Court Racial Goals and Allowed Variations for the Nine Boston School Districts, 1975-1976
(percent)

	School Districts								
	1	2	3	4	5	6	7	8	9
White goal	44	45	56	61	45	53	40	95	51
Highest white	54	55	70	81	56	66	50	99	56
Lowest white	33	34	42	46	34	40	30	71	46
Black goal	33	40	39	35	48	33	35	3	37
Highest black	41	50	49	44	60	41	44	4	42
Lowest black	25	30	29	26	36	25	26	2	32
Other goal	23	15	5	4	7	14	25	2	12[a]
Highest other	29	19	6	5	9	18	31	3	17[a]
Lowest other	17	11	4	3	5	11	19	1	7[a]

Source: Department of Implementation, Boston Public Schools

Note: District composition: 1: Brighton and Back Bay; 2: Jamaica Plain, Roslindale, Roxbury, and West Roxbury; 3: South Dorchester, Roslindale, and West Roxbury; 4. Hyde Park and South Dorchester; 5: North and South Dorchester; 6: South Boston, North Dorchester and Roxbury; 7: Back Bay, Charlestown, North End, South End, and Roxbury; 8: East Boston; 9: Citywide magnet school district.

[a]Recommended but not required by the court.

Table A-2
Racial Goals and Allowed Variations, 1976-1977
(percent)

	School Districts								
	1	*2*	*3*	*4*	*5*	*6*	*7*	*8*	*9*
White goal	39	40	51	53	40	50	31	93	47
Highest white	49	50	63	66	50	62	39	99	52
Lowest white	29	30	38	40	30	38	23	70	42
Black goal	35	43	45	45	53	36	40	4	41
Highest black	44	54	56	56	66	45	50	5	46
Lowest black	26	32	34	34	40	27	30	3	36
Other goal	26	17	4	2	7	14	29	3	12
Highest other	32	21	5	3	9	17	36	4	14
Lowest other	20	13	3	1	5	11	22	1	10

Source: Department of Implementation, Boston Public Schools

Table A-3
Racial Goals and Allowed Variations, 1977-1978
(percent)

	School Districts								
	1	*2*	*3*	*4*	*5*	*6*	*7*	*8*	*9*
White goal	35	37	49	47	36	51	29	94	45
Highest white	44	46	61	59	45	64	36	99	50
Lowest white	26	28	37	35	27	38	22	71	40
Black goal	35	44	46	49	56	35	41	3	43
Highest black	44	55	57	61	70	44	51	4	47
Lowest black	26	33	35	37	42	26	31	2	39
Other goal	30	19	5	4	8	14	30	3	12
Highest other	37	24	6	5	10	17	37	4	14
Lowest other	23	14	4	3	6	11	23	2	10

Source: Department of Implementation, Boston Public Schools

Table A-4
Racial Goals and Allowed Variations, 1978-1979
(percent)

	School Districts								
	1	*2*	*3*	*4*	*5*	*6*	*7*	*8*	*9*
White goal	32	35	48	42	32	50	26	93	45
Highest white	40	44	60	53	40	63	33	99	50
Lowest white	24	26	36	31	27	37	19	70	40
Black goal	35	44	48	55	59	35	42	2	41
Highest black	44	55	60	69	64	44	53	3	45
Lowest black	26	33	36	44	44	26	31	1	37
Other goal	33	21	4	3	9	15	32	5	14
Highest other	41	26	5	4	11	19	40	6	15
Lowest other	25	16	3	2	7	11	24	4	13

Source: Department of Implementation, Boston Public Schools

Table A-5
Racial Goals and Allowed Variations, 1979-1980
(percent)

	School Districts								
	1	*2*	*3*	*4*	*5*	*6*	*7*	*8*	*9*
White goal	30	31	47	37	29	48	25	92	39
Highest white	38	39	59	46	36	60	31	99	43
Lowest white	22	23	35	28	22	36	19	69	35
Black goal	35	44	48	60	61	35	41	2	45
Highest black	44	55	60	75	76	44	51	3	50
Lowest black	26	33	36	45	46	26	31	1	40
Other goal	35	25	5	3	10	17	34	6	16
Highest other	44	31	6	4	13	21	43	8	18
Lowest other	26	19	4	2	7	13	25	4	14

Source: Department of Implementation, Boston Public Schools

Table A-6
Racial Goals and Allowed Variations, 1980-1981
(percent)

	School Districts								
	1	*2*	*3*	*4*	*5*	*6*	*7*	*8*	*9*
White goal	29	29	45	34	26	47	23	92	36
Highest white	36	36	56	43	33	59	29	99	41
Lowest white	22	22	34	25	19	35	17	69	31
Black goal	33	45	50	63	63	36	41	2	46
Highest black	41	56	62	79	79	45	51	3	51
Lowest black	25	34	38	47	47	27	31	1	41
Other goal	38	26	5	3	11	17	36	6	18
Highest other	47	32	6	4	14	21	45	8	20
Lowest other	29	20	4	2	8	13	27	4	16

Source: Department of Implementation, Boston Public Schools

Index

Index

About the Author

Emmet H. Buell, Jr. received the Ph.D. from Vanderbilt University and has taught political science at Denison University since 1969. Dr. Buell was a visiting associate professor at Reed College in 1980-1981. His articles have appeared in *Urban Affairs Quarterly* and *Social Science Quarterly.*

Richard A. Brisbin, Jr., who participated in the data collection and preliminary draft phases of the book, received the Ph.D. from Johns Hopkins University. Dr. Brisbin has taught at Denison Univeristy and Central Michigan University, and is currently at Saint Mary's College in Indiana. His articles have appeared in *Polity,* and *Michigan State Bar Journal,* and the *Ohio Northern University Law Review.*